SWORDFISH

FROM THE COCKPIT, No 10

DONALD PAYNE

Contents

PROLOGUE *Lieutenant (A) Donald Payne* RNVR 4

BEGINNINGS *Lieutenant (A) Donald Payne* RNVR 12

ANATOMY *Chief Aircraft Artificer Bill Banham* 18

WEAPONS, STORES, CAPABILITIES 28

IN THE AIR *Captain Eric Brown* CBE DSC AFC 34

FROM THE COCKPIT *Lieutenant (A) Donald Payne* RNVR 38

Preparing the Targets *Lieutenant-Commander Willie Armstrong* DSM 45

From the Observer's Cockpit *Lieutenant (A) Jock Bevan* RNVR 46

Eagle Eyes *Commander Stan Laurie* 48

A Very Secret Topic *Commander Andy Phillip* 50

Little Touches *CPO (A) Les Sayer* MBE DSM 52

Simplicity Itself *Lieutenant-Commander Bob Selley* VRD RNR 56

Too Clever By Half *Lieutenant Bruce Vibert* 57

Relishing the Experience *Commander Simon Askins* 58

INTO BATTLE *Lieutenant (A) Donald Payne* RNVR 62

Jeopardising the Linear Succession *Sub-Lieutenant (A) Stanley Brand* RNVR 72

The J. C. Wire *Sub-Lieutenant (A) Frank Jackson* MiD* RNVR 74

Floating Bombs *Lieutenant-Commander Tony Tuke* DSC* 92

Two Night Swims *Lieutenant (A) Arthur Towlson* DSC RNVR 94

A Perfect Row of Ships *Captain David Goodwin* CBE DSC 96

Water Spouts Rising *Lieutenant (A) Leslie ('Bill') Bailey* MiD RNVR 98

A Hit Amidships *CPO (A) Les Sayer* MBE DSM 100

First Contact *Lieutenant-Commander Edgar Lee* DSO VRD RNR 102

An Almighty Bang *Lieutenant-Commander Edgar Lee* DSO VRD RNR 104

In a Pickle *Lieutenant-Commander Edgar Lee* DSO VRD RNR 106
No Messing Around *Lieutenant-Commander Mike Langman* DSC CD 108
The Darkest Nights *Lieutenant (A) Don Ridgway* RNVR 110
Devastated *Lieutenant-Commander Brian Bennett* DSC 114
White Knuckle Riders *Lieutenant-Commander (A) Paul Housden* VRD RNVR 116
Closing the Gap *Lieutenant-Commander John Shoebridge* MBE 118
With Alacrity *Lieutenant (A) Bill Penlington* RNVR 122
Morocco-Bound *Chief Aircraft Artificer Bill Banham* 126
Tragedy *Lieutenant (A) Jock Bevan* RNVR 128
No Upper Charlies *Lieutenant (A) Tommy Thomson* DSC RNVR 130
'He's Diving! He's Diving!' *Lieutenant-Commander Bill Henley* DSC* 130

CARE AND MAINTENANCE *Chief Aircraft Artificer Bill Banham* 134
Applied Mathmatics Applied *Sub-Lieutenant (A) Stanley Brand* RNVR 138
Recyclable Stringbag *Sub-Lieutenant (A) Jack Thomas* RNVR 142
The Errant Swordfish *Chief Aircraft Artificer Bill Banham* 144

FRONT-LINE SQUADRONS 146

CATAPULT FLIGHTS 174

ROYAL AIR FORCE FRONT-LINE UNITS 176

FLEET AIR ARM SECOND-LINE UNITS 178

MODIFICATION 408 188

OTHER SWORDFISH UNITS 190

THE LAST WORD *Lieutenant-Commander (A) John Moffat* RNVR 192

SWORDFISH COLOURS 193

PROLOGUE

Lieutenant (A) Donald Payne RNVR

A little before 8 p.m. in the evening, *Illustrious* reached her flying-off position, 120 miles south-east of Taranto. She swung into wind. A light flashed green from her island, and the first of her Swordfish trundled the length of her flight deck, sank momentarily over the bow with the weight of its torpedo, then climbed slowly into the night sky. Soon the first strike of twelve Swordfish was heading in formation into the evening twilight.

The Italians were waiting for them: the RAF reconnaissance flights had put them on the alert. Their Marconi-type radar picked up the Swordfish at a range of thirty miles, and before the aircraft had even got into position to drop their flares, 'ack-ack' was finding their range. With the Italian fleet lit by moonlight and flarelight, the twelve aircraft dived in quick succession through a curtain of fire. It was, according to one pilot, 'like flying into an erupting volcano'. No aircraft type except a Swordfish could have jinked and weaved successfully through such heavy fire, and have been manœuvrable enough to make the split-second adjustments that were needed to avoid the balloons and find the gaps in the anti-torpedo nets. Levelling off close to sea level—one pilot was so low his wheels actually touched the water—the aircraft dropped their torpedoes at point-blank range. Often they were so close to their target that they had no time to break away, instead flying directly over the ship they were attacking. They had to face heavy fire. 'The *Littorio* opened up on us,' wrote one of the observers. 'The flash of her close-range weapons stabbed at us from her whole length. We were coming in on her beam, and were [at] the centre of an incredible mass of crossfire from the cruisers, battleships and shore batteries.' Amazingly, only one Swordfish was lost in the first attack, and one in the second which followed three-quarters of an hour later. And what devastation was caused!

Reconnaissance next morning revealed that three of Italy's six battleships had been put out of action: *Conte di Cavour* had been sunk; *Caio Duilio* was listing and foundering; and the mighty *Littorio*, hit by three torpedoes, was listing steeply, her bows awash with oil, and it would be eighteen months before she

Below: Swordfish of 815 and 819 Squadrons crowd the flight deck of HMS *Illustrious*, autumn 1940. These two units, together with aircraft from 813 and 824 Squadrons, wrought havoc amongst the Italian fleet at Taranto.
Right: *Illustrious* landing-on some of her Swordfish. Two aircraft, their wings folded, have been marshalled forward; a third has just landed, having caught the first wire (the aftermost of the two safety barriers is still raised, and handlers are about to assist with moving the aircraft forward); and two more are making their approach

Left, upper: Swordfish P4131 on board *Ark Royal*, assigned to 810 Squadron and believed to be the aircraft flown by Sub-Lieutenants Pattisson (P) and Meadway (O) and Leading Airman Mulley (TAG) in the attacks on the German battleship *Bismarck* on 26 May 1941. Left, lower: Find, fix and strike: *Ark Royal*'s Swordfish prepare to take off to attack *Bismarck*. Very few of the aircraft engaged in this operation can be identified by means of their serial numbers: as was the general practice at this time, log books and squadron line books tended to quote only the aircraft's call-signs in their records of events and activities. Opposite: Swordfish L2826/'2P' of 810 Squadron, piloted by Sub-Lieutenant A. W. Beale and with Sub-Lieutenant C. Friend as observer and Leading Airman K. Pimlott as TAG, returns to HMS *Ark Royal* following the successful attack on *Bismarck*. The hit scored on the battleship by 825 Squadron from HMS *Victorious* two days earlier (see pages 98–101) had caused the enemy to change his plans; now he was doomed.

was fit to put to sea once more. In addition, two cruisers had been badly damaged, oil storage tanks had been fractured and a seaplane hangar had been destroyed. In the *Supermarina*'s operations room, the Italian top brass stared with horror and in disbelief at the flood of damage reports. 'It was,' one said, 'as though we had lost a great naval battle, and we could not foresee ever being able to recover . . .'

* * *

By midday *Ark Royal* had closed to within fifty miles of the battleship—the ideal range from which to make an air strike. However, getting the Swordfish ready for take-off required superhuman efforts by all concerned, since, with the carrier pitching and rolling, and her flight deck awash and coated with ice, the aircraft slithered this way and that, dragging with them the forty or fifty deck handlers trying to manœuvre them into position. When at last fifteen Swordfish had been ranged, the carrier turned into wind and the first aircraft, heavy with its torpedo, trundled the length of the flight deck. For a moment it looked as though it was flying straight into the sea, but at the last moment the deck pitched upwards

and it was flung into the air, its undercarriage disappearing from sight in the spume of an approaching wave. This near-miracle of take-off was repeated fourteen times, and the Swordfish formed up and headed for their target.

The weather was appalling—thick, low cloud, a buffeting wind and flurries of sleet—and it did not take long for the Swordfish to begin to ice up and become separated from one another. After about an hour the observers picked up a 'blip' on their ASV, exactly where they had been told that *Bismarck* would be found. Diving out of cloud, they attacked the warship beneath them, only to realise at the last moment it was not the German battleship but the cruiser HMS *Sheffield*. The latter had been ordered to shadow *Bismarck* as closely as possible, but unfortunately this vital information had not been passed on correctly to *Ark Royal*. However, good was to come from incompetence: *Sheffield* managed to avoid the torpedoes, many of which were seen to explode on impact with the waves. The Swordfish returned to the 'Ark', three of them crashing in the near-impossible conditions for landing. Another strike force, armed with torpedoes with revised settings, was flown off in the gathering twilight—and this second strike force made no mistake.

The aircraft rendezvoused with *Sheffield* and the cruiser gave them the exact range and bearing of the German battleship. Conditions were too bad to make a co-ordinated attack, so the Swordfish went in individually. Later, *Bismarck*'s gunnery officer, von Mullenheim-Rechberg, praised the courage of the aircrews: '*Bismarck* was a fire-spitting mountain, but the Swordfish came in even more recklessly than the planes from the *Victorious* . . . They were so close, we felt we could reach out and touch them.'

Many Swordfish were hit by the heavy and accurate anti-aircraft fire and several of the aircrew were wounded, but two of the torpedoes struck home, one hitting the battleship abaft her armour belt and close to her stern. With her steering compartment thus flooded and her rudder jammed, her speed dropped and she could steer only erratically. From that moment, her fate was sealed . . .

* * *

What might be described as a typical night anti-shipping strike was led by Lieutenant Whitworth. At 7.30 p.m. it was reported by an RAF Maryland that a convoy was heading south from Cape Spartivento, Sardinia. Within twenty minutes a strike force of nine Swordfish from Malta was airborne. The aircraft formed up in two sub-flights; forming up was always a tricky manœuvre with night fighters in the offing. Each leading aircraft carried ASV and flares and the other aircraft torpedoes; all had long-range fuel tanks. When they had been airborne for about two hours, a faint blue smudge appeared on the

observers' ASV screens. The Swordfish altered course, and soon the convoy began to take shape—ten 'blips', nine close together and the tenth, a guardship, out on its own. They skirted the guardship, and at a range of about five miles spotted the convoy visually. It comprised five destroyers and five merchantmen. The Squadron's orders were, 'Ignore the destroyers; and one merchantman sunk is better than four damaged.' The aircraft therefore attacked singly, so that if one of the ships was damaged, the other Swordfish could, perhaps, finish it off. The pilots came in low, almost feathering the sea. They dropped their torpedoes from close range, and many achieved hits. Ship after ship shuddered to a halt. Suddenly there was the most terrible roar, heard over 100 miles away, as an ammunition ship blew up. The convoy scattered.

When the attack was over, the Swordfish re-formed and headed for home. Many of the aircrew found the return to Malta the most nerve-racking part of their mission. Had their ASV failed, had their navigation not have been spot-on, had the weather closed in, or had they arrived back in the middle of an air raid, they might well have run out of fuel before they could land, but on this occasion all the aircraft got back safely. It is now known that they sank two merchant ships and seriously damaged two others, and, while this may not sound a particularly spectacular achievement, in fact, in less than twenty minutes, Rommel had lost twenty-five engines for his supporting Me 109 fighter-bombers, 3,500 tons of bombs, 4,000 tons of ammunition (mostly shells for the Tiger tanks), 4,000 tons of petrol, over 5,000 tons of food, and, perhaps most

importantly, the component parts of a mobile tank repair unit . . .

* * *

Tom Gleave, the CO at RAF Manston, was one of the last people to see Esmonde alive. 'His face,' he wrote, 'was the face of man already dead. I'd always known him as a vital man, eager and alive, but now his eyes were dulled and his face grey and haggard— the sort of lifeless face you read about but never expect to see. It shocked me, as nothing had done before nor has done since.'

The Swordfish took off and circled Manston, hoping for their promised escort. Eventually ten Spitfires appeared. Esmonde waited as long as he could for more, but with the battlecruisers drawing ever further away he had no option but to head into the skies over the Channel with his pitifully inadequate escort. They never stood a chance.

Before they even sighted their target, they were 'jumped' by over a hundred Me 109s and FW 190s. The Spitfires tried bravely to protect their charges, but were driven away by sheer weight of numbers and suffered heavy losses. The Swordfish then came under a hail of fire both from the German fighters and the German escorts and E-boats. They could have dropped their torpedoes from long range and turned back, but, on the off-chance of getting near

enough to achieve a hit, they continued to head into the solid curtain of fire. No matter how skilfully the pilots jinked, weaved and sideslipped, they were hit again and again. Some had their undercarriage shot away, some had half their wings shot away, some were set on fire. All were shot down. Of the eighteen aircrew who had set out from Manston, thirteen were killed and three seriously injured. The German warships escaped unscathed and, early next morning, dropped anchor in Wilhelmshaven . . .

* * *

'The storm in the North Atlantic had been terrifying in its violence, and our convoy was scattered and battered,' writes Sub-Lieutenant Stanley Brand. 'We took off in Swordfish "Q3" from our MAC ship *Alexia* with orders to round up the stragglers—a job known to aircrew as "The Sheepdog Trials" . . .

'It was some time before, through the gloom and the spindrift, we spotted the most distant of the stragglers. The poor old merchantman was motionless and listing steeply to port. Her stern was low in the water, her mast was broken, her lifeboats had been swept away and there was not the slightest wisp of smoke from her funnel. Flying as low as we could, we circled her. About ten people, frantically waving towels and shirts, were crammed on to her shattered bridge.

'Our TAG used his Aldis lamp to ask what problems they had. It was some time before a reply was slowly flashed back—slowly because signalling by Morse in a foreign language (we thought her crew were probably Greek) has obvious difficulties. When her reply did come it had a terrible simplicity: "Engine broke. Engine room flooded. Fires out. No steer. Pump broke. Mate leg broke. Stokerman arms and ribs broke. No lifeboats. Wireless gone. SOS please." We signalled, "We fetch help soon."

'By this time we were low on fuel, and I would have liked to have reported the merchantman's plight to *Alexia* and have headed straight back to the carrier. However, radio silence was in force, the fear being that, if we used our radios, U-boats might pick up our transmissions and home in on the convoy. I therefore set course for the nearest ship, another straggler to whom we had previously given a bearing to re-join the convoy. We told this ship the position of her fellow merchantman, and had the satisfaction of seeing her alter course to go to the rescue. Then we headed back for *Alexia*, knowing that if the headwind strengthened, or we were even a few degrees off course with our navigation, we would very likely run out of fuel before we could reach her and have to ditch.

At last we spotted the tell-tale signs of a convoy—the contents of a carelessly emptied trash bin, the not-yet-dispersed oil slicks—and a few moments later we sighted *Alexia*. To my great relief, she was turning into wind and was ready for us. We signalled, "Q3 out of fuel and coming straight in" and managed to land safely. When "Q3" was refuelled, it was found that her main tank was empty and her emergency tank held less than a gallon and a half of fuel—enough for about three minutes' flying.

'Not until we arrived a week later in Halifax, Nova Scotia, did we learn that the vessel we had alerted had, by fine seamanship, managed to rescue all the crew of the shattered merchantmen before she had to be scuttled . . .'

* * *

The Fairey Swordfish was unarguably one of the most successful aircraft of World War II. A fabric-covered biplane with a fixed undercarriage and a top speed of only about 120 knots, it looked outdated even in 1936 when it first came into service, yet in the first half of the war, as a torpedo-bomber, it sank

Below: The onerous and frequently humdrum task of convoy escort was the principal operational duty of the Swordfish during the aircraft's final years of service. The magnificent contribution of the aircrews and groundcrews, and indeed of the ships' complements, engaged in this vital work is, regrettably, not always fully recognised in today's history books. Here a rocket-armed Swordfish II from HMS *Chaser* surveys its flock as it joins a Russian convoy sailing, on this occasion, in benign waters. The cruiser at left is *Black Prince*.

more Axis shipping than any other aircraft (over 350,000 tons), crippled the Italian fleet at Taranto and brought about the sinking of the German battleship *Bismarck*. Swordfish were catapulted from warships, and used to reconnoitre and spot for the fall of shot for fleet gunnery. In April 1940 a Swordfish catapulted from HMS *Warspite* sank U 64 (thereby achieving the Fleet Air Arm's first 'kill' of the war) and then went on to direct the battleship's fire so accurately that seven German destroyers were sunk and the *coup de grâce* was administered to an eighth. Swordfish took part in a wide variety of clandestine operations, dropping secret agents in Norway, Greece, Tunisia and Tripolitania. They also participated in the deception of 'The Man Who Never Was'. In West Africa, Swordfish from *Ark Royal* and *Hermes* played a leading rôle in the operations that

were necessary to prevent units of the French fleet from falling into enemy hands. They did valuable work in the desert campaign in North Africa: on one occasion, three Swordfish, led by Captain Patch RM, sank four vessels (including a U-boat) with three torpedoes; on another, a Swordfish flew with a 2,500-pound bomb load to attack Rommel's supply lines (its take-off run was 11½ miles!).

From 1940 until 1945 Swordfish operated almost continuously over the English Channel and southern North Sea. Flying mainly from RAF airfields such as Manston and Bircham Newton, they attacked Axis aerodromes, harbour installations and shipping. They were also used extensively for minelaying, and took part in the D-Day landings. In the Indian Ocean, Swordfish carried out a wide variety of operations, from Bahrain in the north to

Above: A Swordfish Mk I of the Torpedo Trials Unit based at RNAS Gosport, seen in late 1938 or early 1939. As the war clouds gathered, prewar 'silver' finishes quickly disappeared under coats of camouflage paint.

Madagascar in the south, against both the Japanese and the Vichy French. In the second half of the war, as a hunter and harasser of U-boats, they played a major rôle in that most vital struggle of all, the Battle of the Atlantic. In Canada, Swordfish based at Yarmouth, Nova Scotia, were used for TAG training, the aircraft remaining in service with the Royal Canadian Navy until 1948. The Fairey Swordfish's war record is nicely summed up in *The Stringbag Song* (sung to the tune of *My Bonnie Lies over the Ocean*): 'My Stringbag flies over the ocean, / My Stringbag flies over the sea. / If it weren't for King George's Swordfish, / Where the hell would the Royal Navy be?'

As well as being an effective weapon, the 'String-bag'—as the Swordfish was universally nicknamed—won the affection of all who flew her. 'She was a

forgiving aircraft', recalls a pilot of 811 Squadron, 'robust, reliable, versatile and tolerant of pilot error. Of all the planes I flew, she was the most airworthy, and I think it must have been this quality that enabled her to operate throughout the war, day or night, in all weathers, from even the smallest carrier.'

Why were these archaic-looking biplanes so successful? A short answer would be: because of the functional simplicity of their design. And here, unlikely as it sounds, the Swordfish has the same sort of ancestry as the Spitfire. Both were conceived and came into being without official backing. In other words, both were private ventures.

BEGINNINGS

Lieutenant (A) Donald Payne RNVR

IN the early 1930s Clive Rawlings, a Royal Navy officer seconded to the Air Ministry, put forward what was then a revolutionary idea: the Navy needed an aircraft that could not only reconnoitre and spot for the Fleet, but could also deliver a torpedo attack—'a plane with a sting in its tail'. Naval aircraft were, in those days, accorded a low priority in the British armed forces. This was largely because all flying was controlled by the Royal Air Force, who had little enough money to spend on their own aircraft; 'The Air Ministry', read a memo of the early 1930s, 'favours the drastic reduction and limitation of the aircraft-carrying capacity of the fleet'. Rawlings' concept therefore got little official support. So he got in touch with the Fairey Aviation Company, which specialised in the design and production of aircraft for the Navy. It was fortunate indeed that the head of the company, Richard Fairey, had the perspicacity to spot a winner, and the guts to back his judgement. After consulting his design team, and in particular his Chief Designer, Marcel Lobelle, he decided to build an aeroplane that would meet Rawlings' requirements as a private venture.

A prototype, designated F.1875 by the manufacturer and piloted by Chris Staniland, made a successful maiden flight on 21 March 1933. However, on 10 July that year, while flying at 14,000 feet, Staniland put the aircraft into a right-hand spin and was unable to recover. After some dozen rotations, 'spinning round and round like a falling sycamore leaf', Staniland very prudently baled out. He landed safely, but the aircraft crashed on what was then the Bath Road and was a complete write off. This would have been a major setback for an aircraft with Service backing; for a private venture, it might well have been the death blow. However, Fairey and Lobelle modified their design, incorporating over one hundred alterations. These included fitting a metal, three-blade propeller, introducing anti-spin strakes, lengthening the fuselage and increasing by four degrees the sweep of the upper wings. The

result was K4910, which made its maiden flight from Fairey's Great West Aerodrome (now Heathrow) on 17 April the following year. This and subsequent test flights were successful.

Fairey then got a welcome fillip. They had delivered six TSR aircraft, very similar to K4190, to the Greek Navy, and these had proved to be an outstanding success. Reports of their versatility and reliability had filtered back to the Air Ministry and to the Admiralty—and at much the same time it was becoming increasingly likely that there was going to

Below: The progenitor: the Fairey TSR.II, which first flew in April 1935. Production Swordfish were very little different in appearance from Richard Fairey's private venture.

be war. Thus on 23 April 1935 the company was authorised to build three pre-production aircraft based on a modified K4190 design. As soon as these had been successfully tested, an order was placed for 86 production machines, to be built—interchangeably as landplanes and seaplanes—on the assembly lines at Hayes. Following the tradition of naming British naval aircraft after marine creatures, it was agreed to call them 'Swordfish'.

The first production Swordfish were delivered to the Royal Navy in February 1936. In the trials that followed, it was found that the aircraft had serious deficiencies as a seaplane, having too long a take-off run, being prone to 'pounding' in choppy waters and being difficult to turn. However, as a carrier-based torpedo-bomber-reconnaissance vehicle it exceeded all expectations, and Fairey were asked to expedite deliveries. This posed a problem in that Fairey

Opposite: The TSR.II had been preceded into the air—but only just—by Fairey's response to Specification 9/30, for a fleet spotter/reconnaissance aircraft for the Navy. With an optional wheeled or central-float undercarriage, it shared many design features of the later aircraft. It was powered by a Rolls-Royce Kestrel inline engine.

Above: S.9/30 was in turn developed into 'The Greek machine', or TSR.I, the direct forerunner of the TSR.II. It was allocated the company number F.1875.
Below: K4190, the TSR.II, in flight. The company number, F.2038, is stencilled aft of the Air Ministry serial number.

ROYAL NAVY
V 4309

BAE SYSTEMS

COURTESY PHILIP JARRETT

Aviation was a relatively small company, its assembly sheds at Harmondsworth (again, now part of Heathrow) depending largely on manual rather than tooled manufacture. Moreover, as the war developed and the demand for Swordfish increased, the company's contracts to build other aircraft for the Fleet Air Arm—in particular Albacores and Fulmars—meant that it simply could not cope with the demand, and it was therefore decided to share the production of Swordfish with Blackburn Aircraft, who were about to open a new assembly plant at Sherburn-in-Elmet in Yorkshire. Eventually Blackburn took over all production, manufacturing 1,700 Swordfish compared with the parent company's 692.

Left: V4309, a late-production Mk I and one of the first Swordfish built by Blackburn Aircraft at Sherburn-in-Elmet.
Below: K5660 was one of three development aircraft and the first officially to bear the name 'Swordfish'. It flew in December 1935, by which time a production batch of 86 aircraft had been ordered. The major change from the prototype TSR.II was the replacement of the Fairey-Reed propeller by a standard metal propeller.

An employee of Fairey Aviation remembers the early Swordfish: 'They were large, sturdy biplanes, with a wingspan of 45 feet 6 inches. Their fuselage was of rectangular steel-tube construction, faired to an oval section, covered behind the engine with easily detachable metal plates and aft of this by fabric. The wings were built of steel-strip spars and drag struts, with duralumin ribs, also covered with fabric. The oleo legs worked on a simple spring and oil-damped principle, and were of rugged construction and almost maintenance-free. Their powerplant [a Bristol Pegasus III] was equally rugged and easily maintained. There was much to commend this apparently obsolete design. It was simple, and used few sophisticated materials. It involved a large wing area of high lift capability. This gave the plane a short take-off run, and enabled it to carry a heavy load.'

So there they were—sturdy, reliable weightlifters. Time, and the exigencies of war, were to prove what an effective combination this would be.

ANATOMY

Chief Aircraft Artificer Bill Banham

THE Swordfish was, in truth, a relic of the biplane era—an anachronism even before the outbreak of war in September 1939. It was quite a large aeroplane, with wings of unequal span and of single-bay configuration, designed to fold without the use of jury struts. Powered by a single engine of modest horsepower, it combined versatility and load-carrying with robust construction. Unlike many aircraft of its period, it remained in use by both the Royal Navy and the Royal Air Force throughout World War II.

The fuselage, built in four sections for easy assembly, embodied stainless steel tubing, configured on what was known as the Warren braced girder construction principle—rather like the skeleton of a girder bridge. The wings and empennage utilised stainless steel spars and drag braces with duralumin ribs, the interplane and centre-section struts being of steel tubing with fabric-covered, balsa wood fairings to present individual streamlined shapes and wing bracing wires of stainless steel. The whole of the wing and empennage surfaces were fabric covered, as was the fuselage as far forward as the engine and fuel tank bay, which itself was enclosed by duralumin panelling. Later aircraft, modified for the anti-submarine rôle and equipped with rockets and

RATOG (Rocket-Assisted Take-Off Gear), had sections of the undersides of the lower mainplanes and tailplane sheathed in light alloy.

The Pegasus engine fitted to all versions of the Swordfish was generally regarded as a fairly reliable unit, although there were problems. When first specified for the aircraft, the power output was probably just right for the requirements that existed at that time. However, under wartime conditions this output proved barely sufficient as the demands placed upon the aircraft increased, *viz.*:

(a) the ever-increasing weapon load that the aircraft was expected to carry;

(b) the necessity for the aircraft to operate for long periods at near-maximum power output;

(c) the requirement for prolonged running in extreme weather;

(d) the fitting of an additional generator to power new radar systems, thereby placing an additional burden on engine output;

(e) the engine's comparatively obsolete system of valve operation, calling for frequent

Below: Two Swordfish Mk Is fresh from the Blackburn production line at Sherburn; the aircraft in the background, V4320, is running up its Pegasus engine. The photograph illustrates the official camouflage applied to new-built Swordfish at this time (*circa* March 1941), but fresh directives changing the 'standard' paint scheme were issued frequently throughout the war and, in addition, local considerations often dictated variations from the norm. Even brand new machines, as here, often displayed anomalies—notice the discontinuity immediately forward of the serial numbers! Moreover, local repairs and refurbishments often resulted in local interpretations of the official line. The end result was that no two Swordfish were ever precisely identical in terms of their paintwork.

adjustments in order to maintain overall efficiency;

(f) arising from (e), a loss of power as a result of engine overheating following prolonged flying in extreme weather;

(g) arising from (e) and (f), restriction of the lube oil flow through the oil cooler owing to solidification of the oil passing out of the engine through the cooler; and

(h) inefficiency arising from the fact that the standards of manufacture of sparking plugs were never equal to the demands placed on

these very important components, particularly with the high-octane fuel then being utilised (and spares were never plentiful).

The oil cooler was located externally within the airstream, and although various attempts were made to improve its performance these were never entirely satisfactory. It was equipped with a bypass facility, which the pilot could activate if he so wished, to direct engine oil around the Pegasus's lubrication system without passing through the cooler, to help maintain the requisite temperature for the engine. However, there were dangers with this operation,

Left: The Pegasus engine (or 'Peggy' to the maintenance ratings and groundcrews) was a nine-cylinder, air-cooled radial engine and was encircled on the aircraft by what was known as a 'Townend Ring'—a kind of shroud developed by Dr Hubert Townend of Boulton & Paul and designed to reduce the drag induced by the otherwise bare cylinder heads whilst maintaining the cooling efficiency of the airstream acting on the engine. The device found application in a number of aircraft of the 1930s. The engine exhaust pipe can be seen at the foot of the photograph; various configurations could be seen on Swordfish, including, when the aircraft came to be used in night operations, extended 'flame-damping' pipes.

Right: An advanced stage in the assembly of a Swordfish Mk I, with fuselage, tailplane and upper wing centre-section mated together; the mainplanes have yet to be added, along with the undercarriage fairings and much of the metal panelling forward and the fabric covering aft. Notice that the application of paintwork and national markings begins at an early stage in the assembly procedure.

AD HOC PUBLICATIONS

particularly in the intense cold of the Arctic environment. If, after achieving the 'warm up' condition that he required, the pilot forgot to re-open the bypass, any oil in the cooler would freeze solid, thus preventing 'normal' operation for the duration and, eventually, causing complete overheating of the engine's lubrication system, changing the bearing oil's viscosity and possibly resulting in catastrophic engine failure.

The three-bladed, fixed-pitch propeller, manufactured by Fairey Aviation to a US specification (Reed), was of simple construction. Each blade was shaped to obtain maximum aerodynamic efficiency by contouring and twisting, the whole being bolted into a splined hub. It caused few problems. The odd occasion when the tips of the propeller made contact with the flight deck, causing material damage to the blades, could usually be rectified by removing the damaged portion and re-trimming each blade to a consistent length.

The fact that fabric was used to cover the wings, fuselage and empennage of the Swordfish simplified most repair requirements: virtually any perforation or tear in the surface could readily be repaired by the

BAE SYSTEMS

BAE SYSTEMS

APPLEYARDS WORKS (LEEDS)/BAE SYSTEMS

TATE OF LEEDS/BAE SYSTEMS

This spread: Some intimate details of the Swordfish's construction: (clockwise from bottom left) the top centre plane skinning; a completed frame for lower starboard mainplane; a completed fuselage frame with main undercarriage struts installed; and a view of a tailplane assembly shop. These images, all dating from March/April 1941, are of Blackburn-assembled aircraft; as indicated in the credits alongside, various sub-assemblies were contracted out to local companies.

Overleaf: A general view of the production bay at Sherburn-in-Elmet, May 1944. Prominent on the machine in the foreground are the main oil tank, the external oil cooler and an elongated 'flame-damping' exhaust pipe.

application of patches after sewing or stringing, and the subsequent application of quick-drying dope rapidly restored the overall rigidity of the covering. The introduction of RATOG entailed some modifications to the tailplane, principally sheathing the undersides with metal. The rocket assemblies were located half way along the fuselage and inclined downwards at about thirty degrees. When fired, they shot out residual material that could cause serious damage to an aircraft that had not been modified. Similarly, the use of rocket projectiles (R/P) as weapons carried beneath the lower mainplanes required the addition of metal sheathing in those immediate areas.

The internal structure of the Swordfish's fuselage, empennage and mainplanes was accessible for inspection by removing metal panels adjacent to and behind the engine installation, 'screw-in' covers and 'cut-outs' throughout the entire structure of the aircraft and detachable; fabric-covered panels offering access to battery and electrical systems stowage, the deck arrester mechanism and the tail-end shock absorber strut. A large, 'boxed-in' aperture in the centre-section of the upper mainplane gave access to a dinghy which in the event of a water-borne landing would automatically inflate but remain tethered to the aircraft. In the event of a failure of the automatic inflation device, a mechanical override was provided for a member of the crew to activate.

The mainplane assemblies ('wing boxes') were supported by streamlined struts bolted to the upper and lower planes as appropriate. These struts were of fixed length and could not be adjusted. Flying,

landing and incidence wires, and also the tailplane bracing wires, were equipped with adjustable tensioners to enable the wing boxes and other structures to be correctly rigged. The maintenance of the anti-corrosion protection of these components was a vital operation in maintaining aircraft serviceability.

The control surfaces—with the exception of the Handley Page anti-stall slats (located at the leading edges of the port and starboard upper mainplanes)—were fabric-covered, and the operation of each was carried out by means of stainless steel cables, aligned to the pilot's control column and rudder bar. The ailerons were fitted with trailing-edge metallic strips, which could be set manually whilst the aircraft was on the ground to correct any instability in the rolling plane. Both the rudder and the tailplane surfaces were so arranged that the pilot could control and adjust the stability of the aircraft to correct any variations that could occur as a result of differing external weapons loads.

The Swordfish's main undercarriage was of simple 'vee' configuration and comprised two spring-and-coil shock absorber legs, supported by radius rods and bracing struts and equipped with low-pressure tyres. The tail shock-absorber at the rear of the fuselage was designed to rotate over a fixed radius to facilitate differential control whilst the aircraft was taxying; it, too, had a low-pressure tyre. A braking system, installed in the main landing gear wheels, was controlled by air pressure maintained by an engine-driven compressor via a storage tank. Braking was controlled by the pilot through a differential mechanism linked to the rudder bar.

23

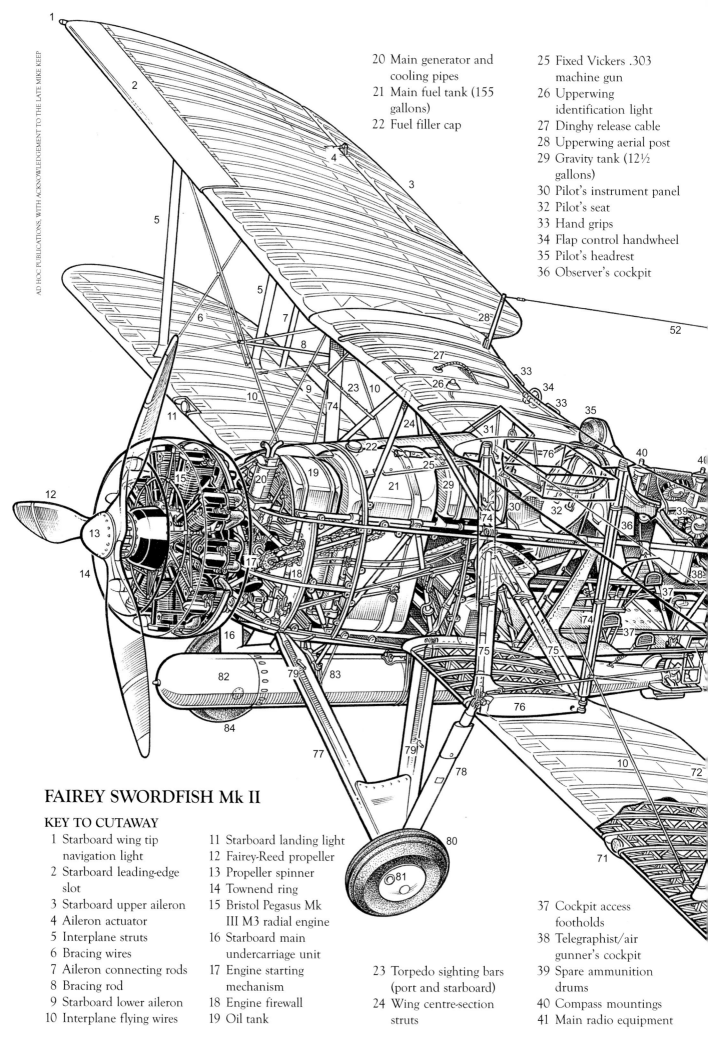

AD HOC PUBLICATIONS, WITH ACKNOWLEDGEMENT TO THE LATE MIKE KEEP

20 Main generator and cooling pipes
21 Main fuel tank (155 gallons)
22 Fuel filler cap

25 Fixed Vickers .303 machine gun
26 Upperwing identification light
27 Dinghy release cable
28 Upperwing aerial post
29 Gravity tank (12½ gallons)
30 Pilot's instrument panel
32 Pilot's seat
33 Hand grips
34 Flap control handwheel
35 Pilot's headrest
36 Observer's cockpit

FAIREY SWORDFISH Mk II

KEY TO CUTAWAY

1 Starboard wing tip navigation light
2 Starboard leading-edge slot
3 Starboard upper aileron
4 Aileron actuator
5 Interplane struts
6 Bracing wires
7 Aileron connecting rods
8 Bracing rod
9 Starboard lower aileron
10 Interplane flying wires

11 Starboard landing light
12 Fairey-Reed propeller
13 Propeller spinner
14 Townend ring
15 Bristol Pegasus Mk III M3 radial engine
16 Starboard main undercarriage unit
17 Engine starting mechanism
18 Engine firewall
19 Oil tank

23 Torpedo sighting bars (port and starboard)
24 Wing centre-section struts

37 Cockpit access footholds
38 Telegraphist/air gunner's cockpit
39 Spare ammunition drums
40 Compass mountings
41 Main radio equipment

SPECIFICATIONS
FAIREY SWORDFISH Mks I–III

Manufacturer:	The Fairey Aviation Company Ltd, Hayes, Middlesex. Production at Hayes and by Blackburn Aircraft Ltd at Sherburn-in-Elmet, Yorkshire.
Chief Designer:	Marcelle Lobelle.
Powerplant:	One Bristol Pegasus Mk III M3 or (most Mk IIs, Mk III) Mk 30 radial developing 775hp.
Dimensions:	Length overall (landplane) 36ft 1in (11.00m) tail down; wing span 45ft 6in (13.87m) spread, 17ft 3in (5.26m) folded; height 12ft 10½in (3.92m) tail down; wing area (gross) 607.0 sq ft (56.39m²).
Weights:	(Mk I) 4,700lb (2,130kg) empty, 8,100lb (3,670kg) loaded.
Armament:	One fixed Vickers .303in machine gun and one flexibly mounted Vickers or Lewis .303in machine gun; one 18in (45.7cm), 1,610lb (730kg) torpedo or maximum external load (bombs, rockets, sea mines or depth charges) of 1,500lb (680kg).
Performance:	Maximum speed 121kts (139mph, 225kph) at 5,000ft (1,500m), economical cruising speed 90 kts (104mph, 165kph); typical time to 5,000ft with maximum load 10mins; service ceiling with maximum load 10,700ft (3,500m); range (clean) 670nm (770 miles, 1,240km).
Number built:	2,392 (992 Mk Is, 1,080 Mk IIs, 320 Mk IIIs).

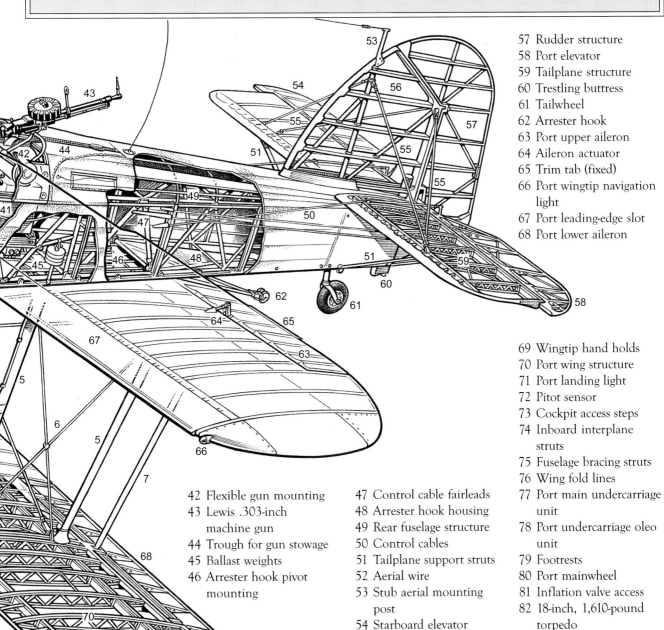

57 Rudder structure
58 Port elevator
59 Tailplane structure
60 Trestling buttress
61 Tailwheel
62 Arrester hook
63 Port upper aileron
64 Aileron actuator
65 Trim tab (fixed)
66 Port wingtip navigation light
67 Port leading-edge slot
68 Port lower aileron

69 Wingtip hand holds
70 Port wing structure
71 Port landing light
72 Pitot sensor
73 Cockpit access steps
74 Inboard interplane struts
75 Fuselage bracing struts
76 Wing fold lines
77 Port main undercarriage unit
78 Port undercarriage oleo unit
79 Footrests
80 Port mainwheel
81 Inflation valve access
82 18-inch, 1,610-pound torpedo
83 Forward torpedo crutch
84 Starboard mainwheel

42 Flexible gun mounting
43 Lewis .303-inch machine gun
44 Trough for gun stowage
45 Ballast weights
46 Arrester hook pivot mounting

47 Control cable fairleads
48 Arrester hook housing
49 Rear fuselage structure
50 Control cables
51 Tailplane support struts
52 Aerial wire
53 Stub aerial mounting post
54 Starboard elevator
55 Tailplane bracing wires
56 Tailfin structure

WEAPONS, STORES, CAPABILITIES

THE Fairey Swordfish was truly a multi-rôle aircraft, although its principal tasks within the Royal Navy evolved as the type moved from being the Fleet's primary torpedo bomber at the outbreak of war to becoming an invaluable convoy escort and anti-submarine aircraft in later years. The heroic and incredibly successful exploits by its crews in the first two years of the conflict notwithstanding, it must be conceded that the mauling the Swordfish received as a result of Operation 'Fuller'—the so-called 'Channel Dash' in February 1942—brought about its swift withdrawal from the torpedo-bombing rôle and its replacement by, first and rather unhappily, the Albacore; then, less disastrously, the Barracuda (which also operated more effectively than its predecessors as a dive-bomber) and finally, and successfully, the American-designed Grumman Tarpon (Avenger).

For its new primary rôle as an anti-submarine aircraft, the Swordfish Mk II had sheet metal underwing panels fitted so that, in addition to carrying light bombs, sea mines, depth charges, flares and so forth (which it had always been capable of carrying), it could also bring a battery of rocket projectiles (R/P) to bear on enemy shipping. So armed, the aircraft was better equipped to tackle both the inshore vessels (both merchant and naval) that were its prey in the English Channel and European coastal waters and the U-boats that it faced up to here and in the Atlantic Ocean.

The introduction to service of the Mk III, with its bulbous radome between the main undercarriage legs, meant that underbelly weapons loads could, in any case, no longer be carried. The fixed, forward-firing machine gun on the starboard fuselage alongside the pilot was eventually dispensed with,

AD HOC COLLECTION

and the hand-held machine gun in the rear cockpit, though not totally abandoned with the demise of the TAG, was rarely carried in the final years of the war.

The Swordfish was used throughout the war (and indeed for some time afterwards) as a weapons trials aircraft; ironically, in fact, the aircraft both started and ended its service career as a torpedo bomber, finally being withdrawn from duties with the Aircraft Torpedo Development Unit at Gosport in 1950, by which time virtually all of the Swordfish that had been used as temporary station 'hacks' had also disappeared from establishment.

Opposite: Groundcrewmen at RNAS Gosport prepare to arm a Swordfish I with an eighteen-inch (1,610-pound) practice torpedo. Notice the connecting leads draped over the main undercarriage struts.
Above: A Swordfish of the Torpedo Trials Unit delivers its 'fish' at the prescribed altitude of fifty feet.

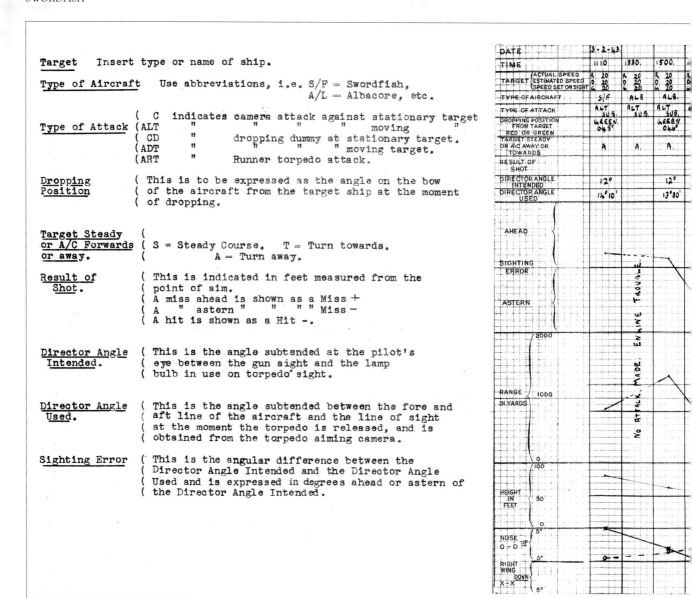

Target   Insert type or name of ship.

Type of Aircraft   Use abbreviations, i.e. S/F = Swordfish,
A/L = Albacore, etc.

Type of Attack   (C   indicates camera attack against stationary target
(ALT   "   "   "   "   moving   "
(CD   "   dropping dummy at stationary target.
(ADT   "   "   "   "   moving target.
(ART   "   Runner torpedo attack.

Dropping Position   (This is to be expressed as the angle on the bow
(of the aircraft from the target ship at the moment
(of dropping.

Target Steady or A/C Forwards or away.   (S = Steady Course.   T = Turn towards.
(A = Turn away.

Result of Shot.   (This is indicated in feet measured from the
(point of aim.
(A miss ahead is shown as a Miss +
(A " astern "   " " " Miss −
(A hit is shown as a Hit −.

Director Angle Intended.   (This is the angle subtended at the pilot's
(eye between the gun sight and the lamp
(bulb in use on torpedo sight.

Director Angle Used.   (This is the angle subtended between the fore and
(aft line of the aircraft and the line of sight
(at the moment the torpedo is released, and is
(obtained from the torpedo aiming camera.

Sighting Error   (This is the angular difference between the
(Director Angle Intended and the Director Angle
(Used and is expressed in degrees ahead or astern of
(the Director Angle Intended.

DATE		3·2·43.		
TIME		1110	1330.	1500.
TARGET (ACTUAL SPEED		R 20	R 20	R 20
(ESTIMATED SPEED		D 20	D 20	D 20
(SPEED SET ON SIGHT		G 20	G 20	G 20
TYPE OF AIRCRAFT		S/F	ALB	ALB.
TYPE OF ATTACK		ALT SUB.	ALT SUB.	ALT SUB.
DROPPING POSITION FROM TARGET RED OR GREEN		GREEN 043°		GREEN 040°
TARGET STEADY OR A/C AWAY OR TOWARDS		A	A.	A.
RESULT OF SHOT				
DIRECTOR ANGLE INTENDED		12°		12°
DIRECTOR ANGLE USED		14°10'		13°30'

Above: A graph from the log book of the late Lieutenant-Commander Douglas Battison showing the results of torpedo-dropping practice carried out during February 1942.

Below and right: The Swordfish was readily convertible to seaplane configuration and in this guise was still capable in the rôle of torpedo bomber. However, in practice it was rarely employed as such.

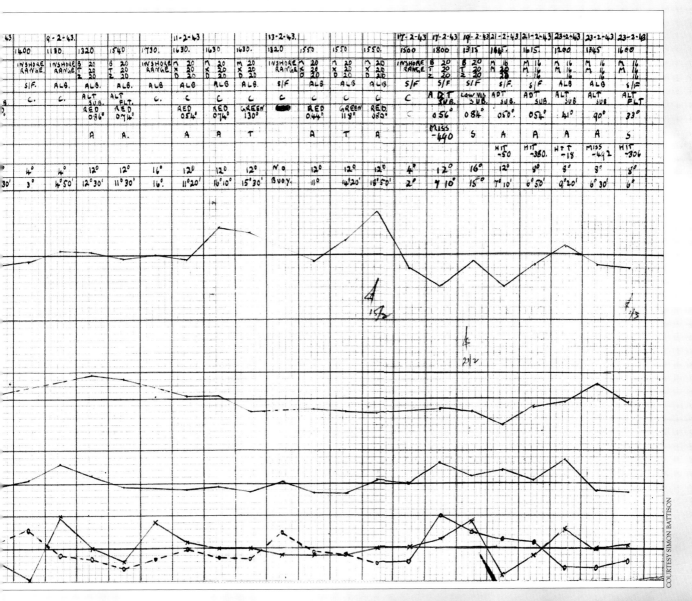

	9·2·43.				11·2·43			13·2·43.				17·2·43	17·2·43	19·2·43	21·2·43	21·2·43	23·2·43	23·2·43	23·2·43
1400	1180.	1320	1540	1750	1630.	1630	1630.	1320	1550	1550	1550.	1500	1800	1315	1645.	1615.	1200	1345	1600
INSHORE RANGE	INSHORE RANGE	B 20 T 20 Z 20	B 20 T 20 Z 20	INSHORE RANGE	M 20 X 20 D 20	M 20 X 20 D 20	M 20 X 20 D 20	INSHORE RANGE	B 20 T 20 Z 20	M 20 X 20 D 20	M 20 X 20 D 20	INSHORE RANGE	B 20 T 20 Z 20	B 20 T 20 Z 20	M 16 M 20 M 28	M 16 M 16 M 16	M 16 M 16 M 16	M 16 M 16 M 16	M 16 M 16 M 16
S/F.	ALB.	ALB.	ALB.	ALB.	ALB.	ALB.	ALB.	S/F	ALB	ALB.	ALB.	S/F	S/F	S/F	S/F	S/F	ALB	ALB	S/F
C.	C.	ALT SUB.	ALT FLT.	C.	C.	C.	C.	C.	RED 0.44°	GREEN 118°	RED 080°	C	A.D.T SUB.	Low Vis. SUB.	A.D.T SUB.	A.D.T SUB.	ALT SUB	ALT SUB	ALT FLT
		RED 084°	RED 074°		RED 084°	RED 074°	GREEN 130°						056°	084°	050°.	054°	41°	90°.	33°
	A.		A.		A	T	A	T	A				MISS –440	S	A	A	A	A	S
														HIT –50	HIT –350.	H T T –18	MISS –492	HIT –306	
4°	4°	12°	12°	16°	12°	12°	12°	N.O.	12°	12°	12°	4°	12°	16°	12°	9°	8°	8°	8°
3°	4°50'	12°30'	11°30'	16°.	11°20'	16°10'	15°30'	BUOY.	11°	4°20'	13°50'	2°	7° 10'	15°0	7°10'	6°50'	9°20'	6°30'	6°

COURTESY SIMON BATTISON

AD HOC COLLECTION

31

Above: Fresh from the Sherburn assembly line, Swordfish Mk II HS158 displays its underwing R/P rails and light stores racks; the metal shielding beneath the wing above the rails can be seen, and the torpedo crutches are also evident, even though by this stage of the war (mid-1942) the torpedo was no longer the aircraft's primary weapon. Notice also the pristine finish of the newly painted flame-damping exhaust pipe and the dark-coloured anti-glare finish of the under surfaces of the upperwing centre-section.

MAIN IMAGE: BAE SYSTEMS

COURTESY PHILIP JARRETT

Left: V4436/'M' of 815 Squadron while based in North Africa on anti-submarine duty in support of British land forces. Flares (outboard) and depth charges are carried underwing.

Below left: Arming a Swordfish with 250-pound bombs.
Below right: Arming an 816 Squadron Swordfish with 60-pound rocket projectiles. Notice the firing leads, yet to be connected.

IN THE AIR

Captain Eric Brown CBE DSC AFC

IN February 1942 I was with a Sea Hurricane squadron, and as our designated carrier was fitted with a catapult we had used a Swordfish at Gosport for catapult launching experience. Each pilot who had not previously flown a Swordfish was given a quick general briefing and an equally hurried circuit in the aircraft before it was loaded on to Gosport's catapult. He was then given two launches with a fellow pilot in the rear cockpit; they changed places and the process was repeated. Later in 1942, I became a deck landing instructor aboard HMS *Argus*. The Swordfish was included in our aircraft stable and was the ideal vehicle with which to impart the rudiments of this difficult art. It was an absurdly simple aeroplane to fly and it was so easy to deck land that it was hard to imagine even first-timers having problems—and they seldom did. The view that its cockpit offered for deck landing was by no means ideal, but the Swordfish had such perfect manners that one could hardly go wrong.

Once the Pegasus had been started, the throttle was opened slowly to 1,000rpm and the engine allowed to warm up until the oil temperature

reached 15°C. Power checks were then performed with one of the matelots lying across the tailplane. The rpm and oil pressure were checked at cruising boost, but with the mixture control at 'Altitude', and then, with mixture control in override position, the throttle was opened fully and take-off boost, static rpm and oil pressure were checked.

Taxying was the essence of simplicity, although the Swordfish had a tendency to weather-cock in high winds and in such conditions it was advisable to have a couple of matelots on the wing tips. For take-off, the elevator was trimmed three degrees nose up, half full port bias was applied to the rudder, the mixture control was set 'Rich' (override), the flaps were raised fully and the oil bypass control was set 'In'. Then the throttle was opened slowly to full power of plus two pounds boost and 2,200rpm. The take-off run was short, any swinging tendency being easily counteracted by the rudder, and climb could be initiated at 70 knots. With the aircraft stabilised in the climb, boost was reduced to plus half a pound. The climb was a long drawn out affair in which, theoretically, one could reach a cruise altitude of 5,000 feet in about ten minutes with a take-off weight of the order of 6,750 pounds.

In cruising flight at 85 knots the Swordfish was very stable about all axes and was very easy to fly on instruments, but harmony of control was somewhat spoiled by over sensitivity of rudder, although this cancelled itself out in aiding the slightly heavy ailerons in endowing this ungainly looking aircraft with an agility totally out of keeping with its appearance and its rate of turn was phenomenal. It has been alleged that the Swordfish was easier to fly than a Tiger Moth, and although this is perhaps an exaggeration in some respects, the aircraft was undeniably viceless and liberties could be taken that

Main image: A Swordfish Mk I of 825 Squadron in the summer of 1940. The observer appears to be photographing the photographer! Opposite: The catapult—technically, an accelerator—at RNAS Gosport, on which Swordfish pilots were given experience before embarking on board HM fleet carriers. The aircraft being hoisted on to the apparatus is one of the few Swordfish that were built specifically as two-seat, dual-control trainers.

although I admit that I never personally confirmed the supposition—that the ideal method of dive bombing was to fly almost immediately above the target and then turn the Swordfish over to the near-vertical, diving until the target could be seen above the upper wing. With a forward CG no real muscle had to be applied in recovery, gentle pressure pulling the Swordfish positively and reasonably rapidly out of the dive, but with the CG aft the elevator called for some physical strength and the response was sluggish. Violent use of the elevator was certainly to be avoided.

There was no warning of a stall other than a gentle sink, which occurred at about 52 knots, and the Swordfish regained flying speed immediately without the least tendency to spin. The rudder bias was somewhat inadequate in a power-off glide, but a normal landing was ridiculously easy. With mixture set 'Rich', carburettor air intake set 'Cold' and brakes checked 'Off', the Swordfish would virtually land itself. This was normally effected without flap at 70 knots on an airfield and at 60 knots on a carrier. Flap—which was just an eight-degree symmetrical drooping of the ailerons by rotation of a knurled wheel set in the trailing edge of the upper mainplane above the pilot's head—was only used for catapulting, its use for a carrier landing not normally being advocated as it encouraged the aircraft to float over the arrester wires.

would have guaranteed any other aircraft stalling and spinning long before. Indeed, this total lack of vice proved the undoing of the occasional pilot, for the Swordfish would forgive most things, but even so ladylike an aeroplane expected its pilot to demonstrate some rudiments of gentlemanliness in handling: no aeroplane may be taken totally for granted.

It was hardly necessary to trim the Swordfish into a dive, and 200 knots could be clocked if the necessary considerable altitude was available, the control forces changing little under these conditions. Dives at torpedo-carrying weight to the maximum permitted engine rpm of 2,860 did not produce undue vibration or flutter. The Swordfish remained stable in all axes, manœuvring precisely in the vertical plane, and it was popularly supposed—

Tutamen et Ultor: 820 Squadron in sunny skies over the South Coast during the last months of peace. Sited against the Swordfish's centre-section struts are the torpedo sights, consisting of a row of bulbs to port and starboard of the centreline. Each space between the lights represented, theoretically, five knots of speed on the part of a moving target vessel, and the apparatus therefore helped the attacking pilot to make the necessary allowances in his aim.

FROM THE COCKPIT

Lieutenant (A) Donald Payne RNVR

SHE was larger than I expected, and sturdier. Her exact measurements were: wingspan 45 feet 6 inches, length 36 feet 1 inch, height 12 feet 10½ inches. She looked, and was to prove, uncomplicated and reliable.

I had been posted to No 9 Advanced Flying Unit at Findo Gask, near Perth, and was clambering into the cockpit of a Swordfish for the very first time. It was reasonably easy to get into, via steps cut in the fuselage, and once you were in it, reasonably roomy and comfortable. Comfortable, that is, when on the ground. Since there was no cockpit canopy and no heating, it was rather less than comfortable when flying in an Arctic blizzard! As soon as I had familiarised myself with the controls, I did a bit of taxying. The Swordfish was easy to taxi; but you had to zigzag, because her large radial engine blocked the view dead ahead.

A couple of days later, I carried out my first Swordfish solo. The Pilot's Notes laid down almost a dozen pre-take-off checks, but in practice we made only four:

T = Trim (roughly central);

T = Throttle nut (tight);

M = Mixture control (rich—override);

F = Fuel (check gauges and switch to Main Only).

The take-off was straightforward, any tendency to swing being countered by a touch of rudder. The Pegasus engine gave plenty of power, and I found myself airborne before I was half way down the runway. She climbed steadily at 70 knots, and cruised comfortably at 85. She seemed amazingly simple to fly: there was no need to bother about things like flaps or undercarriage.

Unless you are a pilot of above-average ability (which I was not), your first solo in a new type of aircraft is usually accompanied by a touch of apprehension, but right from the start I felt at ease in the Swordfish. A fellow pilot described her as 'stalwart, docile, tenacious, responsive, manœuvrable, reliable, slow, sturdy and uncomplicated'. She was all of that.

Below: A factory-fresh Swordfish Mk II. Steps and semi-circular footholds aid entry to the cockpits.

BAE SYSTEMS

AD HOC PUBLICATIONS

BAE SYSTEMS

.Left, upper: Blackburn test pilot H. P. Wilson prepares to take to the air in NS204, the last Swordfish to be built, August 1944. The aircraft is a Mk III: the original observer's cockpit has a streamlined fairing covering the new radar equipment and the observer himself was, accordingly, accommodated further aft than in earlier marks. The cog-like device immediately above the pilot's windscreen is the flap control wheel.

Left, centre and bottom: The pilot's cockpit of the Royal Navy Historic Flight's Swordfish Mk II LS326 (centre) and the main instrument panel in the front cockpit of Mk I W5856 prior to restoration. The Swordfish pilot's cockpit was roomy and in many ways quite comfortable. The panel was well laid out and, to modern eyes, amazingly simple. That of the Mk III was more crowded owing to the need to accommodate instruments associated with night flying and the aircraft's increasingly diverse weaponry—and one or two of the instruments, such as the RATOG jettison switch, were positioned so ingeniously that one needed to be a contortionist in order to reach them! The open cockpits provided the aircrew with a good, uninterrupted view of their surroundings—a big advantage when taking off or landing and when releasing weapons—but flying in winter in Arctic regions was no joke.

Right: Close up to Mk I K5660. The compass pedestals for observer and TAG, the location and trough for the fixed-forward-firing machine gun, details of the pilot's headrest and the configuration of the streamlined flying wires are all clearly seen. Notice, too, the contrast between the aluminium-doped fabric skinning of the aircraft and the darker, 'Cerrux' finish of the metal-clad areas, and the manufacturer's stencilling (which, in service, tended to disappear from the airframe). The torpedo is a dummy.

She was also a wonderfully forgiving aircraft, and in all the time I flew her, I always had the feeling that if I did something wrong she would simply give a sigh of resignation and keep flying straight and level. Landing her posed no problems either—approach at a little over 65 knots, touch down at something under 60—although the big engine cowling did rather restrict the pilot's view and you had either to land off a slight turn or stick your head a bit to port and peer round the windscreen. I enjoyed my first flight in a Swordfish, and it was to prove the start of a long friendship. During the course of the next eighteen months I flew no other type of aircraft.

At Findo Gask we were still under the ægis of the Royal Air Force, who seemed to think that Swordfish pilots needed to be good at navigation, notwithstanding the fact that we usually had an observer in the back to keep us to the straight and narrow. I therefore found myself carrying out a lot of solo map-reading flights to aerodromes such as Donibristle, Crail and Abbotsinch. Flying low and slow in an open-cockpit plane over the beautiful Scottish countryside was a pleasant experience.

We also practised slow flying, formation flying, instrument flying, night flying and ADDLS (Aerodrome Dummy Deck Landings), with the runway marked out like the flight deck of a carrier, and with a batsman to guide us down. We knew that these ADDLS were of particular significance: if we were unable to touch down safely on an eighty-by-eight-hundred-foot runway that was stable, we were unlikely to be able to land safely on an even smaller area that was pitching and rolling. Thus ADDLS, round the clock, were the order of the day.

With some aircraft, pilot and machine develop so close a rapport that they become 'as one'. The Supermarine Spitfire was such an aircraft. The Swordfish was another, although it has to be said that the Swordfish Mk III had shortcomings that sometimes put this rapport to the test. In the first half of the war, most pilots who flew a Swordfish Mk I were enthusiastic about its handling characteristics and performance—apart, obviously, from its speed. It was reliable, adaptable, responsive, amazingly manœuvrable and, quite simply, fun to fly. This was the golden age of the Swordfish—weaving through the flak and the barrage balloons at Taranto, outwitting (and occasionally even shooting down!) Me 109s, C.R.42s and Dewoitines. What an aeroplane! In the second half of the war, however, the Swordfish I was progressively superseded by the Swordfish II and then the III, the last so burdened with weaponry (for example, the 'Oscar' acoustic torpedo) and equipment (such as ASV radar) that its performance deteriorated. Its top speed was reduced from 120 knots to 90 knots, and it lost much of its manœuvrability.

Swordfish were dependable; and, indeed, for an aircraft expected to fly long distances, in all weathers, over the sea, dependability was perhaps the quality that was most important. They were durable, and would fly even when badly damaged. After attacking the German battleship *Bismarck*, one pilot got safely back to HMS *Ark Royal* with 175 bullet and shrapnel holes in his fuselage. They had superb handling characteristics, and their short take-off run, their low landing speed and their stability and responsiveness—even when close to stalling—enabled them to operate from carriers in conditions in which

Below: A Swordfish Mk I photographed in the early months of the war and showing some patchy camouflage on its upper wing. The cable for the dinghy release can be seen on the wing centre-section, flanked by 'prints' painted to indicate safe footfalls for the maintenance crews (these can also be discerned on the port lower mainplane), and the stowage recess for the TAG's hand-held machine gun is clearly in evidence The disposition of the three aircrew can readily be understood from this angle.
Right: Two features of later production Swordfish were the deepened oil cooler on the starboard side of the forward fuselage and the rather more flamboyant generator cooling pipes on top of the nose, as seen here. This aircraft sports some rather dented drag struts, while the fixed 'machine gun' appears to be a dummy.

no other aircraft could have been airborne. Finally, they were adaptable, and this enabled them to carry a diversity of weapons (bombs, depth charges, torpedoes, rockets and mines) and a plethora of equipment (ASV, IFF, homing beacons, etc.) in many different theatres of war.

An incident that brings out both the adaptability of the Swordfish and the spirit in which it was flown is described by Rob Selley, one of the Senior Pilots in 835 Squadron:

'The convoy was returning from Russia to the United Kingdom, when we were spotted late one evening by a German reconnaissance aircraft. The plane, probably a Blohm und Voss, started to shadow the convoy. The weather was bad, with low cloud; it was far too dark even to think of flying off our Wildcats, and we had no night fighters. However, my observer David Newbery and I volunteered to masquerade as a night fighter, and try to drive the shadower away. Armed with an ancient Tommy gun, we took off in our faithful old Swordfish into the night, and were vectored by *Nairana's* Fighter Direction Officer towards the circling plane, which promptly fled! Probably the German pilot picked up the FDO's transmissions, and thought a *bona fide* night fighter was being homed on to him. Anyhow, and for whatever reason, the shadowing aircraft disappeared, and wasn't seen or heard again. David and I returned to the carrier and landed safely, after what must surely be one the most bizarre night-fighter patrols ever flown!'

The Swordfish was also capable of carrying out manoeuvres that otherwise only modern helicopters can realistically perform. R. J. Pickford, a young corvette captain in the Royal Canadian Navy during the war, witnessed the following astonishing feat of airmanship (not to speak of seamanship) involving Swordfish LS320 of 'C' Flight 836 Squadron and the MAC ship and former grain carrier *Empire McCrae* during the passage of westbound convoy HX.274 while negotiating a Force 10 storm: 'We had been assigned as plane-guard when our MAC ship . . . launched a Swordfish to do a patrol. She had no sooner done so than the wind came up with tremendous force—so much so that visibility was greatly reduced by flying scud as the tops were blown off the seas. The "Stringbag" flew low overhead, with the aircrew waving from their cockpits, seemingly quite unconcerned, but I wondered how they could ever be recovered in that howling gale. We were very close to the carrier and could hardly believe what we saw next. The carrier steamed into the wind, as did the Swordfish (which made her ground speed about zero) and the carrier came up under the aircraft from behind and took her on board over the bows! Men leapt on the aircraft as soon as she touched down,

Left: V4374/'2H' and a companion aircraft from 810 Squadron as seen from the observer's cockpit of a third, 1941. A number of early modifications introduced to the Swordfish Mk I's strutwork and rigging are visible here, including the new type of pitot head on the forward outer interplane strut and rigid stays fore-and-aft to help stabilise the flying wires. There appears to be a fresh, unpainted panel of fabric aft of V4374's fuselage roundel and there is evidence of repairs elsewhere on the airframe covering, notably along the rudder hinge line.

COURTESY RICHARD L. WARD

and she was recovered without damage or injury. Incredible!' The pilot of the aircraft was Sub-Lieutenant John Galbraith RNVR.

The rôle of a Swordfish observer was also demanding, and not made easier by the conditions in which he had to work. Jock Bevan, who served in both escort carriers and MAC ships, remembers: 'The two rear cockpits of a Swordfish offered no protection, above shoulder level, against an 80-knot slipstream, rain, snow and occasional hail, while any warmth from the nine cylinders of the radial 'Peggy' engine hardly reached us—only the noise. We had a fold-up, padded seat to sit on, but apart from that there was no "furniture" in the cockpit. There was no chart table, but we were issued with two-foot square laminate boards with attached parallel motions. These were hand- and knee-held, and the chart (Admiralty Hydrographic Department) had to be clipped in place—not an easy task in the slipstream. Literature such as signals information and code books was all part of the juggling act. All of our movable equipment—charts, wind-speed calculator (a sort of white plastic wheel), pencils, etc.—was carried in a flat, green canvas bag about thirty inches square. In the Swordfish III we had to share our cockpit with an ever-increasing amount of technical equipment. Eventually, with the arrival of ASV (which transformed our lives), this equipment became so bulky and so heavy that no room was left for our TAG and his machine gun. The Swordfish became a two-crew plane, with an operating speed of little more than 75 knots.'

The Swordfish was perhaps a more pleasant aircraft to fly than to fly in, though it had, from an observer's point of view, some commendable features. He had, for example, an excellent all-round view, except for dead ahead; he had an excellent and extremely accurate compass; and, because the Swordfish had no cockpit canopy, exit was rapid and straightforward in the event that the aircraft had to ditch. Jock Bevan has a story about this—a story that perhaps brings home something more controversial than the fact that a Swordfish was easy to get out of. He relates it on pages 128–129.

Telegraphist air gunners were 'the élite of the Lower Deck'—young Leading Airmen or Petty Officers who had joined the Royal Navy not to further their careers (it was very rare indeed for a TAG to be commissioned) but to meet an exciting challenge. Over 2,000 TAGs saw service in the war, most of them in Swordfish. They served in 68 carriers and 47 other warships. A total of 445 lost their lives—a high casualty rate—and 297 were decorated. What a record!

A TAG occupied the rearmost of the Swordfish's three cockpits. His principal tasks were to operate the radio and to effect communication either by Morse or Aldis lamp; he also manned the single machine gun (either a Lewis or a gas-operated Vickers .303) that was mounted precariously in his cockpit. He was expected to assist with navigation, and, occasionally, to help swing the propeller as part of the Swordfish's antediluvian starting-up procedure. In capital ships and 'pukka' fleet carriers, TAGs were kept very aware of their Lower Deck status, although this segregation was not universal. In many escort carriers and MAC ships the 'old school' regulations were relaxed, and TAGs were given the recognition they deserved. It was unlucky for them that, just as this was beginning to happen, the three-seat Swordfish Mk I was progressively replaced by the

Preparing the Targets _Lieutenant-Commander Willie Armstrong_ DSM

January 1940 saw my first trip in a 'Stringbag', carrying out air-to-air firing against a towed air target up from RAF Aldergrove over the waters of Lough Neagh. The following month I joined 763 Squadron at RNAS Worthy Down, the unit establishment consisting of six Swordfish and six Albacores. We deployed briefly to Jersey during May, based at the civil airfield at St Helier. We were airborne most days, carrying out W/T exercises. I only ever flew in the Swordfish, the Albacores being reserved for the more senior members of the Squadron. I was responsible for the radio equipment in one aircraft, my duties consisting mainly of ensuring that the main and wet batteries were charged and keeping the Lewis gun clean and the ammunition pans full.

By July that year I was flying in Swordfish with 771 Squadron from RNAS Hatston in the Orkneys. This squadron was a Fleet Requirements Unit, serving the needs of ships in Scapa Flow. Some of the aircraft were fitted with a winch carrying 7,000 feet of steel cable for towing targets, the stability of the 'Stringbag' making it an ideal platform for this task. As well as the standard radio maintenance work, I was now required to prepare all the targets for launching. One other interesting activity was the early-morning Met Flight. We had no observers in the Squadron, so we TAGs took turns for this task. It involved climbing to 10,000 feet and taking a note of the barometer reading every 1,000 feet, sometimes with the aid of an Aldis lamp—a pretty cold experience over Scapa in the winter! On one trip, the aircraft had almost reached its peak altitude when the topmost cylinder of the 'Peggy' exploded . No problem—we had plenty of altitude and just glided back to base. So easy for a Swordfish!

By the end of 1943 I had joined 835 Squadron, embarking in HMS _Nairana_. I made my first flight in a Mk II on 20 December that year and my last in June 1944 when the squadron re-equipped with Mk III. No seats for TAGs! I enjoyed my time as the Senior TAG in the Squadron, especially the thrill of night take-offs and deck landings. The only incident in which I was involved was when Lieutenant-Commander T. T. Miller managed to miss all the wires and clobbered some Hurricanes the other side of the barrier. Luckily, the sturdiness of the 'Stringbag' made sure that none of the crew was injured. It was discovered later that two depth charges rolling about the flight deck were armed, but fortunately there were no big bangs.

As the ratings aircrew of 835 Squadron had the use of their own Ready Room, living conditions on board _Nairana_ were very good. There was one snag: my flying times did not match the ship's routine for meals, so on some occasions my main meal of the day was placed in a heater in the PO's Mess to await my arrival, causing it to dry up, with no hope of replacement. Never mind—we didn't starve!

Below: Three Swordfish engaged on gunnery exercises; the TAG in aircraft 'W', furthest from the camera, is firing at the sleeve target (seen at far left). Part of the winch 'windmill' fitted to the towing aircraft can just be made out, projecting from the cockpit area.

COURTESY PHILIP JARRETT

two-seat Mk III, and their operational opportunities as a result became limited.

What was perhaps a TAG's most telling achievement in the war did not take place in a Swordfish but in a Maryland target-tug. In May 1941 the German warships *Bismarck* and *Prinz Eugen* were known to be moving north up the Norwegian fjords, waiting for a chance to break out undetected into the Atlantic. It was essential the Admiralty be kept informed their movements. For a while, Coastal Command were able to keep the German warships under surveillance, but on 22 May a low front settled over the North Sea and the Norwegian coast became blanketed in cloud and mist. Coastal Command were grounded. At RNAS Hatston in the Orkneys, an experienced Fleet Air Arm pilot and observer volunteered to fly blind to Norway in a second-line Maryland to try to locate the warships, and a TAG, Willie Armstrong, volunteered to go with them to operate their radio. After a hair-raising flight at fifty feet in zero visibility over the North Sea and an equally hair-raising reconnaissance of Bergen and the surrounding fjords, it was established that the enemy warships had sailed. A Maryland had separate cockpits for pilot, navigator and radio operator, and there were no means by which they could make physical contact, so the pilot wrote on a piece of paper, 'Signal C-in-C that the battleship and cruiser have left' and pushed the message through a hole in the fuselage to the TAG. Armstrong tried again and again to contact Coastal Command, to whose

Right: Three Swordfish up from St Merryn in a scene familiar to all trainee aircrew. It can be seen that the aircraft on the left is towing a sleeve target. The Swordfish are from 774 Squadron, an armament training unit where both observers and telegraphist air gunners learnt their trade flying a variety of different second-line and 'retired' types, including Sharks, Rocs and Defiants.

frequency he was tuned, but he could not get through. Realising that he had to improvise, he managed, with no little difficulty, to tune in to the frequency used by the second-line Marylands from Hatston. Target-towing was in full swing when the trainee TAGs, to their amazement, picked up Armstrong's most urgent operational signal, and this was quickly passed up to the C-in-C. The Germans' foray into the Atlantic might well have had a different outcome had this news of their break-out not immediately reached the Admiralty.

It was not often that a TAG's rôle was of such vital significance. Usually his work was unspectacular but essential routine—keeping in radio contact with his carrier or airfield, helping his observer with navigation and making visual contact with aircraft, ships or U-boats. Only very occasionally did he have the opportunity to fire his machine gun—a fact for which pilots and observers were rather thankful, since the gun was wobbly, had no traversing stops and was capable of inflicting as much damage on the Swordfish itself and its occupants as on the enemy. Les Sayer, who was a TAG both before and throughout the war, writes about his experiences on pages 52–54 and 100–101.

From the Observer's Cockpit *Lieutenant (A) Jock Bevan RNVR*

THE honour of waging war in one of the world's last operational biplanes fell to the aircrews of His Majesty's Royal Navy and in particular to those flying the Fairey Swordfish. The Lords of the Admiralty having decided that my place was as one such aircrew, I was able to share in an experience that properly belonged to a bygone era. My own association with the Swordfish came to an end more than sixty years ago and, shamefully, I kept no written record of those days, so that all I have are a few misty memories. Most of my time as an observer in the aircraft was spent in Britain, over the North Atlantic and over the Arctic. The occasional Gibraltar convoy took my squadron to slightly warmer weather, but almost all my flying time seems to have involved trying to keep warm!

When the Swordfish first joined the Fleet Air Arm in the mid-1930s it was designated a TSR (Torpedo-Spotter-Reconnaissance) aircraft. The function of 'spotting' meant observing the existence and movements of an enemy and/or the fall of shells fired by one's own ships. This was, at the

time, the main duty of the observer, who reported his findings by W/T radio (in Morse code) to his home base. Observing the effects of gunfire was virtually impossible from the sea's surface or even from the highest 'fighting top' of a battleship, and so aerial observation played a very important rôle in a fleet engagement. However, the reality of naval warfare in the 1940s seldom involved Nelsonian fleet engagements and it was really difficult to 'observe' a U-boat from the air! The development of radar largely solved this problem, and so the observer's cockpit became filled with ever-increasing electronic equipment and anti-submarine patrols became the primary function of the erstwhile TSR aircraft. These patrols sometimes extended up to 100 miles (up to four hours) in radius and by dead-reckoning we had to find our way home. Thus the observer became the navigator.

Given the length of some of the patrols, bladders were often stretched beyond comfort, but the aircraft designers of those spartan days had not considered it necessary to

include 'pee-tubes' and we were forced to rely upon our own resources for this very basic natural function, the discarded container for a powdered-aluminium sea-marker being an ideal size (about eight inches by six inches) for these purposes.

Communication among the three crew members was never easy. A sort of speaking tube connected face mask and earphones, and one could shout into this before improvements in electromagnetic audio technology made shouting unnecessary. The problem for the most part affected observer/pilot conversation; observer/TAG communications in an open cockpit, tended to be more physical, involving a lot of shoulder-punching and yelling. At about the same time, the introduction of VHF radio and plain-language messaging (in place of Morse code) made the function of the telegraphist redundant. Observers were assumed to be just about capable of loading and operating a single-barrel Lewis gun, and so we bade farewell to our TAGs. A Swordfish crew without the third member, and so lacking his knowledge of the world of naval wireless telegraphy, his valuable liaison with the petty officers' mess deck, his skills with a machine gun and, above all, his

reassuring presence behind us, made a detrimental change to life in the observer's cockpit and the old 'Stringbag' was never the same after the TAG had departed.

Other navigational equipment included the all-important compass, which was attached firmly to the airframe but could be moved from one side to the other of the cockpit. This vital instrument, with its mysteries of 'variation' and 'deviation', had to be understood, and occasionally 'swung' to maintain its accuracy. The gyro compass was for the pilot and not part of our equipment. Parachutes had to be clipped on to our harnesses but were stowed, with all the rest of our gear, along the sides of the cockpit.

The latter days of the Swordfish saw the observer having to share his cockpit with still more technical equipment and the result was the Mk III with its ASV (air-to-surface vessel) radar. Clearly, naval observers welcomed this advance in technology—it transformed our lives, giving us 'super-vision'—but the circuitry in this pre-microchip era was bulky and the huge radome mounted between the undercarriage legs slowed the aircraft's operating speed to an astonishing seventy-five knots.

Eagle Eyes *Commander Stan Laurie*

I loved my time in the old 'Stringbag' and the even older (two-funnelled) *Eagle* from which we operated. Long periods of boredom, occasional excitement and a few scary moments—I wouldn't have missed it!

My first, overwhelming memory as a 'looker' was the amount of 'clobber' with which we clambered on board the aircraft. There was the lap parachute, of course, but also the Bigsworth Board, the cipher machine, the code books, the Very pistol, the Aldis lamp and the course and speed calculator, plus all the operational and weather briefing details, safety signals of the day, etc. Then you plugged in the Gosport tubes to talk to the pilot (if he didn't hear you, then you could reach over his shoulder and shake the stick!), connected your radio jack and attached your 'monkey tail' in case of violent manœuvres.

I suppose one could say that the 'O''s duties were, in order of priority, navigation, communication and observation. Getting back to the ship and knowing where you were was essential, and good wind-finding was the be-all and end-all of this because, although a cruising speed of 90 knots was easy to plot, one was very much affected by changing wind direction and speed. The 'four point' wind-finding method (see page 111) demanded good teamwork between the pilot and the observer and was universally practised.

Communication was by Morse, and situation and other reports had to be sent in cipher. This was easier when one had a TAG, but increasingly, later on, we operated with a Long Range (*sic!*) Tank in the centre cockpit. We operated in radio silence generally, of course, and although the old ship had a rudimentary close-range homing beacon this seemed to be u/s most of the time!

Observation? Well, we were an extra set of eyeballs, although during my last few months in 824 we received ASV Mk I, which cost us a few knots in cruising speed and took up a lot of room in the observer's cockpit. This all seems, and indeed was, so archaic and out-of-date: like our aircraft, it was the result of twenty years at the bottom of the RAF's priority list, until the Admiralty finally achieved control of its own aircraft in 1937.

Below: A Swordfish pilot and observer, parachute packs and Mae Wests donned, await the arming of their Mk I aircraft.
Right: Not the least of the Swordfish observer's talents lay in the field of mathmatics—a good practical knowledge of algebra and geometry was essential, together with the ability to make calculations rapidly and with unfailing accuracy. These diagrams, and those on page 111, give some indication of the sort of workload with which he had to cope in order to ensure that his aircraft was correctly navigated and, by extension, that the effectiveness of his squadron and that of his ship were maximised. These were the days of pencils, rubbers and rulers, with only primitive calculating aids—and all this in a cramped, gale- and rain-swept (and often freezing cold) environment.

COURTESY PHILIP JARRETT

A. TYPICAL BASIC SQUARE SEARCH (right)

v = unit of distance to be flown (the distance depending upon the visibility pertaining)

ETA = (original) estimated time of arrival (i.e., where the aircrew expected to see the objective but failed to do so)

If the aircraft runs out of fuel, the crew will know their position by the wind drift (q.v.) over the time taken on the search.

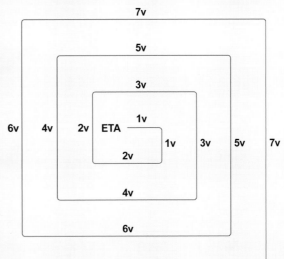

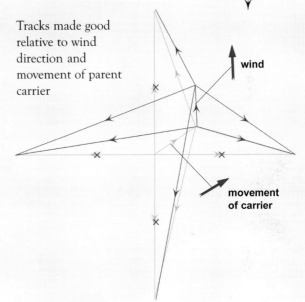

C. SQUARE SEARCH

Tracks made good relative to wind direction and movement of parent carrier

B. SQUARE SEARCH

Tracks made good relative to wind direction

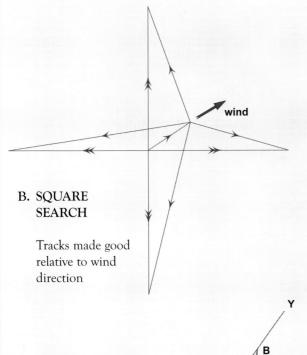

D. CONSTANT RELATIVE BEARING (left)

1. Draw OA to show aircraft carrier's course and speed.
2. Draw OC to show direction of wind.
2. Mark off XY in relative bearing required, with CB and CD = airspeed of aircraft at X and Y in D and B.
3. CB and CD = courses to steer.
4. OB and OD = tracks at ground speed.
5. AB and AD = relative speeds.

To find time to turn (T):

$$T = \frac{P \times S_2}{S_1 + S_2}$$

where P = patrol time in minutes, S_1 = opening ground speed and S_2 = closing ground speed

A Very Secret Topic *Commander Andy Phillip*

My Observer Course, No 60, was undertaken from HMS *Gosling* (RNAS Piarco, Trinidad), and while there we were introduced to a then very secret topic called Anti-Submarine Location (or radar, as we now know it). We were not allowed to keep any notes made during lectures, and flying was carried out in the Grumman Goose. The aircraft were fitted with yagi aerials, electronically connected to a simple cathode-ray tube about seven inches in diameter. Various homing drills were practised, but no tactical use of the equipment was indicated.

The array comprised two aerials—on the Swordfish these were located one on each forward outer wing strut—pointing forward a few degrees off the aircraft's nose-to-tail line. The cathode-ray tube in the observer's (and also frequently the TAG's) cockpit displayed a vertical trace, which, in the event of a contact, would be displaced to right or left of centre, the greatest deflection in the signal showing the direction from which the strongest return was coming. The distance was measured on a scale of zero to 40 miles, and, once a contact has been established, the pilot was instructed to turn the aircraft in order to produce an equal displacement of the signal to the left and right of the centerline, whereupon we could home directly on to the target. The height of operation was about 400 feet, going lower as we neared the target. Ranges were very poor: a coastline might appear at 35 miles, a frigate or destroyer at perhaps five miles and a surfaced submarine at three or four.

On qualifying as an observer I was selected for anti-submarine training and joined HMS *Condor* (RNAS Arbroath) in September 1944 for a month-long course in 796 Squadron, which was equipped with Swordfish fitted with Mk X radar. Thus we now found ourselves using a 'modern' radar set with the new magnetron valve, which enabled the entire scanner to be rotated and thereby give an 'all-round' picture on the screen (still a CRT about ten inches in diameter). The set installed in the Swordfish III was, I believe, a modified version of the H2S carried in the RAF's heavy bombers and used by them for navigation and for improving bombing accuracy.

The set was easy to operate and fairly reliable. We could pick up a coastline at some 45–50 miles, and if we were flying at around 300–400

feet a destroyer could be located at about twenty miles, a submarine with its conning tower showing at five to seven miles and a snorkel-sized object at about two or two and a half. The problem arose when we were operating over a sea state of more than 2 or 3, when the 'clutter' ('noise') around the centre, which could extend across two or three miles, would mask any chance of a small contact being detected. We did have 'clutter control', but this reduced the strength of the outgoing signal and hence the target range. I qualified with a mark of seven and went to RNAS Ronaldsway in the Isle of Man for my Operational Flying Training.

In December, after completing OFT, I parted company with the Swordfish by joining 810 Squadron, where, with my crew of Petty Officer Ron Tyler and Leading Airman Arch Shaw, we flew Barracuda Mk IIIs. The squadron, with eighteen aircraft on establishment, was based at RAF Thorney Island and tasked with anti-submarine patrols down the Channel on a box search starting some eighty miles from Thorney and ranging out as far as 160 miles.

Right: HS315 (left) and HS329—brand new Swordfish recently delivered to 842 Squadron, spring 1943. The port yagi array for the ASV Mk I radar system can clearly be identified, clamped to the outer interplane strut of the photographer's aircraft.

Opposite, top: The 'Pregnant Swordfish'—the Mk III— was characterised by its bulbous radome housing the fully rotatable scanner for the Mk X radar (although redundant, the earlier strut mounted aerials were usually retained). Thus fitted, the Swordfish evolved into a very successful anti-submarine aircraft.

Little Touches CPO (A) Les Sayer MBE DSM

When, before the war, I joined the TAGs' Mess on board HMS *Furious*, I knew immediately that I was in the company of the *élite* of the Lower Deck. My colleagues were all years ahead of me in seniority, in terms not only of their time and experience in the Royal Navy but also of the appointments they held. I had to prove that I was worthy of their company (although, having spent several years in a boarding school, this presented me with few problems!).

The duties of a telegraphist air gunner could vary according to the flight or squadron to which he was attached. A TAG drafted to, for example, a cruiser or a battleship, and flying in a Walrus, might well be the only TAG on board ship, and life was completely different from that in a full squadron where he was one of several. In 811 Squadron, the unit to which I was assigned, his obligations were, however, straightforward: he was concerned with communications, he assisted with radio aids to navigation if required, and he manned the single machine gun in the after cockpit.

The communications equipment we had was reasonably up to date. We could, however far out we were, always reach the ship by Morse. The observer also had a Morse key but I never saw an observer use it; no doubt it was a standby system. Voice, at first in the form of R/T, was a different matter, although the set the pilot used in and near the circuit was not particularly effective. With the introduction of the crystal sets, matters improved, the signals becoming steadier and more reliable. (As an aside, when pilots were

LES SAYER COLLECTION

first trained in 'How to Use the New R/T Equipment', the instructor was none other than Ernest Lush, of 'Oh! For the Wings of a Dove!' fame.) It must be stressed that, for the most part, we operated in R/T silence; the occasions on which we would report events from the air, as it were, were very few indeed. Sometimes, on returning to the carrier but not finding it, and again failing to find it by means of a square search, a bearing would be called for. The TAG would send this request via his Morse key—a request which might or might not be answered by the ship.

There were twelve Swordfish in 811 Squadron in 1938, and after we took off the routine was that we would get into formation, whereupon the ship would call up the Squadron. Each individual aircraft would have to reply with its call-sign. I considered myself to be pretty adept at Morse (and, seventy years later, still am!), but the first time we got airborne I was stunned. I knew that, as they were all 'sparkers', the other TAGs' Morse would be pretty good, but what I heard was not a series of dots and dashes taking a few seconds but, from each aircraft, a 'zipping' sound that lasted less than one! Unbeknown to me, the 'old hands' had each prepared a strip of wood with copper studs tacked into it. When the contacts were wiped, in a single flourish, the aircraft's call-sign was transmitted. Speeds of thirty to forty words a minute—I learned quickly! This system of reporting was hardly 'by the book', to be sure, but it was nevertheless the accepted practice. In the same spirit, if one were flying off on a sortie where medium frequencies were required, one would be expected to leave one's trailing aerial weights on the deck and fly away from them. These little touches, not written down in any handbook, were what identified the *élite* aviators in the prewar Fleet Air Arm.

Other equipment required by the TAG included the collection of plug-in coils required to enable him to change frequencies for transmissions. We had Gosport tubes, of course, but voice communication between either of the officer crewmen and the TAG was rare in my experience. (However, I could generally hear what the pilot said to the observer, and *vice-versa!*) The primitive radar set with which some Swordfish were fitted by 1941 included a little display screen in the TAG's cockpit (the observer had a similar screen); this also was very basic in appearance, comprising merely a horizon line with, on receiving a contact, a 'blip' superimposed. The transmitters and receivers took the form of simple, wing-mounted aerials, and I produced a polar diagram showing the optimum bearings along which the Swordfish might be aligned in order to maximise reception once a contact had been observed. The system, though primitive, worked quite well in practice—we did, after all, pick up a USCG cutter at about sixteen miles en route to the *Bismarck*! Occasionally, with an additional fuel tank in the centre cockpit, the crew would comprise only pilot and either TAG or observer, and then the latter's duties were that much more demanding.

The rearward-mounted gun, either a Lewis or a gas-operated Vickers .303, was not easy to wield—or, rather, the circumstances in which it could be operated effectively rarely

presented themselves. For example, it could not be used in a strafing rôle unless the Swordfish were departing from the scene of an attack on the enemy. Even then, the aircraft was likely to be manœuvring violently and merely keeping one's balance was an achievement! Its main practical function was, in truth, to boost morale. It had an arc of about 90 degrees to port and to starboard, and could be elevated or

Far left: HMS *Furious*, the converted battlecruiser that gave such sterling service throughout two world wars as an aircraft carrier, and on board which Les Sayer served with 811 Squadron during the late 1930s.
Above: 811 Squadron Swordfish on a sortie prewar. Les's 'own' aircraft was coded '610'.
Below: A Swordfish TAG checks his sights. The weapon here is the gas-operated Vickers .303.

depressed to the limits of the TAG's physical capabilities. There were no traversing stops, and so in theory it was possible to damage the structure of the aircraft if the gun was carelessly aimed before being fired. The TAG would normally stand to operate the weapon, a single 'G-string' preventing his falling out in the event of a sudden violent 'jink'. The ammunition was stowed in drums within his cockpit, but what some have identified as 'boxes' for stowing equipment along the port and starboard sides were in fact steps upon which the gunner could stand in order to achieve a more extensive field of fire (particularly greater depression) for the gun. There was a very small, backless and armless seat on which the TAG could sit, secured to the aircraft by means of a single strop. The parachute was stowed in any handy place available.

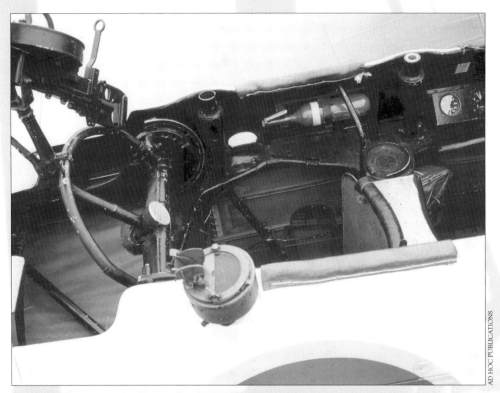

Left: The TAG's 'office', showing the machine gun mounting. Three of the four compass mountings, two for the TAG and two further forward for the observer, are clearly evident. This is the RNHF's LS326: the original TAG's seat was rather less comfortable!

Right, upper: 'A unique and enthralling experience, impossible adequately to describe . . .': grasping for height, a Swordfish departs from HMS *Eagle* somewhere in the Indian Ocean in early 1940.

Right, lower: 'Well done!—but you dare not say so . . .': a Swordfish inches from touch-down. HMS *Eagle* again, with planeguard HMS *Decoy* in attendance.

AD HOC PUBLICATIONS

Swordfish aircrew would sometimes board their aircraft according to a predesignated procedure. Each squadron would have its own routine, and no doubt there were nuances according to the seniority of the TAG involved, and also according to the rank of the officers in the front two cockpits. In some front-line squadrons, TAGs were expected to carry out additional, 'extracurricular' duties such as carrying the observer's chartboard or assisting with the 'wind-up' of the engine prior to take-off.

The commander of the aircraft was generally the pilot, although this was not always so. In one squadron the CO happened to be an observer, and therefore when flying would command whichever aircraft he was in. Similarly, on occasion, no doubt, an observer, not necessarily the Squadron CO, would outrank his pilot.

The TAG took no part in either the landing or take-off procedures in a Swordfish. He strapped himself securely, and might choose to look forward to see what the pilot was doing rather than look aft in his 'normal' attitude, but he had no specific duties during these phases of the sortie. Even so, these aspects of the flight were, for me, always the most exciting, and I always looked forward to them.

There was never, in my experience, any social liaison between the Swordfish TAG and the other aircrew, and to my mind this was a matter of regret. There was some relaxation of these attitudes in one or two squadrons, particularly later in the war, and there is no doubt that the big fleet carriers were more 'pusser' than the smaller escort carriers from the point of view of squadron aircrew, but I was a prewar-trained TAG and therefore tended to be crewed with the more experienced officers—those more in tune with the 'old school'. For example, I never, during the entirety of my career as a TAG in the Navy, entered a wardroom. This was by no means a universal experience: some captains of ships insisted that all TAGs preparatory to a combat sortie take breakfast there. It all depended on the

attitude of those in command. Moreover, during my time in the Navy not once was I briefed or debriefed. For each sortie, I merely clambered into the aircraft, carried out my duties and obeyed my orders, and clambered out when it had been completed. Occasionally the observer would tell me where we were going and what we were going to do, but if he did not I had absolutely no idea. I might also have some liaison with the Senior Observer in the sense that, for example, I might suggest to him that the TAGs under me might benefit from, say, dinghy drill. He would listen, but his was the decision as to whether or not this was carried out, and of course I would never question the decision.

During peacetime, as might be expected, a lot of attention was paid to 'spit and polish', although when war came much of the 'bull' disappeared; there were more important considerations and there simply wasn't the time. Even during the war, however, we TAGs had 'our own' aircraft, and for my part I regarded the rear cockpit of my aircraft as my personal space. I wanted to know who my air mechanic was, and who my airframe engineer was. I got to know them, and this was easier for me than for the other aircrew because they were, like me, 'Lower Deck'. We all had an interest in the appearance of the aircraft, and made sure that it was consistently in good order, clean and neatly turned out.

Facing aft in an open cockpit as one's aircraft leaves a flight deck is a unique and enthralling experience impossible adequately to describe: moving off slowly, the gradual gathering of speed, the change in noise levels as the wheels leave the deck, the gentle dip immediately afterwards, the apparent reluctance of the Swordfish to leave the carrier as it climbs away, grasping the air for height, and then the incredible view of the ship slipping slowly away from beneath one, almost imperceptibly receding . . .

And the landing. A slight tightening of the breath on the approach. Will we catch the first wire? We do. You think, 'Well done!'—but you do not dare to say so to the pilot!

COURTESY MICHAEL GOODWIN

COURTESY PHILIP JARRETT

Simplicity Itself *Lieutenant-Commander (A) Bob Selley VRD RNR*

As far as I am concerned—and I flew nigh on seven hundred hours in one and made two hundred and seven deck landings—the Swordfish can only be described as a simple, sturdy, reliable workhorse. It needed to be, in order to be able to cope with the atrocious weather conditions we flew in, particularly on the Arctic convoys to and from Murmansk. Landing on a carrier which was pitching and tossing and corkscrewing in sixty-knot snowstorms resulted in very heavy landings at times, and it is remarkable that 'prangs' were not more numerous than they were.

It was a delightful aircraft to fly in the summer time and in the warmer climes but perishingly cold in the winter, particularly on the Arctic convoy runs, when, on occasion, aircrews had literally to be lifted out of the cockpits as they were frozen stiff. It seems so ridiculous when one realises that the Mk IV had an enclosed cockpit but was only used for training purposes in Canada. Flying it was simplicity itself. All one had to be bothered with were the control column, the throttle and the rudder bars: there were no retractable undercarriage, no flaps and no variable pitch to worry about. There were no toilet facilities either. If one wanted to 'spend a penny' one had to ask the observer to pass across an empty flame-float tin, into which one duly performed. Unpopularity was guaranteed if one forgot to tell the observer to duck when throwing the tin and its contents over the side! It was alleged that the Swordfish was non-aerobatic, but I have to confess that I did frighten the wits out of my observer Jackie Teasdale by doing a loop in one. He was also none too pleased when I flew through the gap between the Old Man of Hoy and the mainland in the Orkneys.

The Swordfish suffered from the fact that equipment was (or so it seemed) added piecemeal. The original Mk I had a crew of three with a forward-firing gun which was synchronised to fire through the propeller, a telegraphist air gunner with a rear gun and an observer. As extra equipment was added something had to give to reduce the overall weight, and the Mk III ended up with no forward-firing gun, no rear gun and no telegraphist air gunner but with a radio altimeter and extra radar sets causing a large bulge to appear between the oleo legs which housed the scanner, the drag generated by which seriously affected the speed. This resulted in the Mark III being nicknamed the 'Pregnant Swordfish'. All these additions resulted in the top speed being reduced to about ninety knots and the stalling speed to seventy knots when fully loaded with armament. In order to get off the deck and attain flying speed, it was then necessary for Rocket Assisted Take-off Gear to be added. This took the

Above: Swordfish I L9715 from the Torpedo Trials Unit, up from RNAS Gosport in mid-1940 and sporting a decorated propeller spinner. The fixed machine gun on the starboard fuselage is, again, merely a wooden dummy. The aircraft's serial number is hand-written on the outboard underwing stores rack.

form of two rockets positioned behind the main under-carriage oleo legs. The pilot opened up to full throttle and then released the brakes, and when he was abaft the carrier's bridge he pressed the button to activate the RATOG, which gave the necessary 'oomph' to lift the aircraft off the deck.

I can remember only two occasions when the engine packed up on me. The first was no fault of the aircraft. The fitter, when doing his tolerance tests, broke off the end of his feeler gauge and left it in the engine without reporting it. This resulted in my having to force-land in a field the size of a postage stamp on the Mull of Kintyre—which I just about managed, ending up no more than six inches from a deep ditch. Despite denuding the aircraft of all extraneous items to reduce weight, we had to wait three weeks before there was sufficient wind to enable the Swordfish to take off again without hitting the hedge. I was awarded a 'green ink' commendation for this episode.

The other occasion was when we were escorting a convoy from Murmansk back to the United Kingdom. It was on a particularly nasty, stormy, pitch-black night, with a sixty-knot snowstorm howling over the convoy. The Captain ordered an anti-U-boat patrol to sweep ten miles ahead of the convoy. The Squadron CO, Lieutenant-Commander Val Jones, tried to explain to him that flying in those conditions was near suicidal and that no U-boat could exist on the surface in such conditions. Nevertheless, ignoring this advice, the Captain ordered the patrol to be flown. Val refused to send any of his crews but said that he would go if his pilot (me) would take him. I shall never forget the look of anger and despair on Val's face when he told me what had happened. He told me that if I didn't want to go he would tell the Captain that he was refusing to obey his order and would take the court martial himself. What could I say?

We took off and struggled to get to our position ten miles ahead of the convoy. After twenty minutes or so flying flat out into wind, the engine cut out. My immediate reaction was to jettison all my armament to lighten the aircraft and give us more gliding time. When the flares lit up, the convoy was still beneath us: we had hardly made any progress in the howling wind. Somehow I managed to restart the engine as the propeller had continued to windmill, and after several attempts we eventually managed to land back on board the carrier.

When we went to the bridge to report to the Captain, expecting praise for a brilliant piece of airmanship I was torn off a strip for illuminating the convoy with my jettisoned flares. The engine failure was never satisfactorily explained, but it was surmised that the carburettor had frozen up but had defrosted when we lost height, enabling me to restart the engine.

Too Clever By Half *Lieutenant Bruce Vibert*

After almost two years of operational work, the time came for 842 Squadron to disband. Our orders were to leave Thorney Island individually, as one's aircraft became ready, and fly to Maydown in Northern Ireland. With an observer and a TAG in the back, I set off on 15 January 1945, a fine but cold day.

Approaching RAF Hawarden, a grass airfield, I decided to land there and refuel. I saw no other aircraft about, and it therefore seemed to present a good opportunity for 'forced-landing' practice—an opportunity rarely offered to those who spent most of their time over water. Unwisely, however, I did not declare my intentions to those aft. At around 1,200 feet I closed the throttle, fully, and carried out control ring. All this I was about to do myself.

The ring is positioned well below the level of the cockpit coaming, and in order that I could reach it from outside the cockpit I threaded my handkerchief through it and 'cracked' the throttle, leaving the switches on. I then inserted the starting handle and began to wind. Having, finally, reached the required revs I abandoned the handle and, with one foot in a foot port, reached up over the coaming to find the handkerchief and pull. The engine started at once—and so did the aircraft, at a brisk speed and, like my crew, heading for the control tower.

Removing my foot from its port I hoisted myself athwart the coaming to reach the brake. The machine was now bouncing over the grass with the control column jumping about and evading my grasp. Glancing ahead, I saw my crew looking back and running—not an easy task considering a dead-stick landing. When I opened the throttle for taxying in, however, the barely turning propeller came to a stop, and while contemplating my next move I noticed that the two in the back had climbed out, taking their 'chutes and setting off in the direction of the control tower.

The correct drill for starting the engine first calls for 'wheels chocked' and brake 'on', which latter, in the case of the Swordfish, was located on the control column; these two requirements I was to overlook. Most people, on first seeing a Swordfish started, are understandably astonished. Two men are required, and it takes about a minute to wind the starting handle and reach sufficient revs before one calls out 'Contact!' and the pilot pulls the inertia starter clutch what they were carrying. They saw a machine closing on them fast, with a pair of legs sticking out of the cockpit, horizontally. This must also have been an unusual sight for those in the control tower.

Finally realising that serious trouble loomed, I must have regained my wits. Reasoning that turning off the switches would mean more winding later, I closed the throttle fully. That worked, and I was able to resume the correct pilot's position. Taxying past my errant crew without giving them a glance, I shut down next to the control tower.

Not a word of this episode was later mentioned, not even by those who were in the tower. The rest of the trip to Maydown was conducted in utter silence—even when the three of us parted company there to go on our separate ways for whatever the Service had to offer. To my relief, our paths have not crossed since . . .

Relishing the Experience *Commander Simon Askins*

My claim to being a Swordfish pilot is almost fraudulent as, unlike most of the other contributors to this book, I have no gallant wartime experience; instead, I merely came to flying the aircraft, some thirty years after World War II, almost by accident. I was at the time the Station Air Engineering Officer at RNAS Yeovilton, where the Royal Navy Historic Flight was based, and a pilot was required for the 1984 display season. At the time I probably had more propeller hours than most other pilots at the base, who were mostly helicopter crews and Sea Harrier pilots. I had for many years flown and instructed on Chipmunks and Tiger Moths, and I was still current on the Chipmunk, which I flew for glider towing.

The aircraft, LS326, was in 1984 the only airworthy and flying Swordfish in the world, and pilots were selected who would respect its venerability and not indulge in violent manœuvres (although I have talked to several 'old and bold' who claim to have looped and rolled other Swordfish when they, and their aircraft, were much younger!). By 2007 there were three airworthy Swordfish aircraft in Britain, plus a further example, the former HS469, at the Canadian Forces base at Shearwater, Nova Scotia.

The check-out was conducted by having a qualified pilot standing in the rear cockpit and passing encouraging remarks. The trickiest bit was getting the aircraft to start first time, as a mis-start would earn a muted curse from the unfortunate groundcrewman who had just put his all into hand-cranking the flywheel up to speed prior to the pilot engaging the clutch to crank the engine and putting the ignition switches 'on' at the right moment.

There was little that was unique about the Swordfish as it was just a larger and heavier version of a line of biplanes from the 1930s—although it was clearly no fighter aircraft adapted for ground attack! The Swordfish was built as a torpedo/spotter aircraft, and had the strength to carry an 18-inch, 1,610-pound torpedo, and be subjected to evasive manœuvres as it descended to attack height from altitude. It was also very unsophisticated, with basic lever-and-wire controls from stick to surfaces, and a fuel tank ahead of the pilot with a float similar to that of the Tiger Moth to determine fuel state.

The Pegasus Mk 30 was a nine-cylinder radial engine driving a three blade, fixed-pitch propeller, and so there were no worries about feathering in case of failure. The engine would just run . . . or not. When away from base it was a wise precaution to remove the ignition plug from the bottom cylinder to avoid its becoming oiled up overnight. The pilot was allowed to assist in turning over the engine before the first start of the day. This meant pushing the propeller through about one quarter turn at a time and then repeating the procedure until it had completed two or three revolutions.

The throttle response was good, with full power readily available when the pilot opened the throttle from half power or selected the cruise setting. The rate of climb was gentlemanly rather than exciting, the aircraft achieving 10,000 feet in fifteen to twenty minutes depending on the take-off weight. Handling the aircraft for display flying was straightforward. The take-off at around a middle weight of 6,000 pounds was not dissimilar to that for a Sea Prince, and the aircraft reached an unstick speed of around 75 knots after a relatively short run. Flaps were not used for a

Below: The Royal Navy Historic Flight's Swordfish. There are some concessions to modernity, notably in the aircraft's communications equipment and the crew's garb!

COURTESY PHILIP JARRETT

shore take-offs but were deployed for landing, mainly to achieve a lower landing speed and to save wear on the tyres. Stalling held no problems for the pilot and was straight, with little tendency for the wing to drop. The leading-edge slots would pop open a few knots before the stall and give more warning than the buffet that things were getting a bit slow.

For the actual displays, one had to bear in mind that the power-to-weight ratio was much less than for more modern types, be they prop or jet, and care was needed. The display pattern usually consisted of a run up and down the 'crowd line' with rolls of up to thirty degrees' bank either way to show a partial top or bottom view of the aircraft, plus of

course the torpedo (which was only a lightweight dummy). For the final run, we lowered a weighted White Ensign below the aircraft and had the one or two crew members in the rear cockpit standing and saluting the crowd.

I was pleased to take the aircraft to a number of shows, some involving landing and others merely fly-bys. On one of the latter, I remember going to the Royal Marines base at Lympstone in Devon with my son Stephen as one of those saluting in the rear cockpit—which pleased him greatly as a he was a junior RM officer. When landing or staying overnight, I usually had my very knowledgeable and experienced Chief Aircraft Fitter, Ron Gourley, with me to ensure that we did not become stranded on account of a minor snag.

COURTESY SIMON ASKINS

Above: The RNHF Swordfish LS326 has been seen in a number of different colour schemes, not all of them entirely authentic. It bore the code '5A' for a period, commemorating the lead aircraft of those from HMS *Ark Royal* that delivered the attack on the German battleship *Bismarck* in May 1941.

Left: For a period in the 1980s LS326 carried 'invasion stripes' to commemorate the 'D-Day' landings in June 1944. In this photograph, the writer of this article, Commander Simon Askins, is standing on the right; the other gentlemen are CPOs 'Happy' Day (left) and Ron Gourley.

Right, lower: Return to sea: LS326, on a visit to HMS *Hermes*, prepares for take-off with plenty of human muscle in close attendance.

COURTESY PHILIP JARRETT

COURTESY PHILIP JARRETT

Right, upper: After the war, and before being transferred to the RNHF, LS326 had been purchased and operated by Fairey Aviation with the civil registration G-AJVH. It was handsomely finished in a striking silver and blue colour scheme.

Right, lower: The aircraft as it first appeared when flown by the RNHF in the early 1960s. By the late 1980s LS326 was finished in a scheme very close to that which it actually carried during wartime service when serving with 836 Squadron in board MV *Empire MacCallum*.

At Biggin Hill in May 1984 we were on the ground and were attracting the usual crowd of the curious when one lady stepped forward to tell us that she had been a fabric worker at Blackburn (Brough) on the original production line during the war. She duly admired the stitching and the general workmanship on the mainplanes and pronounced it 'up to standard'! Many ex-RN aircrew and groundcrew made themselves known to us as well, only too keen to tell us of their own experiences. At RNAS Culdrose, landing in a very heavy rain shower, I discovered one problem about which I had not been warned: when taxying in rain, the water would pour off the upper mainplane into the pilot's lap, leading to an undignified wet crotch and general

embarrassment when disembarking! My final display was at the SBAC event at Farnborough that year, demonstrating as one of the 'veterans' that usually end the show.

All these shows were free of incident—thank goodness! I suspect that, as the Station AEO, I would have been the target of some ribbing had anything untoward occurred. I genuinely relished the experience of flying the Swordfish, albeit for only about twenty hours. I felt that, afterwards, I had a better understanding of how demanding some of the wartime exploits must have been, and I take my hat off to those involved in the Taranto attack, the *Bismarck* sinking, the 'Channel Dash', the Atlantic and Russian convoys and all the other operations in which the aircraft was involved.

COURTESY BRIAN LOWE

INTO BATTLE

Lieutenant (A) Donald Payne RNVR

'WHY do you want to fly a Swordfish?' In January 1944, after a year of flying training, first at Sealand near Liverpool and then at Kingston in Ontario, I was awarded my wings. I was also, I hoped, about to be awarded a commission. I was standing in front of the usual top-brass Selection Board, and thought I was probably doing all right, when suddenly one of them asked the question—the Swordfish being the aircraft for which I had stated a preference. I was unsure what to say. Truth to tell, one of my reasons for asking to fly Swordfish was that I reckoned that they would be safer and easier to fly than any of the other torpedo-bomber-reconnaissance aircraft the Fleet Air Arm had to offer. However, I doubted whether this answer would convince the Board that I had the officer-like qualities that they were seeking. I decided to compromise. 'Because,' I said, 'I think Swordfish are the best planes the Air Arm has got.' I did not realise what a

good answer this was: although I had no idea of this at the time, two of the Board were Swordfish pilots. I got my commission—and a couple of weeks later I got my Swordfish.

After a month at Findo Gask, I was posted to 766 Squadron, based at Inskip, near Blackpool. Up to this point, my flying had been controlled by the Royal Air Force; from now on it would be controlled by the Navy.

Inskip gave me my first experience of life in a naval air squadron, albeit a second-line (non-operational) one. About a dozen pilots, a dozen observers and a dozen telegraphist air gunners were brought together, and, as well as being taught the niceties of anti-U-boat warfare, we were told to sort ourselves out, by mutual agreement, into crews. The individual members of a Swordfish crew had, on an almost daily basis, to put their lives in one another's hands, and it was therefore important that they had

COURTESY PHILIP JARRETT

Left: 820 Squadron's CO, Lieutenant-Commander A. C. G. Ermen, briefs some of his aircrew on board HMS *Ark Royal* in 1939. The photograph provides a good illustration of Royal Navy flying clothing of the period. A minor airframe detail concerns the formation lights clamped to the Swordfish's after outboard interplane struts, the starboard item being clearly visible here: when war came they were rapidly dispensed with. Opposite: A Swordfish Mk II of 766 Squadron (otherwise known as No 1 Naval Operational Training Unit), to which the writer was posted in early 1944. The aircraft, its paint finish somewhat weatherbeaten, is armed with a full suite of rocket projectiles, and it is noticeable that the horizontal sighting bars, generally evident on all operational Swordfish in their customary position forward of the wing centre-section struts, are absent in this instance.

faith in one another's ability. It was also a great help if they got on well. If you are low on fuel, in the middle of the Atlantic, and cannot find the convoy, that is not the time even to think of personal recrimination.

After flying with several observers, I went up one afternoon with Reggie Holland, who, I learned later, had been the Public Schools Fencing (Sabre) champion. He seemed very capable, and I reckoned that we would get on all right. After two or three flights, I asked him, jokingly, (a) if he could swim (this not being one of my accomplishments) and (b) if he understood that an observer's first duty on ditching was to rescue his pilot (!). When I got a couple of nods, we agreed tentatively to team up. Over the next few weeks, I flew the courses he gave me with particular care, and did my best to ensure that my landings were neither bouncy nor heavy, while he—he told me later—took extra care with his D/R plot, his ASV readings and his wind-finding.

Eventually, he suggested that we make our provisional arrangement a permanent one. I made a point of reminding him that I was a pilot of only average ability, and that several pilots in our group had more experience, and more hours in their log books. (Quite a few of us had come to Inskip not direct from Advanced Flying School but via a second-line squadron.) However, Reggie took the view that a pilot who was trying to make it first time into an operational squadron was a better bet than one who was, so to speak, having a second bite at the cherry. Sadly, this was to prove prophetic, for in the next couple of months we lost two crews, one disappearing during a night navigation exercise over the Irish Sea and the other going over the side during deck-landing trials. Both aircraft were being flown by pilots who has come from a second-line squadron.

Teaming up with a telegraphist air gunner was more of a problem. Pilots and observers, in those days, were officers; TAGs were 'Lower Deck', either petty officers or leading airmen. At the time, I thought this wrong; sixty-five years later, I still think it wrong. We all flew in the same aircraft. We were chilled by the same winds, bludgeoned by the same seas, fired at by the same 'ack-ack'. Why should TAGs have been denied officer status? 'This segregation,' one of our observers has remarked, 'was a great pity. The enforced class distinction made frank communication between the aircrew less easy.' One of our TAGs, Willie Armstrong, gives his opinion: 'Personally, I accepted the difference between rating and officer aircrew because I was

Regular Navy, but I think the other TAGs, who were Hostilities Only, thought there should have been a closer working arrangement, similar to that enjoyed in the RAF.' Reggie and I eventually teamed up with Leading Airman Burkinshaw. However, since we slept, ate, worked and spent our leisure time in different parts of the ship or airfield, and were not supposed to fraternise when we went ashore in uniform, we never really got to know him, nor he us. The only time we met was when we clambered into the cockpits of our Swordfish. My recollection is that he was young, quiet, pleasant and efficient. During training, he did whatever was asked of him with a minimum of fuss, and I am sure he would have done the same on operations.

In 1943 the rôle of the Swordfish was beginning to change: torpedo strikes against enemy shipping were giving way to protecting convoys against U-boats. To cope with this, the Swordfish Mks I and II were gradually being replaced by the Mk III. In the latter, the lower mainframe was strengthened to carry depth charges or rocket projectiles, an ASV (air-to-surface-vessel) Mk 10 radar was housed in a dome beneath the fuselage, and the rear cockpits

were modified to carry not both observer and TAG but an observer only, together with his complex new equipment—ASV screen, homing beacon, IFF etc. Thus, for many TAGs, the advent of the Swordfish III marked if not the end of the road, then at least the beginning of the end of the road.

* * *

Our training at Inskip was designed to prepare us for the rôle we were about to play in the war against the U-boats. We flew on navigation exercises, practised depth-charge dropping and rocket-firing, carried out bad-weather, formation and night flying and, whenever we had a spare moment, continued with our ADDLS. It was all pretty intensive—usually two or three flights a day.

The navigation exercises were often at night, over the Irish Sea. These, of course involved instrument flying, with my having to follow accurately the courses and airspeeds that Reggie gave me. They also sometimes involved 'finding a wind'. Because of the slow cruising speed of the Swordfish, navigation depended to an unusual degree on making the right allowance for the wind. Every time a Swordfish took off from a carrier, the observer had with him the latest Met report. However, weather in the Atlantic alters swiftly. Met reports were sometimes inaccurate,

and on these occasions a Swordfish crew needed to be able to find the speed and direction of the wind themselves. The pilot would jettison a marker—an aluminium dust marker in a smooth sea, a smoke float in a rough sea or a flame float at night. He would then carry out a 'rate one turn' and fly away from the marker on a prearranged course for one minute. Next, he would perform another 'rate one turn' and fly on a reciprocal course for another minute. If there was no wind, he would then find himself back immediately above the marker. If there *was* wind, it would have blown the aircraft off course, and by taking a couple of bearings, half a minute apart, on the marker, the observer would be able to delineate on his chart board a triangle, from which he could calculate the strength and direction of the wind. This may sound a bit of rigmarole, but when flying long distances over a featureless sea, often with radio silence in force, it was imperative that the Swordfish crew knew exactly where they were. Heaven knows how many aircrew owe their lives to their being able accurately to 'find a wind'.

Our depth-charge dropping was carried out off Heysham at the entrance to Morecambe Bay. We did our best to straddle a towed target, ideally placing three depth charges in front of it and one behind, from a height of about fifty feet. If we came in much lower than this when doing the real thing, we would be in danger of blowing off the Swordfish's tail! Photographic evidence later revealed our prowess (or lack of it) and enabled us to see where we went wrong. This was fun by day, but it was not so much fun by night, when it was not unheard of for pilots to misjudge their height and fly straight into the sea.

R/P firing was also carried out off Heysham This, again, was fun by day, but involved quite complicated manoeuvring by night. Reggie would use his ASV to home me on to the target. At a range of about a mile, I would climb to 1,000 feet, then go into a shallow dive, and at 500 feet release parachute flares.

Crewed only by the pilot, a Swordfish of 810 Squadron takes the wire on board HMS *Illustrious*, *circa* 1942. Deck handlers are sprinting forward to assist with moving the aircraft once it has come to a halt. The aircraft's call-sign appears to have been applied to a replacement panel of fabric.

Left and below: Landing an aircraft, however well adapted, on an acre or so of pitching and rolling flight deck (and that refers to the deck of a big *fleet* carrier) has always been a challenge, and accidents have, unsurprisingly, been frequent. The identity of the Swordfish depicted here has not been established beyond doubt, but the angle of approach and the broken starboard undercarriage unit suggests a brush with the round-down of the carrier, HMS *Glorious*, in 1939 or 1940.

Right: The aircraft carrier *Argus*, on which the author conducted his first deck-landing practice. The 'smudge' at left is smoke rising from her boilers. Four-inch HA/LA guns are carried at the stern. This elderly, 14,500-ton converted passenger liner—the prototype flush-decked aircraft carrier, dating from World War I—performed valiant service through the second world conflict, not only in the training rôle but also, on occasion, in the thick of the action, as in the Mediterranean in 1941–42 when she was a component of Force 'H' and also supported the Allied landings during Operation 'Torch'. She survived until 1947, when she was broken up.

These, it was hoped, would illuminate the target. I would then go into a 15-degree dive and fire my rockets, aiming a little short of the target (obviously, everything over the target was useless, whereas anything short of it at least had a chance of running underwater and achieving a hit). Most of us got fair results, but we all had the feeling that in mid-Atlantic, with high winds, low cloud, poor visibility and a U-boat firing at us, things would not be quite so easy.

Apart from the intensive flying, I particularly remember two things about our time at Inskip. The first was when we met our sparring partners from the base at Heysham. They took us down in their submarine, and we took them up in our Swordfish. We ended up not only full of gin and beer, but full of admiration for one another, and vowing that nothing would ever induce us to exchange our lot for theirs. I also enjoyed the camaraderie of life in a squadron. We knew, however, that we had one last hurdle to get over before we could join a 'proper' (that is, an operational) squadron. We had to be able to land on a carrier.

We conducted our deck-landing training on HMS *Argus*, a former Italian passenger liner converted in 1918 to a flush-deck carrier—one without the usual island superstructure. She was not much to look at. One observer reported her as a 'wreck floating bottom up', and another as 'a small dismasted hulk on fire aft'. (She looked as though she was on fire aft because she had no funnel, and the smoke from her

engines streamed out behind her through ducts at her stern.) She had been used for deck-landing trials in the 1920s, in some years suffering thirty accidents in every hundred landings, a statistic of which, fortunately, we were not aware at the time. She spent much of 1943 and 1944 steaming up and down the Clyde, with Ailsa Craig either dead ahead or dead astern and aspiring operational sub-lieutenants (A) queuing up to land on her. The Clyde was a good place for deck-landing training: it was reasonably safe from attack by U-boats or bombers, was sheltered from the high winds and heavy seas of the Atlantic by Kintyre and Arran, and was close to a number of Fleet Air Arm aerodromes, including Ayr, Machrihanish and Abbotsinch.

For many of us, our week on board *Argus* was our first experience of life in a warship—the tedium of the aircrew ready-room, the hierarchy of the wardroom, and the wonderful sense of belonging, albeit only temporarily, to a ship's company. However, our programme was so intensive that we had little time to think of anything except flying. While at sea we practised bomb and rocket attacks on towed targets, machine-gun attacks on a dust marker, night flying, formation flying, compass swinging, photographic reconnaissance and, of course, deck landings—about twenty by day and ten by night.

The three basic rules for landing on a carrier are: (a) concentrate (b) obey the batsman and (c) complete the landing as soon as you can. During training, speed was not an issue. However, on operations,

COURTESY JOHN ROBERTS

whenever a carrier landed-on her aircraft, she had to steer directly into the wind. This jeopardised her position relative to other ships, and made her vulnerable. Some pilots favoured landing off a sharp turn. This saved time, and was liked by the ship's Captain and Commander (Flying), but it left little room for pilot error, or for him to be able to cope with last-moment gyrations by the carrier. I favoured a longer and straighter approach, a preference that later saved my life. Whatever type of landing a pilot attempted, however, he was in the hands of the batsman.

The task of the batsman—more correctly, the Deck Landing Control Officer, or DLCO—was to help carrier-borne aircraft to land safely. He had a pair of

Above: A Swordfish Mk I about to cross the round-down of one of the fleet carriers, *circa* 1938. The aircraft's arrester hook has not been deployed: the use of this aid was eschewed by many prewar pilots, who held that the device was for those of a nervous disposition only.

Below: Safely down, nevertheless. These views give a good indication of the rise and fall of the surface of the flight deck aft, a design feature intended to assist the absorption of a landing.

'bats', rather like big-headed squash racquets, with which he signalled his instructions to the pilot. These bats were illuminated at night and when visibility was poor. When an aircraft was ready to land, the batsman would take up his position on a small platform on the carrier's port quarter. From here he would watch the plane as it approached the

Above: A Swordfish, its arrester hook trailing, comes in to land on board the escort carrier HMS *Tracker*. The batsman is giving the 'steady' signal; in seconds, this will be changed to 'cut', indicating to the pilot that he should switch off his engine, whereupon the pilot will drop the last few feet under forward momentum (and gravity) only. A second aircraft is following, its pilot hoping fervently that his predecessor will have an incident-free touch-down.

flight deck, and give the pilot visual signals (which were the same for all types of aircraft).

It was essential that pilots obey the batsman. This was particularly important at night and in heavy seas, when the stern of a carrier might be rising and falling thirty feet or more and all a pilot could see was two lines of landing lights dimly outlining a heaving flight deck. In such conditions a batsman was better able than a pilot to judge whether an approach was likely to result in a safe landing. Without the help of batsmen, many of the Swordfish's greatest achievements—crippling the *Bismarck*, protecting our Atlantic and Russian convoys—would not have been possible; these men were a vital if seldom-remembered aspect of the Swordfish story. Luckily for us, we had an excellent batsman on board *Argus*.

A first deck-landing is a little like a first solo—a mix of excitement and apprehension. It was, I remember, a dull, slightly misty day, with a quiet sea (that was good), but not much wind (that was *not* so good). From 300 feet the flight deck looked depressingly small and, like most novice pilots, I initially approached too low, not being used to the landing area moving away from me at something like twelve knots. 'Bats' signalled me 'higher'. I obeyed him, my

LES SAYER COLLECTION

COURTESY BILL PENLINGTON/BRUCE VIBERT

COURTESY BILL PENLINGTON/BRUCE VIBERT

Above: Training brought with it the inevitable mishaps—some of them on land and some of them no fault of the Swordfish crews. Here a Blackburn Skua target-tug has had a serious disagreement with a Mk II, rather spoiling the flying capabilities of both aircraft.

Left, upper and lower: An errant deck landing involving a Swordfish of 842 Squadron, rather too far to starboard and clipping *Fencer*'s island. The aircraft slewed before coming to a halt and, happily, the crew were unhurt. Despite the camera-shake in the first picture—for which the photographer can be entirely forgiven considering the circumstances—the censor has assiduously erased the still hush-hush strut-mounted ASV array.

Opposite, top: A Swordfish safely down on board the carrier HMS *Argus* during deck-landing practice. The vital 'batsman' is positioned in front of his screen at left. The immediate effect when the arrester cable tensioned was the raising of the aircraft's tail.

Opposite, bottom: The Swordfish occasionally spread its undercarriage legs a little too violently when landing-on. There was not much that could be to prevent it from 'doing the splits' when it was employed as a torpedo bomber, but later in the war, when weapons loads were generally confined to the wings, it proved possible to rig a restraining cable connecting the two main wheel struts. The device can be made out in this view of an 836 Squadron Mk III.

Swordfish instantly obeyed me, and I managed a very reasonable landing, catching the second out of the six arrester wires. Not everyone was so lucky. Most of us, at the end of the week, were judged sufficiently competent to be posted to an operational squadron, but for a couple of unfortunates it was back to second-line flying.

* * *

Reggie and I were posted to 836 Squadron, which was based at Maydown, near Londonderry. 836— discussed in detail by John Shoebridge on pages 118–123—was the largest squadron in the Fleet Air Arm: it had been formed in March 1942 with six Swordfish, but by the time it was disbanded in July 1945 it could boast 92, all operational and all engaged in the vital Battle of the Atlantic. This resulted in a little-known record: Swordfish were the only aircraft of any of the combatants in World War II to be operational in greater numbers on the last day of war than on the first. There were 140 operational Swordfish in September 1939 and 198 in May 1945—hence the aircraft's epithet 'Obsolescent but never obsolete'.

Jeopardising the Linear Succession *Sub-Lieutenant (A) Stanley Brand* RNVR

The DLCO (Deck Landing Control Officer) was informally referred to as 'Bats', a name not derived from his mental condition but from the distinctive tools of his trade, which were a pair of luminescent, handled discs like ping-pong bats. These were held in outstretched arms—and, with another disc fastened to the chest, the arm position was made obvious, even in half-light conditions—to give orders to a pilot as to how to adjust his speed and aircraft attitude on the approach to land on the ship, then when to cut the engine or to open up and go round again. To convey this information during the operation of landing, Bats stood on a five foot by five platform projecting from the deck on the port side, level with the first arrester wire, surrounded with rope nets stretched horizontally into which he could—and frequently did—hurl himself if danger threatened. Originally an ungrateful Admiralty provided nets with six-inch square spaces, into which Bats were hesitant to jump, firstly because although the rope was stout enough, it gave too good a view of the unwelcoming ocean thirty feet below, and secondly because of the tendency for feet to go through the mesh but not in adjacent squares, without reducing Bats' velocity, until the rope met his private parts, causing some anguish and jeopardising the linear succession of future Bats. Lining the frames with a small mesh net was not good enough, and so a mattress was found to serve two purposes, the second being that whenever we caught a glimpse of the sun, we knew where to find Bats.

Bats' signals were an order, and failure to comply brought down the wrath of My Lords of the Admiralty of a severity reserved for the disobedient, since disobedience undermined Good Order And Naval Discipline thus challenging the Authority of My Lords themselves. Fortunately, keel-hauling and flogging had gone out of fashion and there was nowhere on a MAC ship for a yardarm to hang people because it would be a hazard to aviators. To make sure that the culprit was branded for all to see, short of applying a red-hot iron, an entry was made IN RED INK in the offender's Flying Log Book so that it would be taken into consideration in the unlikely event of the subject of promotion of the criminal ever being raised. This was a procedure to which the Navy strictly adhered, even on one occasion where, in the opinion of a Captain RN, the DLCO had made a stupid mistake and the pilot had disobeyed it and had had to take risky action to save his aircraft and himself. This, however, was on a straight-laced RN ship and it was unlikely to be carried out in the realistic atmosphere of a MAC ship, where a mixture of Merchant Navy, RN, RNR, RNVR, RNZVR and RCN officers would no doubt pass vociferous comment.

Often the best DLCOs were pilots of long flying experience who had developed a nervous disposition because of stress caused by over-exposure to dangerous activity without relief. Unlike the RAF, which gave seven days' leave every eight weeks to operational aircrew and also a second-line posting after thirty operational flights, the Fleet Air Arm had insufficient manpower, or willpower, to adopt a similar policy. If aircrew were given this improvement to conditions of service, it would also have to apply to submariners, to corvette and frigate crews and, logically, to all front-line personnel facing appalling

Left: Deck landing practice for Swordfish pilots on board an escort carrier in the Clyde; Ailsa Craig is in the mist on the horizon. The luminescent 'bats' being brandished by the DLCO are very noticeable: the pilot is being advised that he is 'steady'. Quite what has been deleted from the flight deck by the official wartime censor is unclear.

Opposite: The variety of signals displayed to incoming pilots by a World War II Royal Navy 'batsman', and their meanings. The signalling system was modified in later years in order to achieve commonality with the practice in the United states Navy.

COURTESY BRIAN BENNETT

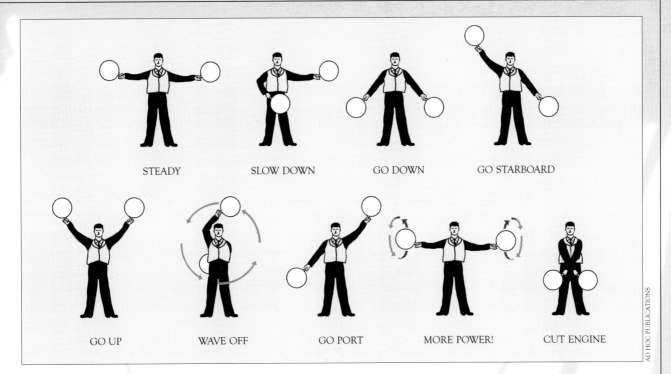

STEADY SLOW DOWN GO DOWN GO STARBOARD

GO UP WAVE OFF GO PORT MORE POWER! CUT ENGINE

AD HOC PUBLICATIONS

conditions at the risk of losing their lives. Such a concession would in effect reduce available manpower by about ten per cent—in the middle of a struggle for the life of a nation, which was a fight for right against great injustice. We had to tolerate a smaller injustice until the fight was over. So, Fleet Air Arm aircrews had to endure stress without a glimmer of relief on the horizon, not just until they cracked, but until it became obvious not only to their peers but also to their Commanding Officers that they had had more than they could stand. Even then, it was not always convenient to release them for a rest.

Men of great experience, living on their nerves but with the courage to carry on in spite of their misgivings were ideal candidates to become DLCOs, and an inappropriate comment sometimes made by the insensitive was, 'He may be a new DLCO but it's obvious that be has been Bats for ages.' There is no doubt that heightened reaction to danger with abnormally rapid response time was an essential qualification to control an incoming aircraft. With practice, a rapport soon established between Bats and pilots. If not, it was necessary to appoint a new Bats or there would soon be a shortage of serviceable aircraft. A good Bats could convey information by movements which could be felt rather than be defined, like those of a ballerina.

Bringing in a Swordfish to land on a deck with the ship rising and falling through thirty feet (forget the added complications of rolling twenty degrees each side of vertical if you can) was no mean task even for an experienced batsman. Timing was the be-all and end-all. The aircraft had to be sinking steadily on its approach to the stern, to arrive there as the stern was also sinking but about three feet above its lowest point of movement. There was always a steady moment at the lowest point before the stem started to rise again and it was during this 'steady' that the 'cut' signal was given and the hook engaged to arrest the aircraft, and because the bow was at its highest the uphill slope on the deck helped to bring the machine to a halt and reduce the load on the arrester wire. It was not the best situation to 'go round again' because the aircraft was then at its lowest and any obstruction forward was at its highest, so the timing of the approach to land was further complicated by the need to include consideration of the roll. The arrival of the aircraft at touch-down was best timed to coincide with the middle of a roll from starboard to port so that the port side was going down, not up: in this way an escape route free from obstruction (except for batsmen) was available to the pilot, who could swing violently left over the side of the ship. Poor old Bats! Into the net again!

Certain calamity awaited when the 'cut' was given to a Swordfish which was too high as the stem was rising. Think of a tennis ball falling vertically and being hit by a horizontal racquet brought up underneath it. The force of impact usually rammed the undercarriage up through the lower mainplanes, presenting the ground crew with the task of moving a deadweight of up to five tons (and in a hurry if another Swordfish short of fuel at the end of its patrol was waiting to land) a hundred yards up a heaving and rolling deck without any lifting gear other than willing hands. This is where the rapport between the Services showed how good it was. Every man off duty would suddenly appear, even before the tannoy instructions could be made, and the wreckage would get up and walk like Lazarus. In extreme conditions, with life at stake, the wreckage would be ditched over the side with a pause only to puncture the fabric enough to make sure it wouldn't float to give a tell-tale message to any shadowing submarine. During this short pause it was amazing how much equipment could be salvaged or looted by eager hands with spanners and hacksaws!

The J. C. Wire *Sub-Lieutenant (A) Frank Jackson MiD* RNVR*

Following my training to be a FAA observer at HMS *Goshawk*, Piarco, Trinidad, I was instructed to join 825 Squadron at Lee-on-Solent in August 1943. Before the war this Squadron had been the first to be equipped with the Swordfish, and by 1943 the aircraft was supposed to be obsolete. However, it was still flying operationally in 1945 when the war ended! The 'String-bag' could carry a torpedo, for attacks on shipping, or bombs, or rockets or depth charges for attacks on submarines. It was also used on occasions for mine-laying operations and as a 'spotter' or reconnaissance aircraft. Towards the end of war we sometimes carried 'Oscar', a type of torpedo that, when dropped astern of a submarine as it dived, had the ability to home on the submarine's screws.

825 Squadron had been employed in many theatres, and among its exploits had been the attack on the German battleship *Bismarck* in May 1941 and the attack on the *Scharnhorst* and *Gneisenau* as these ships had made their 'dash' through the English Channel in February 1942.

The Squadron, which by the end of 1943 was also equipped with Sea Hurricanes, flew from Inskip in Lancashire to join HMS *Vindex* in the Clyde on 14 December that year. The Hurricanes were landing-on while the Swordfish were still in the area of the Lake District when, over the airwaves, one of the Hurricane pilots was heard to say, 'Jesus Christ!' Apparently, he had managed to miss all the arrester wires until the last one before the barrier, which had dramatically reduced his speed to zero in just a few feet. This particular arrester wire became known as the 'J. C. Wire'. I was flying with my pilot, Sub-Lieutenant Peter Cumberland, but our landing on *Vindex* got nowhere near as far as the first arrester wire: we stalled too soon, hit the round-down with the underside of the fuselage and slid to a standstill with a bent fuselage! Over the next fourteen months on *Vindex* during which Peter Cumberland and I flew together, there were many crashes—some more serious than others—but, thankfully, Peter managed to keep a clean sheet.

It was soon very evident that life on board *Vindex* was never going to be dull. 'Wings', Lieutenant-Commander Percy Gick, had taken part in the attack on the *Bismarck*, while 'Ops', Lieutenant-Commander Stovin-Bradford, had been involved in the night attack on at Taranto. They seemed very determined that this bunch of aviators would be the first carrier-borne anti-submarine night flying unit, and that they would be very efficient at their job and capable of flying day or night in all kinds of weather. We had a number of extemporary aids to assist us. To prevent the undercarriage of the Swordfish from doing the splits when landing-on in rough seas, for example, a wire cable was strung between the wheels of the aircraft. When the carrier was immersed in a sea fog at night, a searchlight pointing vertically was sometimes used to assist aircraft in locating the ship. Again, in bad visibility, the carrier could make smoke, and when the ship turned into wind a pilot would follow the smoke until it came into view. Then he would dive down to the deck—although he did not always make a successful landing!

Below: Well wrapped-up deck handlers engage in last-minute preparations before a Swordfish takes off from the flight deck of an escort carrier. The wartime censor has not only deleted the radar antennæ but, in his enthusiasm, most of the outer interplane strutwork as well.

Opposite, top: A Swordfish Mk I having just come on board HMS *Courageous*, September/October 1938. Two men are freeing the arrester hook, one of them apparently the DCLO as he is clutching a 'bat'! The prominent aircraft homing beacon atop the ship's mainmast is a recent installation.

COURTESY RICHARD L. WARD

Maydown served two purposes. It provided the aircrew for Merchant Aircraft Carriers—the so-called 'MAC ships'—and it also acted as a pool for aircrew who, like Reggie and myself, were waiting to be sent to a squadron operating from an escort carrier. It was not so much a home as a staging post—a large, rural, sprawling, outdated air station. The officers slept in Nissen huts, and some of the Wrens had to put up with no running water and chemical toilets. It was informal and vaguely chaotic—the antithesis of what one would expect from an RN establishment, and symptomatic of the fact that the composition of the air arm was changing—changing from RN (Royal Navy) to RNVR (Royal Naval Volunteer Reserve).

In the early years of the war, almost all Swordfish aircrew were RN. For example, of the men who in 1940 had crippled the Italian fleet at Taranto, only four out of 42 aircrew involved were RNVR. The RN aircrew were dedicated enthusiasts who had joined an unfashionable branch of the Service because they believed in the future of naval aviation and wanted to make it their career. They achieved a very high standard of airmanship that set a benchmark for those who came after them. Aircrew like Reggie and I were vaguely aware that we were following in the footsteps of brave men of legendary expertise. However, unlike our predecessors, were not wedded to the Navy. We did not want to make our career in it; in fact, some of us could hardly wait to get out! We marched to the beat of a different drum—less formal, less traditional, less tied to the past. Inevitably there was sometimes friction, most (but by no means all) of it good-humoured, and summed up in the ditty, 'There's a balls-up on the flight deck and the Wavy Navy's making it!' By the time I joined my last squadron, towards the end of 1944, only two out of our forty-odd aircrew were RN.

836 Squadron was particularly distanced from the ways of the old Navy because those of its pilots and observers who served in MAC ships were required to sign Ship's Articles as Supernumerary Deck Officers in the Merchant Navy. They therefore owed allegiance not to the Senior Naval Officer of a convoy, but to the Master of their MAC ship—a point

COURTESY PHILIP JARRETT

brought home by the Merchant Navy badge they wore on their uniform. Perhaps nothing indicated this change from old to new more clearly than the dress code. In the early days of the war, pilots and observers were often required to dress formally for dinner in the wardroom in their white, stiff-necked, No 10, 'death-by-choking' uniform; towards the end of the war, dress for 836 pilots and observers was frequently pyjamas, 'Scapa Scanties', battledress trousers, a long-sleeved vest and a woollen, roll-neck sweater. It is little wonder that, after a while, many 836 aircrew felt that they had a greater affinity with

the Merchant Navy than with the Royal Navy. When protecting a convoy, we came to think of its merchantmen as our responsibility, our 'flock', which looked to us to protect it from the wolf-packs of the U-boats.

Reggie and I were soon to learn what convoy protection was all about. One day we were told to fly to Hatston in the Orkneys, and from there to 'proceed' to HMS *Vindex*, where we would join 811 Squadron as a replacement aircrew.

* * *

A view of part of HMS *Sparrowhawk*—alias RNAS Hatston—in early 1942 with Swordfish of 822 Squadron (V4438 nearest) visible. Notice that the aircraft have handlers at each wing tip to assist the pilot with taxying; each of the aircraft's lower mainplanes had 'cut-out' hand-holds for this very purpose.

We landed at Hatston late one autumn afternoon and were told to report post-haste to HMS *Vindex* in Scapa Flow. Hatston is adjacent to Scapa, and within a few minutes of take-off we were over the main base of the Home Fleet. There were some couple of dozen ships at anchor, and it did not take me long to spot *Vindex*. She had turned into wind but was not under way, and I realised with some consternation that I was going to have to land, for the first time, on a carrier that was stationary. An Aldis lamp flashed green from her island, and, short of signalling 'I'm a beginner. Would you please get under way?', there was nothing I could do but land. Feeling, quite erroneously, that the eyes of the entire Home Fleet were on me, I started my favoured long, straight approach. 'Bats' made no signals until he gave me the cut, and I touched down safely. An hour later *Vindex* was standing north out of Scapa Flow. We were about to escort a convoy to Russia.

The carrier rendezvoused with the merchantmen the next morning. By now the weather had deteriorated. There was a heavy sea, a strong wind and seven-

COURTESY PHILIP JARRETT

tenths cloud, and it was raining. In the afternoon Reggie and I took off on our first operational patrol, a 'Cobra 15', that is, circling round and round the convoy at a radius of fifteen miles. From 400 feet we could see the ships in convoy more clearly than from *Vindex*'s flight deck. There were about twenty merchantmen and almost as many warships , the latter comprising two carriers, two cruisers and over a dozen destroyers and corvettes. We had a fleeting glimpse of dark grey ships butting into a pale grey sea, beneath grey clouds and a grey sky; then, with visibility no more than two or three miles, the convoy disappeared from sight and we were on our own.

Our first patrol was uneventful, and of a pattern to be repeated many times in the months ahead. Reggie concentrated on his ASV; I concentrated on keeping to the courses he gave me. Flying in bad weather in an aircraft with an open cockpit is windy, wet and cold; but at least a Swordfish pilot had a good all-round view, particularly of the horizon, and this made possible a combination of instrument flying and visual flying. At the end of two and a half hours we were back over the convoy and ready to land. I made my usual approach, and right up to the last moments 'Bats' indicated 'Keep coming as you are'. Then, unexpectedly, he signalled 'Higher and faster'. I quickly obeyed him. My Swordfish quickly obeyed me—and this was just as well, because I suddenly realised that, in the aftermath of a bigger

than usual wave, *Vindex*'s stern was swinging up in front of me. With additional power and height, I scraped over the round-down and landed heavily but safely.

A couple of days later, I made my first operational night deck-landing. Because Reggie and I were the least experienced members of the Squadron, the CO did his best to ease us in gently, giving us a couple of day patrols to start with. However, the second of these had to be cancelled because of bad weather, and, as luck would have it, our first night patrol coincided with weather that was bad, but not quite bad enough to prevent flying. When we took off at 2 a.m. it was blowing a near gale and sleeting. Our patrol this time was a 'Cobra 10'.

It has been suggested that flying in bad weather is twice as stressful as flying in good weather, and that flying by night is three times as stressful as by day. I do not recall, that night, feeling stressed: I was too busy keeping to the courses Reggie gave me, and trying to avoid icing up or flying into the sea. With the cloud base at 300 feet there little room for error. However, I do recall feeling physically and mentally

Below: Space is always at a premium on board aircraft carriers, and the wing-fold facility of the Swordfish reduced the aircraft's width by over fifty per cent. Here an 816 Squadron 'Stringbag' is being marshalled by flight deck handlers on board the escort carrier HMS *Tracker*.

COURTESY MICHAEL GOODWIN

Above: Swordfish were rarely called upon to guard convoys away from the Atlantic and Mediterranean regions, but in February 1940 aircraft from 813 and 824 Squadrons on board HMS *Eagle* shepherded the first troop convoy of Australians and New Zealanders from Colombo to Aden. These two units were the last to retain their smart prewar 'silver' finishes.

exhausted, and mightily relieved when, at the end of sortie, we were back above the convoy, without Reggie having detected the merest hint of a U-boat's 'blip' on his ASV. None of the merchantmen, of course, were showing any lights, and in the darkness it was impossible to see either them or the carrier, but after a few minutes a dozen pinheads of blue appeared beneath us. *Vindex* had turned into wind and switched on her landing lights. I told myself that we had made it, and I came into land with the enthusiasm of a homing pigeon to roost. Of course, I thought I was concentrating, but with hindsight I believe my overriding emotion was thankfulness—thankfulness that we had found our way home and that everything was going to be all right.

I remember the sleet plastering into my goggles. I remember the welcoming yellow bats. Then, suddenly, there were no longer two yellow bats but only one. I was coming in too fast—'like a bat out of hell,' the batsman told me later, apparently without irony. I was too close to touch-down to risk a downward glance at my airspeed indicator, but my instinct told me 'Bats' was right. I throttled back, and my good old Swordfish almost instantly lost speed. I was conscious of the flight deck rushing towards me. As the batsman signalled 'Cut', I hit the deck hard, made an ungainly bounce, and thought I

was heading for the barrier. Then came an almighty jerk as we picked up the last arrester wire and, within a dozen feet, were brought to a halt, literally inches from the safety net. Never again, not even when landing on a beautiful afternoon in the still waters of the Clyde, did I give any deck landing anything less that one hundred and one per cent concentration.

For the next few days we flew round-the-clock patrols, round and round the convoy. By now we were well north of the Arctic Circle. It was winter, and dark for nineteen hours out of twenty-four. The weather was unpleasant, with strong winds, heavy seas, low cloud and sleet. Flying was not much fun. At least our efforts were rewarded: during the whole of our passage to Russia, no U-boat ever got close enough to the convoy to made an attack. Not one of our 'flock' of merchantmen was lost. After eight days we dropped anchor off Vaenga, the port of Murmansk.

We spent a little less than a week in Russia. My recollection is of low, snow-covered hills, skiing with

COURTESY PHILIP JARRETT

Left: RATOG—Rocket-Assisted Take-Off Gear—was a facility available to the Swordfish though infrequently used. The extra 'push' it provided helped shorten take-off runs. One rocket pack was fitted each side of the fuselage, angled away from the airframe and the vulnerable fabric surfaces.

convoy), etc. On the very rare occasions when Reggie thought he might have had a contact on his ASV and we had homed on it, the contact had disappeared before we got near it, signifying either a false alarm or a U-boat that had been forced to submerge. During the whole of this return voyage, *Vindex*'s Swordfish made only two definite attacks, and failed to make a single confirmed kill. Not much, you might think, to write home about. Yet by our constant, round-the-clock patrolling, we prevented the U-boats from getting close enough to the convoy to *make* an attack. Not one of our 'flock' was lost, or even fired at—and this at a time when convoys not protected by carrier-borne aircraft were still often losing fifteen or even twenty per cent of their merchantmen.

I stayed with 811 until, at the end of 1944, the Squadron was disbanded. Reggie and I then found ourselves back at Maydown, awaiting another posting. We wouldn't have said no to a MAC ship, but it was not to be.

* * *

equipment borrowed from the RN Hospital, the hard-bargaining Russian children, who offered us debased roubles in exchange for clothes or cigarettes, and a visit to nearby Murmansk. I had some knowledge of the effects of German bombing—my parents lived in south-east London—but never before had I seen such total devastation. The city was rubble, with families living in open trenches beside what had once been their homes. It gave us a glimpse of what life must be like on the Eastern Front. My last recollection is of the magnificent concert given in *Vindex*'s hangar by the Red Fleet Choir. I reckon their singing and Cossack dancing would have won applause in the Albert Hall. And the party afterwards in the wardroom wasn't bad either!

Our return voyage was officially described as 'uneventful', although that was not the way we aircrew saw it. The weather, once again, was foul—heavy seas, strong winds, a lot of rain. Most of the time it was pitch dark. There were U-boats in the offing, and our Swordfish needed to be airborne continually, circling the convoy in conditions no other aircraft could possibly have tolerated. My log book records a succession of patrols—'Cobra 15', 'Adder 10' (ten miles ahead of the advancing convoy), 'Alligator port' (up and down the port side of the

Rumour had it that in Western Approaches Headquarters in Liverpool there was a board on which the names of all 836 Squadron aircrew were neatly pigeon-holed. Sometimes at night a window would accidentally be left open, and in the morning the office cleaners would find that the wind had blown half the documents out of their repositories and on to the floor. The cleaners would then put them back at random. Reggie and I had reason to believe this, since, after only a few days at Maydown, he was posted as a replacement observer to 813 Squadron in *Campania* and I was posted as a replacement pilot to 835 in *Nairana*.

The highlights of my time in 835 were a shipping strike off Norway and another convoy to Russia. At the time, our night strike against ships in the Norwegian fjords had an air of Hollywood unreality about it. It seemed strange to risk sending a carrier strike force into enemy-controlled waters just to attack a few merchantmen; strange, too, to expect a couple of dozen obsolescent Swordfish to do a job that was seemingly beyond the RAF. However, four years after Taranto, the faithful old Swordfish were still proving their worth, albeit in much less spectacular fashion. I do not believe that any other operational aircraft were successfully doing in 1945 the same job as they did in 1940.

We were given escape kits, revolvers and hidden compasses; we were taught some useful Norwegian phrases and how to build an igloo; and on the night of 28 January *Nairana* and *Campania* turned into the wind at their flying-off point, some eighty miles off the Norwegian coast. I remember hoping that Reggie had a good pilot.

It was a beautiful night, with a full moon, a quiet sea, only the odd patch of cloud and little wind. The lack of wind meant that our Swordfish, laden with bombs or rockets, had to use RATOG. When we activated the booster rockets—usually about three-quarters of the way through our take-off run—we were catapulted into the air. Common sense told us to fire the gear when the flight deck was as horizontal as possible. If it was tilting steeply downward, we were likely to find ourselves flung straight into

the sea; if it was sloping steeply upward, were likely to find ourselves, with insufficient flying speed, hanging, and stalling, over the carrier's bow. Common sense also told us that it was better to fire fractionally late than fractionally early; and many pilots, myself included, liked to be level with the island before we fired. This was because, if one of our rockets malfunctioned, or if the carrier cork-screwed, we might find ourselves catapulted not over the bow but into the island.

The sea was calm that night and the flight deck level, so RATOG posed no problems, and a little after 8 p.m. a dozen Swordfish from *Nairana* and a dozen from *Campania* were heading *en echelon* for Norway. We were told that our targets would be found in Rovdefjord and theirs in Romsdalefjord, a little to the north. After some three-quarters of an hour we sighted the Norwegian coast—snow-covered mountains, fringed by a dark sea and bathed in moonlight. We made our intended landfall off the little island of Riste and were about to enter the fjords when there was a sudden burst of 'ack-ack', the tracer coming up slowly at first, then with sudden acceleration as it passed well ahead of us— well ahead because the German gunners, used to

Below: An inkling of the sort of conditions under which Swordfish aircrews engaged in the protection of Russian convoys sometimes had to operate may be gathered from this view of HMS *Fencer*, the flight deck of which is being cleared of snow and ice in order to permit flying.

COURTESY TOMMY THOMSON

firing at 300mph Mosquitos, had overestimated our speed. We broke formation and made for the safety of sea level, where we presented a less obvious target, and the 'ack-ack' died away.

As we entered the fjords a wonderful thing happened; just how wonderful I do not think we fully appreciated at the time. The scene had a Tolkien-esque grandeur—the big gold disc of the moon, the snow-white mountains and the dark, twisting lanes of water. There was no sign of life. Suddenly, and unexpectedly, one by one little pinheads of light began to appear on the lower slopes of the mountains. Norwegian homesteaders were risking the wrath of the Germans, and perhaps their lives, by switching on lights in their homes to guide us through the fjords.

However, before what was happening had dawned on us, we spotted a target—a small, solitary merchantman. Three of us climbed to 800 feet, the ideal height from which to make an attack with rockets, while the rest of the Squadron headed up-fjord in search of more exciting prey. The first aircraft to attack scored at least four hits, and the ship came to an abrupt stop. This should have made my job easy as I was the next to attack, but I remember thinking, as I started my shallow dive, that the ship looked very small. I hoped

it was indeed a German merchantman carrying iron ore and not a Norwegian ferry carrying women and children. My foolish thoughts upset my concentration, and my first salvo sailed harmlessly over the target. Given the lack of opposition this was unforgivable, and not at all in the Taranto tradition. I lost airspeed and altered my angle of dive, and my second salvo of rockets hit the luckless vessel amidships. Fire broke out, and my observer and I could see her crew trying frantically to lower their ship's lifeboats. Our third aircraft administered the *coup de grâce*.

The rest of the Squadron, meanwhile, had found more satisfying targets in the shape of two decent-sized merchant ships. They attacked with bombs and rockets. One ship was sunk, the other set on fire and beached. Targets ashore, such as anti-aircraft positions, were also identified and attacked. Then, individually, we were heading for home, and by a little after midnight all our Swordfish were safely back on board *Nairana*.

The operation had been a minor success—and it may, perhaps, have achieved more than we realised. At the time, we were told that the ships we attacked were carrying iron ore, but research suggests that they may have been carrying

something more important—the heavy water (deuterium oxide) that was being processed near Narvik and then taken by night through the fjords to the German V-2 rocket base at Peenemünde.

A week later we were escorting JW.64, one of the largest-ever convoys to Russia. It consisted of twenty-six merchantmen escorted by almost as many warships—two aircraft carriers, two cruisers and some twenty destroyers and corvettes. Two things I particularly remember about this operation are the difficulty and discomfort of flying an open-cockpit plane in the Arctic and the ferocity of the storm that hit us on the way home.

On our fourth day out from Scapa, I flew a particularly unpleasant 'Crocodile 20'. By this time we were some way north of the Arctic Circle. Each day there were about seventeen hours of total darkness, about four of sepulchral twilight and only a couple of hours of anæmic daylight. When we took off, at 5 a.m., it was blowing a near-gale and *Nairana* was pitching into a heavy sea. At least the strong, 30-knot wind meant that we did not need RATOG. Once airborne, I had to fly almost all the time on instruments. The cloud was eight-tenths at 500 feet, with patches at sea level, and we needed to fly below

the cloud base to avoid icing up. My observer kept his eyes on his ASV. I kept mine on my instruments—especially the altimeter—and only very occasionally did I get a blurred glimpse of white-capped waves uncomfortably close beneath us. After about an hour I began to feel cold. I was wearing vest and pants, Scapa Scanties, pyjamas, battledress trousers, a pullover, a kapok inner suit and an Irvine immersion suit, but with flurries of snow and the torque from the propeller all the time streaming over the windshield and into the cockpit, even this plethora of clothing failed to ward off increasing numbness. Soon there was another problem: Swordfish did not have a 'pee-tube'. (Even if there had been such a facility, when one was flying in the Arctic the member concerned is usually so shrunken with cold that not even the most boastful aircrew were confident of finding a way through half a dozen diverse layers of clothing.) At such times, it did not

Below: With seagulls screaming overhead, the escort carrier HMS *Chaser* prepares to leave Scapa Flow to accompany another convoy bound for the Soviet Union, March 1944. As well as Swordfish (of 816 Squadron), Grumman Martlet fighters are embarked and are visible right aft. Notice that aircraft 'G' has its call-sign painted on the wing-fold end rib. A barrage balloon may be discerned along the shoreline.

Above: An 842 Squadron Swordfish II having crash-landed on board HMS *Fencer* in December 1943. The pilot, Sub-Lieutenant Bruce Vibert, and his observer, seen here about to disembark, were unhurt. The aircraft was written off. See photograph on page 123.

help to know that if the engine failed we would have to ditch, and that if we had to ditch it would almost certainly be the end of us. The life expectancy of those who come down in the Arctic is about two minutes. In our immersion suits this was increased to about twenty minutes, but we all knew that if we came down in the sea at any distance from the convoy we were not going to be picked up in twenty minutes. No wonder, then, that in the small hours of that morning I listened attentively to the throb of our engine. Our Pegasus did not fail us—a tribute both to those who designed it and to those who serviced it—and after two hours forty minutes we were back over the convoy.

Next day the weather worsened, bringing heavy seas, a gale force wind and patches of cloud at sea level. Of the twelve Swordfish that took off over the next twenty-four hours, two had to return with ASV or engine failure, one ended in the catwalk and one went over the side. The crew of the last had an almost miraculous escape. The pilot, Ron Brown, was half way through his take-off run when *Nairana* corkscrewed violently and the aircraft was flung straight into the carrier's island. The Swordfish hit the Oerlikon gun mountings, performed a spectacular half-roll, plummeted vertically into the sea and sank like a stone. We thought it had spelt the end of Ron Brown and his observer Jock Bevan, but, against all the odds, their Swordfish dinghy broke free and inflated and Ron and Jock were seen struggling to climb into it. They then were swirled away into the darkness. The Captain of HMS *Onslaught* risked his ship and the lives of his crew to comb the sea for them with his searchlight, and after fifteen minutes they were picked up. In those fifteen minutes, however, they had become almost literally frozen solid, and were in the final stages of hypothermia. To quote the official report, 'Their limbs wouldn't bend, and their clothes had to be cut away from their frozen bodies.' But they survived! Four days later, we dropped anchor—very thankfully—in Kola Bay.

Our voyage home, with Convoy RA.64, was equally eventful, since we were hit by what has become known to meteorologists simply as 'The Great Gale'—one of the worst storms ever recorded. On 4 February the weather began to deteriorate. By midday the wind was a steady 60 knots and the waves were steepening and forming into huge, wide-spaced rollers, half-a-mile apart, the spume from their crests blown in a solid, horizontal sheet over the sea. Flying was out of the question, and for this we were thankful, but as the conditions worsened we began to wonder if the weather was not more to be feared than the U-boats. Next morning our Met Officer pinned up this forecast (on top of which some wag had scribbled, 'Fly off all the Swordfish!'): 'Weather Forecast. Monday 19th February. Intense depression over Spitzbergen continues to move rapidly NE. Strong SWly gale will continue today with cloudy conditions and intermittent rain; wind decreasing and veering slowly this evening. Grade "C" forecast till 2000/19: Wind SWly, averaging 50–60 knots but gusting considerably over. Weather cloudy with intermittent rain. Cloud 8/10–10/10 at 800 feet, patches at sea level. Visibility 3–5 miles. Sea very rough. Swell heavy SWly.' This turned out to be

Below: Landing accidents were not irregular occurrences even on big carriers in peacetime. Here L7682 of 810 Squadron has come to grief on HMS *Ark Royal*, May 1939. The aircrew escaped unhurt.

AD HOC COLLECTION

an underestimate because the wind that evening did not decrease: it increased. By midnight our anemometer was recording an almost constant speed of over 80mph, and, as the wind strengthened, the waves steepened into huge rollers, sixty feet from trough to crest, surging endlessly out of the southwest. Some ships were so badly battered they were in danger of foundering. To quote the official publication *Convoys to Russia*, 'Other convoys suffered serious weather damage but none so bad as this. The convoy became scattered, numerous ships suffering severe damage. Several merchant ships were reduced to steering with block and tackle on the rudder head, and, on return to Britain, twelve warships had to be docked for repairs.'

In the small hours the convoy split into two. About half the merchantmen and half the warships, including *Campania*, thought it safer to heave-to; the other half, including *Nairana*, thought it safer to hold course at four knots. Carriers are not good sea boats, and I was not alone that night in thinking that we were in very real danger of capsizing. We would roll 45 degrees to port, hang there for a moment as though about to turn turtle, then roll 45 to starboard, to end with another sickening pause.

Suddenly, there was a terrific crash. In the hangar, an American Heyster fork-lift truck, weighing nearly a ton, had broken free from the wire lashings that held it in place. As *Nairana* rolled, the truck went careering across the deck, colliding with two

Left: Lifts forward and aft permitted aircraft to be struck below, freeing flight-deck space and allowing maintenance to be carried out under cover. Few MAC ships had these facilities, and, on those that did not, all work had to be carried out topside, often in appalling weather.

Right, upper: A Swordfish takes off from HMS *Biter*. The ship's disruptive camouflage is typical of that for escort carriers during the second half of the war, the objective being to break up the outline and confuse the enemy—in particular the enemy's U-boats.

Below: The escort carrier HMS *Puncher*, with Swordfish on deck, sets off on another voyage. The raised windbreaks offer some measure of protection against the elements.

AD HOC COLLECTION

Swordfish. The duty watch flung themselves on to it to try to bring it under control, but there were not enough of them. Again the truck hurtled across the deck, crashing into the parked aircraft. The tannoy blared 'Emergency! Emergency!' and mechanics and handlers, pilots and observers, came streaming into the hangar. By sheer weight of numbers they managed to hold the truck down. A cargo net was flung over it, and blocks of timber were rammed beneath it to lift its wheels off the deck. At last it was secured. But what a scene of devastation it left in its wake! Two Swordfish were completely written off, and another four badly damaged. However, both watches worked through the rest of the night, and by dawn all four of the damaged aircraft had been made

serviceable—a tribute both to the skill and commitment of our groundcrew, and to the adaptability of our Swordfish.

In the Inquiry that inevitably followed, it was found that the hangar personnel had done everything right. The truck had been correctly stowed, and correctly secured with wire lashings. What had caused the accident was that whereas in American

COURTESY PHILIP JARRETT

87

carriers the securing wires would have been held in place by bolts housed in dished apertures below deck level, in *Nairana* the wires were held in place by screw-in bolts that protruded above deck level. The solid tyres of the American Heyster, continually passing over these bolts, had weakened them, and so when, that night, *Nairana* gave a particularly vicious roll the strain was too great, a bolt had snapped and the wires had parted. Mayhem ensued. On such apparently trivial technicalities could depend the fate of aircraft and, by extension, that of aircraft carriers—and, by extension again, the fate of convoys.

Next day the weather improved a little, although the seas were still enormous and the wind still 50 knots, gusting to 90. With the convoy scattered, we anticipated an attack by the Junkers 88s that were based in northern Norway. Sure enough, a little before midday, 'bogeys' appeared on our radar. There were about two dozen Junkers, some, it seemed, carrying torpedoes, some mines. A group of the latter flew low across the path of the advancing convoy. Their leader was hit by 'ack-ack' and set on fire. He flew more and more slowly, lower and lower, until he hit the sea and disintegrated. Quite a few Swordfish aircrew, myself included, were watching from the catwalk. My first reaction was a *Boy's Own Paper* 'Got him!', but then I remember thinking, 'There, but for the grace of God, go I'. Perhaps this is the time to say something about the relationship that, I believe, usually existed between Fleet Air Arm aircrew and our German adversaries.

I know that some of those who fought in the Battle of the Atlantic hated the Germans. I know that sometimes, when a U-boat was sunk, pieces of dismembered bodies would be put in buckets and displayed as trophies on the decks of destroyers. I do not believe most Fleet Air Arm aircrew would have

thought much of that. When, for example, Harry Horrocks sank a U-boat, he dropped his Swordfish dinghy for the survivors to climb into, then circled overhead until they were picked up. When George Gordon shot down a Blohm und Voss and it ditched, he called up one of our Swordfish and the latter found and circled the German airmen until they were rescued. When *Nairana* brought U-boat survivors back to Britain for internment, our Commander circulated a memo: 'We have German prisoners on board. If you meet then, please treat them as you yourself would wish to be treated if *you* were a prisoner of war.' 'Chivalry' is an out-of-date, out-of-fashion word. It never, of course, justifies war; but it does sometimes mitigate it.

As if to prove this, there was an unexpected sequel to that Junkers attack on our convoy. Fifty years later, quite by chance, one of our Swordfish pilots who had been watching from the catwalk met one of the very few surviving Junkers pilots who had been carrying out the attack. They became friends. Eventually, the German pilot, Hans-Werner Grosse, came to one of our Squadron's annual reunion dinners. Here he made so many friends that he was invited to become an honorary member of 835 Squadron. Many of us, today, exchange Christmas cards with him, and one or two of us have visited him and his wife at their home in Lübeck.

The Junkers' attack that morning was the Germans' last major attempt to disrupt RA.64. This may have been partly because of the heavy losses they suffered, and partly because we were hit by another storm which made flying, for any aircraft, impossible. Again, the convoy was scattered. When we did at last reach home waters, half our warships and more than half our merchant ships had to be docked to repair damage caused by the storm.

Left: A black-painted Swordfish III with its underbelly ASV radome clearly evident and a searchlight fitted beneath the starboard wing—both systems avid consumers of generating capacity.

Opposite, top: Unspectacular but vital convoy work: Swordfish Mk II HS644, in service with 836 Squadron in the early months of 1944, with wing leading-edge slots deployed and arrester hook lowered as it banks sharply to port in order to land on board a MAC ship.

COURTESY PHILIP JARRETT

COURTESY BRIAN LOWE

This was our last convoy. With the end of the war against Germany in sight, and our Swordfish not being suitable for the war against Japan, 835 Squadron was disbanded on 28 March 1945.

* * *

When my grandchildren ask, 'How many U-boats did you sink in the war, Grand-daddy?', and I reply 'None', I do not think they are very impressed. However, sinking U-boats was not our top priority: our main objective was preventing them from sinking our merchant ships, and in this task we were successful.

Before convoys were protected by carrier-borne aircraft, our Merchant Navy suffered horrific losses. Even in a 'good' transatlantic convoy of, say, twenty merchantmen, two or three would usually be lost, while in a 'bad' convoy as many as eight or ten might succumb (one convoy, HX.229, lost over half of its merchant ships). As soon as convoys were protected by carrier-borne aircraft—most of them Swordfish—these losses were dramatically reduced: now, in a 'good' convoy no ships at all would be lost and even in a 'bad' convoy the losses usually amounted to no more than one, or at the most two, vessels.

In this work of convoy protection 835 Squadron has a proud record. During the fifteen months we served in *Nairana*, we escorted thirteen convoys comprising over 300 merchantmen in total. Thanks to our constantly circling Swordfish, not a single one of these ships was lost to a U-boat. No shepherds could have guarded their flock more assiduously nor more successfully.

This unspectacular work attracted little attention at the time, and has received little since: convoy code-names such as JW.64 and RA.64 do not conjure up visions of great victories. However, one incident shows how much our efforts were appreciated by our friends in the Merchant Navy. On 4 March 1944 one of our Swordfish, coming in to land at night in a heavy swell, went over the side. The pilot, Lou Wilmot, and the TAG, George Ferguson, were killed. Next morning they were buried at sea. It was a moving ceremony, taking place against a vast sky, a gentle wind and a pale sun. As the bodies of our friends slid over the side and into the sea, a strange thing happened. There was sudden silence. For perhaps twenty seconds there was not a sound, because every merchant ship in the convoy had stopped its engines. Then the engines picked up, the propellers again churned up the water, and the convoy and the Battle of the Atlantic went on.

* * *

When 835 Squadron disbanded, I thought I had probably flown my last Swordfish. How wrong I was! After a welcome spell of leave, I found myself, together with quite a few other Swordfish pilots, back at Maydown as, we reckoned, part of a sort of transit camp while the Admiralty decided what to do with us. Anxious to avoid the dreaded Barracuda—which most pilots regarded as the antithesis of our reliable old 'Stringbag'—I put in a request to fly Sea Otters on air–sea rescue duties. As it was going to be several months before there was a place for me on the Sea Otter conversion course at Lee-on-Solent, I and three or four other fortunate pilots were given the job of collecting Swordfish from Fleet Air Arm aerodromes all over Scotland and taking them to Barton, near Manchester, to be broken up.

D. ROLPHE/LES SAYER COLLECTION

We had barely started this assignment when we witnessed a historic event—the surrender of the German U-boat fleet in Loch Foyle. During the afternoon of 14 May a formation of Swordfish took off from Maydown and flew to the mouth of the loch. We saw their wakes first, like aircraft vapour trails in the sea. Then we saw the U-boats themselves, looking for all the world like slim, black pencils. For years, armed with rockets and depth charges, we had searched for them, most of the time without ever seeing them. It seemed strange, now that we had them in our sight, to be flying passively past. From 100 feet we could see the crews lounging about on deck, some of them enjoying a cigarette, most of them, I expect, wondering what life in a prisoner-of-war camp was going to be like. It may be surprising, but I felt no elation, only a profound thankfulness that, for all of us, the Battle of the Atlantic was, at last, over.

It did not take the Admiralty long to realise that Maydown—out on a limb, so to speak, in Northern Ireland—was not the best base from which to ferry aircraft around Scotland, and towards the end of May we were transferred to Donibristle, near Edinburgh. I doubt whether I realised how lucky I was. The war against Germany was over. The odds were that by the time I had finished my Sea Otter conversion course and arrived in the Pacific, the war against Japan would be over too. Meanwhile, it was summer. The Powers That Be at Donibristle accepted that our exclusive job was ferrying Swordfish, and we were left to do this in our way and in our own time. No wonder we came to know Edinburgh so well!

Over the course of the next couple of months, I collected literally dozens of Swordfish, some of which had not flown for years, from airfields all over

Above: Swordfish continued in service in Canada until the end of 1948; well into 1945, they were still being used for TAG training. This photograph shows officers and airmen of No 1 Canadian Course that year. The aircraft is of the enclosed cockpit type—still actually a Mk II if generally referred to as a 'Mk IV' (see pages 188–189).

Scotland, and took them to Barton. Here, I was told to taxi each one fast between a couple of posts that looked like goal posts; this knocked off the wings. The fuselage was then doused with petrol and torched. Finally, the metal components were compressed into a coffin-like cube, dropped into a pit and buried. At the time I thought this to be vandalism and a crying shame, but, looking back, I suppose it was a good thing that as much surplus war equipment as possible was destroyed. Moreover, the job did have compensations: there can be few more splendid sights than the Scottish Highlands on a beautiful summer's day, seen from the open cockpit of a slow-flying aircraft. It is also worth recording that, although many of the Swordfish were old and had not been in the air for years, and indeed had 'dodgy' service sheets, when it came to their final flights I experienced not a single engine or airframe failure. This dependability was their hallmark.

* * *

On 24 July 1945 the Admiralty promulgated a signal: 'All Swordfish are downgraded to training.' This sparked off a spate of obituaries: 'The Fairey Swordfish was the only aircraft, of any of the combatants, to remain fully operational throughout the entire war . . .'; 'A handful of these famous planes crippled the Italian fleet at Taranto . . .'; 'Their work was more varied and more profitable than that of any other type of aircraft . . .'; ' Swordfish sank or caused heavy damage to nearly a million tons of enemy

Right: After the war, a number of Swordfish were saved from destruction in Canada. This Mk III, lacking a radome, was acquired by the National Museum in Ottawa. It sports the serial number NS122, although the aircraft's precise provenance is unconfirmed. Below: NF389, a Mk III, was used for various trials after the war and was later retained at RNAS Lee-on-Solent as a static display aircraft. It still exists, one of three Swordfish on charge to the Royal Navy Historic Flight.

shipping. They helped win the Battle of the Atlantic . . .'; 'They kept flying with a cylinder head missing from their Pegasus engine, and with every bit of fabric stripped off their lower wings . . .'

In the Far East, and a small number of FAA aircrew flew the Swordfish until the very end. Richard Griffiths, a fighter pilot, recalls: 'My squadron, 733, had a variety of aircraft and most of my flying was in Grumman Wildcats and Avengers, but we had a couple of Swordfish which we used for various tasks such as aerial photography. A major (and to us young aviators a most important) rôle was carrying passengers in the observer's and air gunner's seats on various trips round Ceylon, and especially from 'Trinco' to Colombo and back again for the occasional weekend. However, I flew the Swordfish for fun and not in anger. It was, of course, a great joy to fly, especially in the very hot and humid climate of Ceylon: just to be able to climb up to a few thousand feet—it was rarely more than five thousand—and feel the cool fresh air in one's face and body . . . was a rare pleasure.'

Other aircraft may also have been fun—and a lot more comfortable to fly (I believe the two most popular with their pilots were the Spitfire and the Japanese Zero)—but if it is pitch dark, sleeting and blowing a gale and the deck of the carrier is rising and falling like a dummy horse on a roundabout, the only aeroplane in which I would ever wish to be is a 'Stringbag'.

Floating Bombs *Lieutenant-Commander Tony Tuke* DSC*

From time to time during World War II, Royal Navy squadrons were detached to undertake unusual duties, and from surprising locations. Although, looking back, the fact that Swordfish were frequently flown from land bases that were under the operational command of the Royal Air Force is well understood, during the months immediately following the establishment of 826 Squadron its personnel could be forgiven for wondering whether they had enlisted for service with RAF Coastal Command instead of the Fleet Air Arm. But these were desperate times. France, Belgium and the Netherlands had fallen under the Nazi jackboot and the Battle of Britain was being fought out in the summer skies over south-eastern England. Every available resource was being committed in the frantic endeavour to keep the enemy at bay.

826 Squadron had originally been earmarked to operate out of RNAS Lee-on-Solent as a traditional torpedo-spotter-reconnaissance unit, flying the Fairey Albacore and training in the rôle that would eventually see it embarked in aircraft carriers to defend the Fleet; instead, it was hastily

commissioned at RNAS Ford and very quickly found itself covering the evacuation of the British Expeditionary Force from France in the face of the German advance. On the fall of France, it was dispatched to Norfolk in order to conduct offensive operations against the enemy's North Sea coast, taking with it a handful of Swordfish as insurance against the non-availability of the Albacores. This proved to be a wise precaution, for not only did the Albacore's Taurus engines prove troublesome, the difficulties were such that the powerplants had to be returned to Bristol for modifications, imposing an additional workload on a factory already operating at near-full capacity and rendering individual aircraft *hors de combat* for considerable periods of time.

Thus we found ourselves based at Bircham Newton and its satellite airfield at nearby Langham, placing extraordinary demands upon our obsolete Swordfish, the ridiculous ease with which they could be flown hardly compensation for the hazardous duties to which they were put. Each aircraft was armed with a dozen or so 14-pound floating

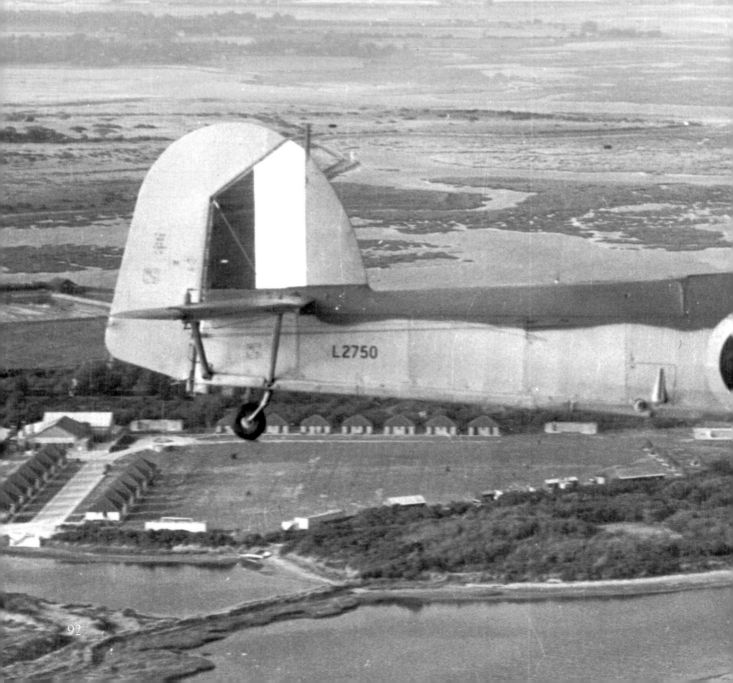

bombs—they could hardly be called mines, although they performed a similar function—and we would take off for the Dutch canals at Rotterdam and elsewhere, the object being to disrupt German waterborne traffic. The mines would, it was envisaged, drift against the lock gates and detonate, although after the first few sorties we found that fishing nets would be strung across the surface of the water to arrest their progress. We had no air cover, of course, owing to the titanic battle with the *Luftwaffe* going on back home, and we often flew at night in order to reduce the risks, but, even so, weaving around at low level over enemy-held territory at a sedate 70 or 80 knots was an interesting challenge.

These operations lasted a few weeks and we were then posted to Jersey Airport in the Channel Islands, no doubt with similar night-flying sorties on the agenda, but we managed to evacuate the Squadron and its equipment before the Germans arrived. We were dispatched temporarily to St Merryn, having lost, over the previous few months, eleven aircraft (Albacores and Swordfish) and

thirteen crewmen. St Merryn had just been completed, and the aircraft were dispersed; even so, Jerry managed to find us, dropping his bombs, I remember, one tea-time! By early November 1940 we had moved north to RNAS Campbeltown, ready to begin training for our deployment on board the new fleet carrier HMS *Formidable*. It had been an interesting baptism for a new FAA squadron!

Below: A Swordfish Mk I on a training flight in the summer of 1940, illustrating typical camouflage paintwork and markings of the era The magnificent efforts of the Royal Air Force during the summer that year tend to overshadow the contributions by the other services during this desperate fight for survival. Swordfish taking part in the Battle of Britain? Certainly!

Two Night Swims *Lieutenant (A) Arthur Towlson* DSC RNVR

Having volunteered for the Fleet Air Arm in 1940, I joined some one hundred Naval Airmen 2nd Class, half of them New Zealanders, as No 22 Pilots' Course at HMS *Vincent* (Gosport) for preliminary seamanship training, followed by Elementary Flying at No 24 EFTS Luton in Miles Magisters and Service Flying Training at RAF Netheravon, No 1 SFTS, in Hawker Harts, Hinds and Audaxes to reach 'Wings' standard and Commissioned Rank as a Sub-Lieutenant RNVR. Next followed Specialised Naval Flying Training at RNAS Crail (HMS *Jackdaw*) in Swordfish and Albacores, and Deck Landing at RNAS Arbroath (HMS *Condor*). However, expecting a first appointment to a squadron, I and others were not overjoyed to join 823 Squadron at RNAS Machrihanish for a night torpedo course which would inevitably lead to a posting to Malta, where 830 Squadron were enjoying great success but also many sad losses. It was during this torpedo course in February 1942 that, on the night of the 17th, flying solo and returning to Strath, my Swordfish experienced a failure of the throttle linkage system to the engine, forcing me to land in the sea.

Flying solo at that time meant that there was no W/T communication with base—the only radio in the Swordfish was that operated by the TAG—and a long, black night seemed inevitable. The Swordfish with me having settled in the water, I was able to scramble on to the upper wing and was relieved to see that the aircraft dinghy had burst from its stowage and was floating by the fuselage, attached by a lanyard of designed breaking strength so that it would part when the aircraft sank—which it did a few minutes later. Having managed to get into the half-submerged dinghy and somehow baled out some seawater, the valise of pyrotechnics attracted my attention. This included six red star distress signals; how I wish I had paid better attention at lectures as to how to activate these. I took the first and gently removed the sticky tape and the cap, and nothing happened. A second signal brought same result. Then to the third, and, ripping off the tape, I achieved success as a stream of red stars soared into the sky, followed by still more from the previous signals, which had been activated by the still flaming third. It was all to no avail: nobody observed my firework display. I settled down for a long wait, thinking of home, Mother, Jesus Christ and Davy Jones' Locker.

Six hours later the coaster *Busaris* sailed so close to me in the night that the mate on the bridge heard me shout. Locating me with an Aldis lamp, he stopped the ship and had me picked up. I was treated suspiciously as a possible enemy and my rescuers were not at all convinced by any papers I had in English. The skipper refused to break W/T silence to report my survival, but he finally discharged me at Oban to await naval transport back to Machrihanish.

On completion of our course, we pilots were joined by observers and our CO, Lieutenant M. E. Lashmore RN, and Senior Pilot, Lieutenant Maund RN, as 828 Squadron at North Front, Gibraltar, awaiting transfer to Malta, during which time we were kept busy flying anti-submarine patrols for HMS *Eagle* when ferrying Spitfires to Malta and also the night A/S 'Spartel' patrols between Cape Spartel on the North African coast and Cape Trafalgar in Spain. I was on one of these patrols, with Sub-Lieutenant Jones and a telegraphist air gunner, when my Swordfish was blown

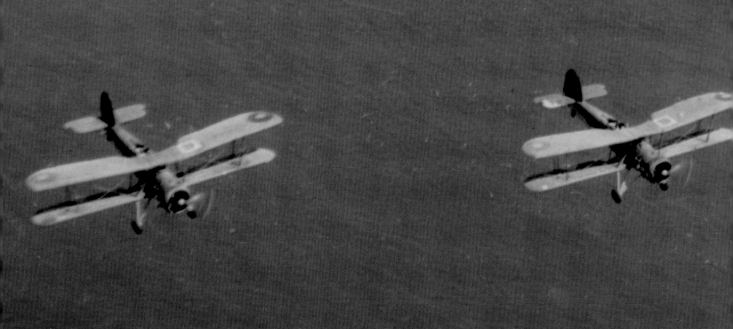

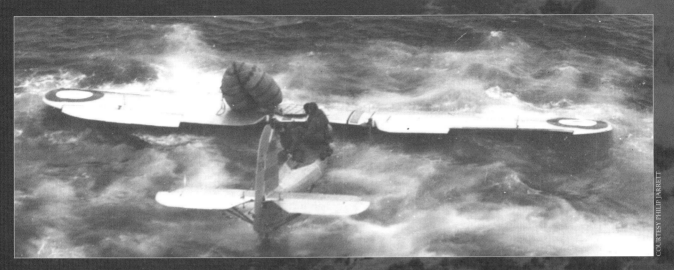

into the Atlantic; a signal warning of deteriorating weather had come from the aircraft we were to relieve, but we were already airborne and were navigating on an inaccurately forecast wind. We could not make the return to Gibraltar, finally ditching 135 degrees and five miles off Trafalgar. Our situation had not been assisted by our position being off the chart available to my observer, and he had no details of the Group Flashing Lights we saw. (Was it Ceuta? Cadiz?)

As I had a crew, Gibraltar had been informed of our ditching location, and the dinghy drill and knowledge of pyrotechnics were no problem following my first

Above: The aircrew of an 821 Squadron Swordfish Mk I scramble clear after ditching during a prewar exercise. The dinghy, housed in the aircraft's upper wing centre-section, is inflating and, with luck, will be ready for use just in time.
Below: A flight of five Swordfish on a training exercise over the Scottish coast.

experience. We were picked up by the asdic trawler *Lady Hogarth* and returned to The Rock to be transferred with the rest of our party to Malta by the convoy Operation 'Harpoon' . . . but that is another story!

A Perfect Row of Ships *Captain David Goodwin* CBE DSC

At 2040 exactly our wheels left the deck and I gave Olly Patch a course to the flame float. Twelve of us—the first wave—took departure from there at 2057, and set course for Taranto Bay, immediately starting to climb. We had about 170 miles to go, so it was not very encouraging when we ran into cloud at 4,000 feet after only twenty minutes. At first it was patchy and we managed to keep the leading sub-flight in view—although we lost our left-hand man almost immediately—but by 2140 we had climbed into dense cumulus and then there was no hope of seeing anything.

We went on climbing through that bloody cloud, and it took us twenty minutes, while Olly's courses were all over the place and I had horrible visions of colliding with other aircraft. Eventually we came out of it, at 7,000 feet—to see nothing. There were a thousand stars and a bright moon shining down on those billows of whiteness sliding astern under our wheels, but of other aircraft not a sign.

I must admit that this moment was my worst in the whole trip, and my nearest to panic. I have never felt so utterly alone: it was cold and unearthly up there, we had lost all the others, we did not know when they were going to attack, the sea was down below and the ship was 100 miles astern. Ahead was Taranto's welcome, and it looked as if we might have to meet it alone. I afterwards discovered that quite a few of the others had also been separated, though the majority of the torpedo-droppers and flare-droppers had managed to stick together.

We, incidentally, were supposed to be leading the dive-bombers on the cruisers and destroyers moored alongside the Mar Piccolo. At 2215 we sighted the 'heel' of Italy, having come down again through the cloud to see if the others had done the same. At that time we were flying at

4,000 feet and the wash of the sea along the Italian coast was clearly visible at eight miles. We soon left it, striking north-east to hit the western coast of Taranto Bay. The clouds by now had thinned, so we climbed again so as to get a good height for our bombing. I reckoned we would see the coast again at 2300, and we did, within a few minutes of this estimate. Taranto was about eight miles to the north-ward, and we turned towards it. By this time there were already guns putting up a barrage (but no tracer); presumably they had heard us (or the others) on their sound locators, so there wasn't much doubt that our objective lay ahead of us.

I reeled in, tidied up the cockpit, loosened my parachute in its stowage, and kept on my feet to look ahead. We were within a mile of Paulo Island (at the entrance to the harbour) at 2305—and then the whole sky seemed to burst into flames. Red, green and white tracer came up in front of us and curved over in beautiful arcs, while lower down the small guns were casting a hundred triumphant arches over the surface of the water. But as we passed over the island I saw the first flares dropping away to starboard, and so, after all, we had arrived at the same time as the others: it was perfect. We were at 7,500 feet and some of the HA was coming up to about 8,000: I couldn't decide whether it was a barrage or aimed directly at us. We had four miles to go across the harbour to our target, and it seemed an eternity. I looked over the side at the water below and we hardly seemed to be moving. This was obviously my imagination, for Olly was now gliding shallow at about 110 knots, and taking a good deal of avoiding action when he saw a particularly vicious tracer ahead of us. I had time to look down and see the cruisers in the outer harbour firing vast

Left: Pilot and observer stride towards their Swordfish as an air mechanic makes some last-minute adjustments to their steed on board HMS *Illustrious*; the vacant torpedo crutches are clearly evident. Aircraft from four different squadrons took part in the Taranto raid—nine from 815 and seven from 819, the carrier's own units, and three from 824 and a pair from 813, 'borrowed' from the complement on board HMS *Eagle*.

Opposite: HMS *Illustrious* photographed probably on the same occasion as that featured on page 5, with aircraft from 815 Squadron forward. Flying operations are again being conducted: notice that both barriers are raised, and that the forward lift has just been sent up again, having deposited its occupant in the hangar below.

LES SAYER COLLECTION

quantities of small stuff, and I knew the torpedo aircraft must be attacking. Then we got over the lock, and there in the light of the moon lay our target—a perfect row of ships, packed like sardines.

We were ideally placed to start our dive, and I screamed at Olly and pointed. But instead he turned to port—away from them. God! He hadn't seen them, and we were losing height rapidly and soon it would be too late. I shouted down the voicepipe like a madman, and could have wept for the longing to take his arm and point. That bloody long range tank again! At last he heard, and round we came and shot across the inner harbour, going into a dive for 2,000 feet and passing over the line of ships obliquely.

When he released his bombs I don't know, but I don't see how they could have missed anyway. We went on down until we were skimming over the houses, and I thought all hell had been let loose. We were being fired at by the cruisers and destroyers, and by guns of every description on the wharves just below us. I got my Lewis gun in my hands, with some crazy idea of hitting back at them, but almost immediately it shot out of my grasp and I was thrown out of the cockpit to the end of my strap. Olly was taking violent avoiding action, and I'm sure he saved our lives by doing so. I could distinctly hear the sharp crackle of machine guns and louder crack of Breda or Bofors underneath us, and all the time those coloured streams of fire seemed to weave a fantastic web all around us.

As we passed the seaplane base I gave the anchored aircraft some bursts from my gun, but I was feeling vindictive at the time. And then, quite suddenly, I realised that we were no longer being fired at. We had been under fire for fourteen minutes, and we had got away with it! We laughed.

Turning south, we made over the countryside for the coast at about 600 feet, but we had one more scare before we left Italy. I was watching a big fire astern of us (the seaplane hangar and someone's bombs had got connected) when suddenly a beastly little gun started pooping off at us from what seemed only a few yards away. We were glad of a friendly hill which Olly dived behind, and that hid us: perhaps they thought we had been shot down, and ran like mad to pick up the pieces.

The journey back of 190 miles might seem an anticlimax; it wasn't for me personally. At one time we thought we were running out of petrol, until Olly realised he had read the gauge wrong. At another moment we suddenly found ourselves over our own battle fleet: the visibility was not very good, and there were an ugly lot of thunder clouds hanging about just over us.

My beacon wasn't working, so I had to rely on navigation, and it was a great relief to sight *Illustrious* at 0135. This business of getting back may be all very well in daylight, but when you have to find a ship at night at that distance it isn't always funny. You draw lines and rub them out; and sweat blood because you think you've made a mistake; and listen to the wireless and wonder if you've missed a signal; and cock an eye out for enemy fighters near their coast; and try and make the beacon work; and then, when you're buried at the bottom of the cockpit in an attitude never devised for the human body, your pilot shouts at you and you struggle out to say 'Yes', and all he says is, 'Wasn't it bloody?'

Olly did a perfect landing on deck at 0200. We were safe at last, and I suddenly realised how much we wanted a cigarette . . .

97

Water Spouts Rising *Lieutenant (A) Leslie ('Bill') Bailey MiD RNVR*

The only scene in HMS *Victorious*'s operations room that I recall is of Captain Bovell standing in a gloomy light, part way down a ladder from the bridge, wishing us well and reassuring us that 'few casualties were to be expected in this kind of operation'. Shortly afterwards, in my aircraft, which was due to leave second after Esmonde's, I saw the third aircraft of the sub-flight lurch towards us and stop with its propeller within a whisker of our tail unit. The pilot caught my startled look and gave me a wry grimace. What had happened? I never knew, but assumed he had fumbled his brakes or, perhaps more likely, his aircraft had slid with a roll of the deck, which was running wet with rain. Anyway, we very nearly had an early night after all.

Then we were away, to give me my first sight of a carrier deck and island slipping away astern. Still moist—at least, behind the ears from observer training—and obsessed with trying not to do anything stupid, my main anxiety was to keep an accurate plot soon after we formed up, but I quickly found my compasses and ASI swinging and lurching like a trio of drunks. This, I eventually decided, was due to our constant jinking to keep formation, a form of flying that I had experienced only once or twice and then had no need to keep a plot. So I settled for the course and speed arranged before we left; but then it nagged at me that Colin Ennever (Senior Observer) might have made changes on viewing the sea surface and thinking better of the Met wind. (No orthodox wind-finding was done, presumably because of the difficulties of breaking formation and possibly losing touch in rain squalls.) But wouldn't he have 'zogged' (hand-signalled) any changes to us? Should I ask? He seemed permanently head-down in the 'office', probably peering down the tube of one of the two radar (ASV) sets in the squadron; and his TAG never seemed to look my way.

Anyway, he had got it right. After something over the hour we encountered *Norfolk* in company with the now somewhat disabled *Prince of Wales* and I was reading the message being flashed to us from the flagship:

'Enemy bearing [I forget] 15 miles [I think].' The reality of the day sank into my mind as I read the first word.

Away we all went, just beneath the overcast, and after a few minutes I saw *Bismarck*. She seemed alone. *Prinz Eugen* had slipped away, unbeknown to us, under cover of rain squalls some four hours earlier. Of the US coastguard vessel *Modoc*, which features in various postwar accounts, I saw nothing and heard nothing subsequently. For all I know, she may have been detected by Ennever's ASV on our way, and he, among others, may have seen her, but *Bismarck* was all that Jack Thompson, my pilot, and I saw. Soon Jack said, in a rather offended tone, 'She's pooping at us!' as I saw salvos begin flashing over her. The gunnery was impressive, with shells bursting at exactly our height, but mainly ahead. Esmonde, whose aircraft suffered slight damage, promptly rose into the cloud just above with the rest of us following, whereupon I lost sight of everything. We bumbled along for maybe less than a minute when one Swordfish suddenly emerged, heading towards us but crossing our track from right to left, in a shallow dive, missing us, it seemed, by less than a span and then vanishing back into cloud. Being in cloud was becoming more dangerous than being shot at, so after another very short while we broke out and found ourselves alone, with *Bismarck* below, slightly to our starboard and heading the opposite way. Another brief hesitation and then Jack said, 'I'm going in', pushing over into a steep dive. As we began to level out I heard loud firecrackers about my ears and saw white streaks of tracer passing by. At first I thought the crackers were strikes on the aircraft, but they must have been the sounds of near-misses: we suffered no damage.

As we turned away, after what seemed an interminable run in, I had a full view of the starboard side of the ship,

which seemed to have gone surprisingly quiet. I called to Jack, who was now waltzing the aircraft about, 'She has stopped firing—we seem to be all right now', or some such inanity, and he replied, 'She's chucking big stuff at us ahead.' Looking forward, I saw water spouts rising, around which Jack had begun his slaloms. At that moment I received two great blows on my back. 'This is it!' I thought, but it was only Don Bunce tactfully drawing my attention back astern to see a high water spout rising from the waterline of the ship, about amidships. Otherwise she still seemed strangely quiet. There was no sign of other aircraft nearby, but we saw a gaggle against the grey sky, some way off.

As we reached the others and formed up again on the left of Esmonde, Colin Ennever immediately 'zogged' me for my information and I signalled back that we had seen one hit on the starboard side. Our clocks now showed about midnight, although it was still daylight. However, we had about an hour to go, provided we intercepted well, and then it would be after sunset in gloomy weather. After about an hour, I seem to recall some large changes in our headings before sighting the wash of *Victorious*, now in near darkness, sometime before 0200. We must have been searching around for her, perhaps for half an hour or so. One postwar account tells of us overflying the ship in the rain squalls and gloom, which may well be true; others speak of searchlights switched on by *Victorious*, where Captain Bovell was becoming anxious (there was no radio beacon throughout the operation), but we saw nothing of them. Esmonde first saw red signalling lamps from our cruiser escort. Anyway, we were soon down, with no mishaps. All I can then remember is being called up to the bridge, alone, where Captain Bovell asked for my report. He thanked and dismissed me without comment after I told him virtually what I had signalled to Ennever. Of three Fulmars that flew off later than us to shadow *Bismarck*, two (crews Campbell and Goodger, and Furlong and Hoare) failed to return, but I heard nothing of

this at the time—nor, of course, of the fact that Furlong and Hoare were later rescued by a merchantman.

After turning in, I seemed to be awakened immediately. It was about dawn and we had to be away on a diverging search by seven aircraft to the north-west, towards the pack ice. One of the aircraft was piloted by D. P. B. ('Pat') Jackson with Observer D. A. ('Dapper') Berrill and TAG Leading Airman Sparkes. Pat Jackson has recounted the astonishing experience that he and his crew had of becoming lost on this search. They sighted a swamped lifeboat, ditched by it, baled it out with their flying boots and sailed it for over nine freezing days, living the life of Riley on a beaker of water and some ship's biscuits that they found in the boat along with its masts and sails, before being rescued by an Icelandic vessel. The rest of us found nothing. *Bismarck* had slipped from the shadowing cruisers at about 0330 and was heading south-east. Had we searched in that direction—which, as I read later, was the wish of Captain Bovell and Rear-Admiral Curteis in our escorting cruiser squadron—we would have had every chance of finding her again . . .

We were off again, at about 2100 on another diverging search of six aircraft to the south-east, but by now, had we known it, *Bismarck* was too far south. We returned at about midnight, and again my head hardly seemed to hit the pillow than I was roused. It was about 0500. The sea seemed rough. The ship had quite a roll on, and one of the others in the bunk house who had also been roused was trying to put a sock on while standing. He was sent hopping at high speed, first all the way to one end of the large space and then back, still grasping his sock half on. It was so ludicrous I was unable to suppress a guffaw, although I wasn't really amused and suspect my reaction was largely due to renewed tension. It didn't amuse the hopper.

There were only three aircraft this time. One was to search astern and the other two, including mine, ahead. The light and weather were poor, and as I clambered into the

This spread: HMS *Victorious*, 24 May 1941, *circa* 2145 hours: fully armed, the nine Swordfish of 825 Squadron are readied for their attack on the German battleship *Bismarck*. The aircraft in which the writer flew was coded '5C' and is seen in the right foreground; the CO's aircraft, coded '5A', occupies the centreline alongside. Fulmar fighters of 800Z Flight are ranged right astern.

aircraft there seemed to be something unfamiliar in the gloom about the helmeted pilot's head gazing down at his instruments. As I plugged in the speaking tube I was startled to hear Esmonde announce himself. He made no mention of Jack Thompson's absence, but, to put me at ease I suppose (or maybe to ensure that I wouldn't sit back and assume he knew the way round anyway), he said I would be in charge in the air and would be giving the orders. He seemed very relaxed and confident. (After our

Left: Back at Greenock on *Victorious*'s flight deck a few days after the action: (left to right) Midshipman (A) Leslie Bailey RNVR, Lieutenant (A) W. F. C. Garthwaite RNVR, Lieutenant Percy Gick (SP, 825 Squadron) and, with cat, Lieutenant Colin Ennever (SObs, 825 Squadron. The Swordfish in the background carries the intriguing inscription 'Atlantic . . .' just beneath the observer's compass, while the hole in the fairing for the TAG's compass mount bears testimony to *Bismarck*'s flak.

COURTESY LESLIE BAILEY

A Hit Amidships *Chief Petty Officer (A) Les Sayer MBE DSM*

I had been in 811 Squadron on board HMS *Furious* for about a year when the war broke out. I was a brand new TAG when I joined 811, and so I was introduced to all the exercises that were taking place at that time, and to all the rôles that the Swordfish undertook–torpedo-dropping, dive-bombing. When hostilities began I was drafted to Ford to assist with the training of TAGs and also of observers–teaching them Morse, W/T procedures, and so forth. When Ford was bombed, the entire training unit was moved to Arbroath, where, for some ten months, I continued the same sort of work as part of the Royal Naval Signals School.

In May 1941, after my spell at Arbroath, I went to join 825 Squadron at Campbeltown, preparatory to embarking in *Ark Royal*. The Chief TAG was leaving to go on a course and I took over the position. We fully expected to spend

several months working-up, but this did not happen. Instead, the German battleship *Bismarck* was on the move and we were hurriedly put on board HMS *Victorious*. This was a brand new carrier, half full of dismantled Hurricane fighters in packing cases bound for Malta, and conditions were somewhat chaotic. Nobody knew where anything was; I did not know the Squadron. Six of the TAGs had just come out of training; another three had varying degrees of experience. I was desperately trying to get them together, and here we were doing thirty knots in awful weather, chasing after the most formidable warship in the enemy fleet–although we had not been briefed as to what was expected of us.

At 22.10 in the evening of 24 May 1941, forty-eight hours after leaving Scapa Flow, our nine Swordfish, led by the

FLEET AIR ARM MUSEUM

return, I learned from a disconsolate Jack that Esmonde had replaced him at the last minute because of the bad conditions.) I continued my policy of finding the wind on each of our scheduled tracks, and he followed all my directions without demur, although I suspected he may well have thought I was fussing and would have preferred his own very experienced observer. A few minutes before my ETA he suddenly announced 'Ships ahead', whereupon I stupidly blurted out 'Are they ours?' before looking. He gave no reply, but I could just make out the blur of one of our four escorting cruisers through a curtain of light rain and then, a few minutes later, the carrier.

After we were down Esmonde sent for me to report to him in the hangar. There he gave me a gentle rocket—not, as I was expecting, for making daft remarks or some such, but for disconnecting my speaking tube just before we landed. I did this in the fond belief that it was standard practice in case we went into the sea. Heaven knows where I got the idea. Faintly amused, Esmonde quietly disabused me and quickly went on to say how much he appreciated my effort, especially finding a wind on each leg, and how well it had gone. They were kind words; and his nerve to trust me that morning seems even more extraordinary to me now than it did then.

Soon we were all depressed with the news that one of the other two aircraft was overdue . . . and before long it was clear that it was the fourth to have gone in the past thirty-six hours. So far, during this period five aircrew members of 825, of whom three were lost, had each flown four times for some fifteen hours. Everyone else, including the three who were lost but eventually rescued, had flown two or three times for up to twelve hours. The sombre mood was lifted considerably when we heard that *Bismarck* had been sighted, shortly after our last flight, some 500 miles to the south.

CO, Lieutenant-Commander Eugene Esmonde, took off, formed up and departed. We were fitted with a primitive radar system, and when we got within what we thought would be striking distance of the battleship, we got a 'blip'. Thinking this to be the *Bismarck*, we descended through cloud, but it turned out to be the *Modoc*, a US Coast Guard cutter, and we had given away our position; the *Bismarck* herself was only about six miles away.

We went in. My pilot was Lieutenant Percy Gick, who was the No 1 torpedo attack instructor in the FAA: if anybody was going to score a hit, it would surely be he. They started throwing everything at us, of course, but we got away with it, allegedly because the German rangefinders were not calibrated for enemy aircraft approach speeds below 100 knots. It is also said that we were flying so low that the German guns could not achieve the necessary depression. At first I thought that our torpedo had got hung up, but, as if in answer, back came this Dartmouth voice: 'I am not lined up properly. I am going in again.' We therefore wheeled away to a distance of about fifteen miles.

The Germans must have thought that the attack was over and that the Swordfish had all departed. They did not see us; they did not know that we were there. So we dropped the 'fish' from about 500 yards and at a height of about twenty feet. We turned away, but by the time the gun crews had woken up we were twenty miles away. They then opened up with their fifteen-inch main armament. They did not hit us, but we could not avoid the spouts of water thrown up by the shell splashes and when we hit one of them all the fabric from the bottom of the aircraft was torn away. We had a rather cold trip back! As we approached *Victorious* she put on a searchlight and, amazingly, we all got back on board—three of the pilots had never carried out a deck landing at night before. We were probably the least prepared torpedo squadron to do the job required of us, but our No 1 aircraft did hit the *Bismarck* amidships.

Left: Though not known for certain, this photograph is said to show Lieutenant-Commander Eugene Esmonde and his crew, Lieutenant C. C. Ennever and Petty Officer (A) S. E. Parker, taking off from *Victorious* for the first attack on *Bismarck*. The vessel off the port bow is presumably one of the carrier's escorting cruisers.
Right: Honoured: (left to right) Lieutenant Percy Gick, Lieutenant-Commander Eugene Esmonde, Sub-Lieutenant V. Norfolk, Petty Officer (A) Les Sayer and Leading Airman A. L. Johnson on the occasion of their awards of, respectively, the DSC, DSO, DSC, DSM and DSM, on board *Ark Royal* in October 1941. The 'spit-and-polished' Swordfish in the background is fitted with a Long Range Tank in the observer's cockpit.

First Contact *Lieutenant-Commander (A) Edgar Lee DSO VRD RNR*

On returning from my observer's training course in Canada I found myself with a fortnight's leave, following which I went off to St Merryn to do my gunnery course. I had a fortnight there, and shortly after this I reached the age of twenty and was 'promoted' from Midshipman to acting, temporary, probationary (and more or less unpaid) Sub-Lieutenant and was told that I had been appointed to HMS *Ark Royal*, although no squadron was mentioned at the time. This happened during the weekend of the German attack on Russia in June 1941. So I went up to Greenock to join the SS *Pasteur*, and during the train journey met one of the course who was also going out there. I had no idea of our ultimate destination when we boarded the *Pasteur*, but three or four days later we arrived in Gibraltar. The first thing I had to do was to get some tropical kit!

We sailed after two or three days, bound for Cagliari, Sardinia, to attack the airfield there. The newcomers—there were five of us—did not fly, but I went on to the catwalk alongside the flight deck to watch the aircraft landing-on. One of the Swordfish appeared to have something hanging down from under the wing. It was a bomb, and when the aircraft touched down it fell off and exploded. I dived down the nearest companionway! The Flight Deck Officer, Lieutenant-Commander Stringer, ex-RAF and later to become a Captain RN, rushed straight into the blazing wreck in a attempt to save the crew: the pilot and observer were hauled out, but the TAG was dead. Once the body had been removed, the wreck of the Swordfish was pushed over the stern into the Mediterranean. The pilot and observer died in the Sick Bay shortly afterwards.

My introduction to operational Swordfish flying had shaken me somewhat. As a result of this incident, crews were instructed that, in the event of hang-ups involving fragmentation bombs, they were either to bale out or to attempt a forced landing in the sea.

As I was sipping a hot coffee the tannoy sounded. 'Sub-Lieutenant Lee report to the AIO.' Percy Gick, 825 Squadron's Senior Pilot, announced that we were going off on an A/S patrol, so it was straight into flying kit and take off.

Anti-submarine patrols were a regular feature of our days in the Med. However, with sunrise in this part of the world coming early, and because of the insistence that we ate breakfast before we took off, we were obliged to get up at about 3 or 4 o'clock in the morning. With a depth charge under each wing, we would patrol forwards and backwards ahead of the Fleet, at a radius of some ten to twenty miles, searching in a predetermined pattern for any hint of enemy submarine activity. Usually, of course, nothing would be seen, and we had to resist the dangers of boredom. Occasionally we would be ordered to search *astern*, and this was something I really hated—your home was moving away from you, not coming towards you or, at the very least, keeping more or less constant station! On one of these sweeps the weather was particularly bad, and we were told to return to the ship if things got too much. The Squadron had been equipped with ASV radar although, as I was the 'sprog' in the unit, my particular aircraft did not have it. We took off, and I completed the first leg of the search, went to a quarter bearing and then went astern. Unfortunately, when we were being briefed in the Air Intelligence Office, I had failed to pay attention to the course of the ship and had recorded it as one-eight-zero (which would have taken her right into the Tunisian coast) instead of two-eight-zero.

We came across one of the liners that used to do the run from Genoa to the United States. Being a Swedish neutral, she was all lit up, and she became our turning point. Later,

Below: Swordfish '4C' off HMS *Ark Royal*'s starboard quarter with a heavy underwing load. The aircraft has full-fin red, white and blue striping, which suggests that the photograph was taken during the summer or autumn of 1940.

Above: 810 Squadron's Swordfish P4123, bombed up and awaiting clearance to fly, receives attention from maintenance personnel on *Ark Royal*'s flight deck to correct a technical problem during a hot Mediterranean day in 1940.

on the new course, I was steering 280 degrees when the YG beacon enabled me to see the bearing on the ship, I discovered to my horror that it was one-eight-zero and here we were flogging away on two-eight-zero. Beginning to panic, I asked the air gunner to get a D/F bearing, and, fortunately for me, the ship's captain, Captain L. E. H. Maund, broke radio silence. I got on to the new bearing, and we just made it back to *Ark Royal* before running out of fuel. We landed-on.

'Sub-Lieutenant Lee and Sub-Lieutenant So-and-So report to the bridge!'

I was for the chop. Commander (Flying) questioned the pilot and Commander Bentick, the Observer Commander, questioned me in the company of the Captain.

'Well, Lee, you made a bit of a mess of that!'

'Yes, sir. Entirely my own fault.'

'Well, never mind. You were one of the crews who actually completed the trip. The others returned early because of the weather.'

So I was sent on my way, not exactly rejoicing but certainly relieved!

Each search patrol would generally involve the entire squadron (as opposed to separate sub-flights). We had an establishment of nine aircraft in 825, although from time to time not all would be serviceable. If we were really lucky, there might be some Fulmars around as fighter escort, but this was rare as these aircraft were primarily there for the defence of the Fleet, not us. Following take-off we would fan out, each aircraft being just about within visual distance of the next. We did make one abortive attack on the Italian Fleet, which, on our approach, decided not to get involved

with the likes of *Ark Royal* and the battlecruiser *Renown*. We also had that wonderful little beast HMS *Manxman*, a mine-layer capable of forty knots, the sight of which thundering towards them probably made the enemy commanders think twice too! There was never much chance of our intercepting the Italians in fact, as we had a headwind of about 50 knots. The Italians were disappearing at a rate of 30 knots, and thus the Swordfish had something of a struggle even keeping up. C.R.42s appeared, and we played hide-and-seek with them in the cloud for a while. We set course back for *Ark Royal*, but now she was not where she ought to have been because she had had to take evasive action when set upon by Italian bombers. We were therefore obliged to conduct a search, and by the time we landed-on we had practically no fuel left, some of our aircraft having had to jettison their torpedoes also. However, all made it back safely in the end.

One very valuable lesson had been learned as a result of the serious damage inflicted by Axis bombers on the carrier *Illustrious* in the Mediterranean. When she had been bombed, the (non-flying) pilots and observers of the torpedo-bomber squadrons were down in the Wardroom and a lot of them had been killed when a bomb came through the flight deck. *Ark Royal* had a different regime: while the fighters were airborne, the Swordfish observers (and perhaps the pilots too) were made Captains of guns. I had the starboard forward heavy machine guns under my command in these circumstances. We were now in the open, although the 4.5 just above did not do the hearing a lot of good! Thus non-flying aircrew were not only occupied, they were in the open and dispersed about the ship. I must confess to being impressed by the big Italian trimotor bombers. The Italians may not have had a very good reputation as a fighting force generally, but those aircrews were extremely brave men: some were shot down at *very* close quarters.

An Almighty Bang *Lieutenant-Commander Edgar Lee DSO VRD RNR*

We had put on a show of force off Barcelona, landing-on and taking off—outside Spanish territorial waters, naturally. Later, on 13 November 1941, *Ark Royal* was returning to Gibraltar with most of the torpedo bombers airborne on exercises, and my Swordfish was one of the last to land-on. We had not, of course, seen a submarine. We landed on, the pilot and the air gunner got out on deck, and the aircraft was struck down into the upper hangar with me still on board (I had all my navigation equipment to offload). My aircraft had been parked forward and the lift had gone back up.

I had just collected together my gear and was standing alongside the aircraft when there was an almighty bang. Everything went black. My first thought was that a depth charge had gone off on deck; if ever a Swordfish had to use the barrier, a depth charge would sometimes fall off and go skating along the flight deck in a shower of sparks. Immediately, however, the carrier started to heel.

Clearly, it was time to get out. In the darkness, I cautiously made my way to the side bulkhead, having lined myself up with the aircraft's propeller and walking in what I calculated to be a straight line at right angles from it. The first door I came across opened out into the Air Gunners' Mess, and from there I was able to go down to the Wardroom. By this time the list had increased to some 10–12 degrees and everything in the Wardroom had slid into the scuppers. I decided to try to get to my cabin to collect my 'rabbits', but this was in the lower steering flat I changed my mind and went up to the quarterdeck.

Eventually the destroyer *Laforey* came alongside. She had to be careful because *Ark Royal*'s aerial masts, which were normally upright, were still lowered following our landing-on, and had also to keep her quarter well away from our port propeller, which by this time was out of the water. All the non-essential crew were ordered to abandon ship; the huge loss of life when *Courageous* had gone down was still fresh in the memory. Some people jumped down on to the destroyer's deck, others slid down on ropes. When she had completed her task, *Laforey* went back on patrol, and eventually we were returned to Gibraltar.

The Board of Inquiry blamed Captain Maund, citing a lack of effective damage control, although the Board knew very well that the loss of the carrier was not his fault. He was dismissed his ship and later sent to Egypt to look after the aerodromes there. Apparently, however, the actual cause of the loss was entirely physical, a design fault: the transfer ducts carrying air for the boilers were sited too low in the ship, so the water rushed in, cutting off the air supply to the boilers and lowering the air pressure in the boiler rooms—extinguishing the fires in the starboard boiler room and then the amidships room. There was no electrical power for the fans, and there were flashbacks in the port boilers and a general loss of power throughout the ship.

There was an outside chance of saving the carrier, but the torpedo had struck in the vicinity of the switchroom, putting the main pumps out of action. One of the destroyers cam alongside to supply power, and in fact the port engine room was got running. A tug was on its way, but *Ark Royal* was making only about two knots and conditions in the boiler rooms were fast becoming impossible. Thus, after some hours, the Captain gave the second order to abandon ship and the latter was left to her fate. Vice-

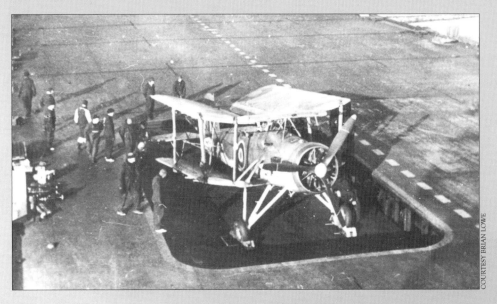

Right: A Swordfish, chocked and folded, on *Ark Royal*'s aftermost (of three) lifts; notice the arrester wires aft and the eight-barrelled 'pom-pom' AA mounting at left. It was not unusual for aircrews to 'ride' the lift before disembarking—all in the interests of a brisk flight-deck cycle that got all the returning aircraft down in the shortest possible time.
Below: With the destroyer *Laforey* alongside, the carrier's personnel abandon the doomed carrier following her torpedoing by the German submarine U 81. The Swordfish parked forward are already beginning to slip from the flight deck.

COURTESY BRIAN LOWE

Admiral Somerville came out from Gibraltar and stood with Maund in the deck of his destroyer as the 'Ark' went down. Maund was later exonerated of all blame, and eventually became a Rear-Admiral, but he was never to command a ship again.

Discounting HMS *Hermes*, which, in any case, was in reality a prototype, *Ark Royal* was the first genuinely purpose-built carrier in the Royal Navy, all her predecessors having been conversions or adaptation of other types of ship; *Courageous*, *Glorious* and *Furious*, for example, were originally battlecruisers, *Eagle* a Chilean battleship and *Argus* an Italian passenger liner. The 'Ark', nevertheless, had shortcomings in terms of her design, as was proved on that fateful day in November 1941. It has to be said that she was, in comparison with her predecessors, an extremely comfortable ship. Being a very junior officer, my cabin was rather noisy and claustrophobic, but on the other hand, while at sea we were given low camp beds and allowed to sleep on the quarterdeck—not at all an unpleasant experience in a Mediterranean summer, especially with my wind-up gramophone nearby, playing my favourite music! From war to pleasure cruising in a matter of hours!

As a squadron, 825 had now lost all its aircraft, although happily, of course, all its personnel were intact. I returned with some of the other officers in the battleship *Nelson*, which had just emerged from a period in drydock at Gibraltar for some patching up following a torpedo hit forward. We came back, incidentally, through a full hurricane. The ship was reduced to steering speed, and, standing on the after conning tower, some fifty feet above the waterline, the crests of the waves were at eye level or above. Quite an experience! We made it to Greenock, and thence to a fortnight's survivors' leave.

IMPERIAL WAR MUSEUM

In a Pickle *Lieutenant-Commander (A) Edgar Lee DSO VRD RNR*

I was told to report back to 825 Squadron, which had been re-formed on New Year's Day 1942 with six Swordfish at Lee-on-Solent. However, the CO and the Senior Pilot were the only two with wide experience; the other two, Sub-Lieutenants Wood and Brian Rose (my pilot), had joined the Squadron much later. Among the observers, only the SO and the SP's observer had very much experience. It had been decided that we would train to become an army co-operation squadron—presumably for the 'Torch' landings in North Africa.

One day the COs of the three resident squadrons were called to the Captain's office and they were asked for volunteers for carrying out an attack on the German battlecuisers *Scharnhorst* and *Gneisenau*, which were expected to make an attempt to return to Germany from their French base via the English Channel. (The French *Résistance*, chiefly in the form of the incredibly brave Lieutenant Phillipon, had been transmitting details of what was taking place at Brest at regular intervals.) Esmonde told us what was happening. The Germans were expected to leave port between 10 and 14 February, when virtually moonless nights and a spring tide would offer the best conditions for a successful breakthrough. It might be a night attack, carried out from RAF Manston further along the coast, but, from the Germans' point of view, sailing through the Strait of Dover at dawn would have required a departure in the late morning, and during the early part of the passage north the ships would most certainly have been spotted as there were regular air patrols every day. Sensibly, the Germans decided to leave under cover of darkness, at around 2100 hours, even though this meant that Dover would be passed at around midday. It also meant that a strong and effective fighter 'umbrella' could be organised.

Meanwhile we carried out some night patrols. We were equipped only with W/T at that time; the RAF at Manston, however, being a fighter-bomber aerodrome, had R/T, as did the radar station at Swingate, near Dover. Unfortunately, there was only one spare R/T set at Manston, and so this was installed in the CO's Swordfish. Thus anyone doing a night patrol controlled by Swingate had to use this particular machine. We were up every morning at five, well before dawn, to get ready, but the wait continued and we carried on with our patrols for about a week.

On 11 February Esmonde was summoned to the Palace to receive his DSO, and he returned at about 11 o'clock. The following day Brian Rose and I were detailed to go out to Deal Bay to carry out some dummy torpedo attacks, and while we were engaged in this we were suddenly recalled. The German ships had been spotted. When we

returned we were briefed by Esmonde, who explained that we would be flying in line astern at 50 feet, and that we would have fighter top cover. However, as is now known but was not known at the briefing, senior RN and RAF officers—not, it must be stressed, the RAF squadrons—managed to make rather a mess of things; for example, one plan that had been vetoed by an Admiral was that to send one of the 'R' class battleships to a position off the Humber estuary, ready to intercept the German ships as they made their way north-eastwards. Moreover, the COs of the squadrons in No 11 Group RAF had no idea what was afoot: the Intelligence Officer at Biggin Hill was on leave, and his safe was locked. The upshot was that the RAF were asked to escort a squadron of Swordfish in an attack on 'German shipping' in the Channel. None of the light blues at squadron level had been informed that this shipping constituted a rather more potent force than they had been meeting in the past. Indeed, the first inkling the RAF squadrons had that this operation was rather different was when the fighter escort arrived over the German warships, went in closer to salute them in the belief that such wonderful looking vessels could only belong to His Majesty's Royal Navy . . . and promptly got peppered!

Esmonde had thus decided to go in, ignorant of the fact that the proposed fighter cover would not materialise. We took off and did some circuits over Manston, waiting for the fighters to appear. We were joined by No 72 Squadron with only ten Spitfires and then set course for the enemy warships. About ten minutes from the coast, we were intercepted by German fighters. The Spitfires had problems, firstly in flying slowly enough in order to provide an effective escort for us and secondly in flying in such a way as to be in a position to counter the German Messerschmitts. The RAF managed to drive off the first attack, although some damage was inflicted on our Swordfish. A few minutes later, a swarm of aircraft appeared, not only Me 109s but also FW 190s—a real match for the Spitfires. We were now in a pickle.

My air gunner was killed in the next attack. I tried to climb into his cockpit—something I had done before, though in calmer circumstances—but I could not move him. I therefore concentrated on assisting the pilot. The attack had come on from astern, but almost immediately the enemy started to attack from the beam also. My job was therefore to watch the attacking aircraft carefully, estimate when each might open fire and advise the pilot as to how the aircraft might be jinked hard a-starboard or a-port to evade the streams of shells. We survived in this way for a while, carrying out violent manœuvres, but then a cannon shell, which must have missed me by a whisker, hit the back of Brian Rose's seat, putting a lot of splinters into his back and depriving him of the full use of his arms. By this time we were on the approach of our run-in. The CO's Swordfish ahead of us dropped his torpedo and crashed into the sea; I noticed that he had had his port lower mainplane shot away. We thus found ourselves in the van of the first sub-flight, with Kingsmill behind us. The second sub-flight, for some reason, were about 500 feet above us, in 'vic' formation rather than line astern. I know now, from German reports, that they were shortly afterwards met by a squadron of Me 109s head-on and blown out of the sky.

As a result of the attack in which Rose was injured, we had lost station on *Gneisenau* but were nevertheless in a position to go for *Prinz Eugen*. We dropped at about 1,200 yards, not far away from the designated range. The German cruiser turned into our torpedo track (so as to present a more difficult target) and we nearly flew into her stern as we broke away. As our main fuel tank had been holed—although there was, fortunately, no fire—Rose announced that he was going to attempt to ditch our injured Swordfish astern of the German fleet. We flew over the aftermost destroyer of the escort, and after they had given us a stream of lead we were looking like a flying colander.

The pilot made a very good emergency landing, but he was unable to get out of the cockpit. The dinghy was tethered to one of the wing struts. My pilot was a biggish chap—about six feet tall and probably some twelve stone; I was rather smaller, but fortunately pretty fit, and as he pushed with his feet I managed to raise him and tip him overboard into the dinghy (which must have been extremely painful for him). I went back to try to get our air gunner, Johnson's, body out, but, with the water rising fast as I struggled, it was a forlorn enterprise. I got into the dinghy but then realised that the it was still lashed to the aircraft and that there was every possibility that we would be dragged down with it as it sank. Despite the freezing conditions, I managed to free the dinghy and as we got under way the aircraft went down.

We were now bobbing around on the choppy waves, waiting for something to happen. After about an hour and a half I heard a roar of engines and a torpedo boat approached us. My first thoughts were that it was an E-boat, but, clearly, it was better to become a PoW than to drown, so I reached for the flare. Now the visitor saw us and began to draw alongside. I was still unclear as to its identity, but then spotted that it was flying the Jolly Roger—something that, I calculated, would be beyond the German sense of humour. The crew of the boat first tried to get Rose on board, but, badly injured, he was unable to help himself. With no thought for themselves, two of the crewmen jumped into the icy water and managed to manœuvre him on to the boat. Then they helped me on board.

It was fortuitous that we had been spotted. The Dover MTBs had been ordered to intercept the German fleet, but, in the rush to get into the fray, had been unable to warm their Merlin engines, with the result that several suffered failures. The skipper of this MTB had been unable to reach the Germans, but he had seen us going down and had decided to steer south to look for us—assisted by one of the young pilots from the fighter escort, who had seen us go in and had made a 'Mayday'. We were taken to Dover. Rose was rushed off to hospital, and I was taken in and placed in a marvellous piece of kit—what looked like a corrugated-iron shelter with rows of 100-Watt light bulbs inside to help thaw me out! I was then escorted to Dover Castle and spent about 45 minutes with Admiral Ramsay. He was absolutely splendid: here was a very senior officer, surrounded by general mayhem, who still took time off to put me at my ease. I was put through on the phone to Admiral (Air) at Lee-on-Solent to report events, and then I went back to Manston.

By the early evening, back at Manston, it began to dawn on me that I was the only chap in the Squadron to have returned. In the Mess I learned that Rose was in hospital in Dover. The CO at Manston, Tom Gleave, was extremely good to me, arranging a 'Tilly' so that I could drive over to see my pilot. When I returned, I had the dreary task of packing up all the belongings. Next day the Press descended, and, again, Tom Gleave did me a great service by fending off the most persistent reporters. Gleave and Esmonde had got on very well together, and indeed it was the former who recommended that the latter should be awarded the VC—as far as I am aware, the first and only occasion when an RAF officer has recommended an RN officer (albeit one who was a former RAF officer) for this award.

Rose must have had nearly a year off flying because of his injuries, but he eventually returned to service, flying Swordfish from Bircham Newton on minelaying sorties off the Dutch coast. He later did some instruction in torpedo-bombing at Crail flying Barracudas and subsequently did the Bats course. At Machrahanish one day, a flight of Barracudas arrived, their pilots detailed to fly off in new Avengers as replacements. One of the Barracudas was unserviceable, and Rose volunteered to take it across the water to Northern Ireland following repairs. For some reason he decided to go via Abbotsinch, and while approaching the runway 'appeared to be having difficulty with his undercarriage'. Possibly because the pilot was distracted and lost sight of his airspeed, the aircraft stalled and spun in. Rose was killed.

Background image: The battlecruisers *Scharnhorst* and, in the distance, *Gneisenau*, photographed from the heavy cruiser *Prinz Eugen* during the 'Channel Dash'.

No Messing Around *Lieutenant-Commander Mike Langman* DSC CD

I had not met the new Commanding Officer of 815 Squadron, Lieutenant-Commander Gick, before, but when I did, I was most impressed. There was no messing around. He asked me to make a dummy attack on a target at sea using R.3030 radar and then told me to make another one with the Senior Observer on board to check out my new observer, Peter Woodham. They must have been okay. We repeated this exercise the next night, but the air gunner preparing to fire his Very pistol to illuminate the target must have mistaken the height of the rim of the cockpit, because the cartridge ignited inside the cockpit, setting the fuselage fabric alight. I had no idea what was happening behind me, so I turned the aircraft around to the shore as quickly as possible and landed back on the aerodrome as the fire went out. Fortunately, neither of the people in the back was injured.

We joined the main part of 815 at Baggush, approximately 100 miles west of Dekheila, on 15 April 1942, but, knowing that the Squadron did not stay in one place very long, we were surprised at the number of vehicles needed to service the operation of twelve Swordfish aircraft and to provide for 100-plus men. There were tents everywhere, some partially dug into the sand, and all in a semblance of some order. The aerodrome itself was simply a levelled part of the desert, not far from the only road and single railway line which existed (and ended) in this part of Egypt. The most used runway was marked by 45-gallon drums for daylight flying, and, at night, cans the shape of watering cans full of paraffin with a rag hanging out of the nose were used. It appeared to be very primitive, but it worked.

The Swordfish was a remarkable aeroplane. It could carry a number of different weapons such as a torpedo, rockets, 250-pound bombs or depth charges and parachute flares, or, like the CO's aircraft, a motorbike on the torpedo rack, between the front wheels. The cockpits were open to all kinds of weather, and, when we were not flying,

the engine and cockpit had to be covered in canvas tarpaulins to keep out the sand and rain. The Bristol nine-cylinder radial engine could drive the aeroplane for about three and a half hours using 167 gallons of fuel. When a sixty-gallon tank of fuel was fitted in the back of the cockpit, the endurance was increased, permitting flight between five and six hours, sometimes more.

Although 815 was a naval squadron, the operational flying was dictated by No 201 Group Royal Air Force, based in Cairo or Alexandria. Each day the RAF officer attached to the Squadron would receive details of requirements for the next night, and we would do our best to carry them out. We would think nothing of being sent away to, say, Sidi Barrani (about 90 miles to the west) to carry out a particular search, and then return to base the next morning.

On 22 May we picked up a radar return on our ASV and saw, in the moonlight, a submarine on the surface. We immediately attacked it with depth charges as it was diving and saw its stern rise out of the water. Unfortunately, only three of the four depth charges came off the racks and later on we were told that no submarine in that locality had been reported as sunk, although we heard later that a submarine had been attacked and sunk by destroyers six days after our sighting near Tobruk.

I would never say that we were overworked, but flying our searches at night and then having the day off (except for flight testing your own aircraft for the next night's work) took a bit of getting used to. Furthermore, flying the Swordfish was great fun, although sitting in the front cockpit on your parachute waiting for a radar contact, which seldom appeared, did become rather tiring now and then. For this reason, aircrew were allowed one week's leave

Above: An 815 Squadron Swordfish, armed with depth charges and flares, at RNAS Baggush in 1942. An RAF Vickers Wellesley can just be seen at the extreme right of the photograph.

for every six weeks' operational flying. Normally in 815 we had twelve Swordfish and a full crew of three for each, so we were not particularly stretched.

The period from 15 April to 26 June, spent at Baggush and Sidi Barrani, was mostly taken up with anti-submarine and surface vessel searches. If we were looking for submarines we would carry four depth charges, or, in the case of shipping, 250-pound bombs. If no target was found in the search area and we were carrying bombs, we would, on the way home, drop them on enemy camps and vehicles, usually to be found on, or near, the desert road. This used to cause quite a lot of anti-aircraft response, but it was not very concentrated and I do not remember any of our aircraft being damaged by it.

On 26 June we were informed that the German Army had made a strong push to the east and that we should get out of Baggush as quickly as possible and return to Dekheila. We were all ready to go, and could see the German tanks passing along the desert road, when the CO noticed the White Ensign still flying. He sent his air gunner to lower it and bring it back to his aircraft. Then we all took off. The Germans must have thought we were mad!

On arrival at Dekheila, the Squadron was split into two groups. Four aircraft and crews (I was one of them) would remain where they were and the other eight with their crews went somewhere near the Suez Canal. The Dekheila aircraft were immediately fitted with long-range fuel tanks and we started anti-shipping operations at once. The task now was to prevent the enemy bringing food, ammunition, more troops etc. into El Alamein and harbours to the west. Dekheila was kept operational with a reduced staff and provided everything we needed to keep the Squadron going. The next four months were the most exciting, demanding and satisfying experience in my time in the Middle East. Our sorties were arranged so as to last between five and six hours, and for a change, we could use our initiative when we came upon the enemy.

On 27 September we were carrying out a search and the wind must have changed because it blew us further out to sea than we intended. We became lost and, after finding our way back to the coast, realised that we would not be able to get as far as the aerodrome at Dekheila because our fuel was getting very low and we should perhaps make a forced landing. The trouble was, it was night and we could not see what the ground below us was like. This did not matter really because the engine cut and we had to land. Luck was on our side and the Swordfish came to a stop, knocking off the undercarriage and releasing four parachute flares, which burst into flames behind us as we skidded along the ground. In the morning we heard voices in the distance and saw a small group of soldiers whom we recognised as British, shouting to us not to move because we were on the edge of a minefield! Shortly after this the Army, having won the battle at El Alamein, took off in hot pursuit of what was left of the Germans.

The Squadron, by now a single unit again, set up camp at Marsa Matruh, halfway between Alexandria and Tobruk, and carried on searching for submarines and surface vessels—which we did not find.

Above: A page from Lieutenant-Commander Langman's log book for May 1942, illustrating the varied tasks allocated to 815 Squadron aircrew in North Africa at that time.
Below: Maid of all work—including transporting the CO's motorcycle! Notice the Swordfish's black-painted undersurfaces and, at left beneath the Townend ring, the special dust filter that typified aircraft working in these environments.

COURTESY MIKE LANGMAN

COURTESY MIKE LANGMAN

The Darkest Nights *Lieutenant (A) Don Ridgway RNVR*

In May 1942, their Lordships took the very sensible decision to remove both aircraft and hangars from cruisers operating in the North Atlantic. At last I was to be liberated from HMS *Berwick*. Apart from being lonely, it had been a very boring time, enlivened by just two 'panics' when reports came that the *Tirpitz* (our *raison d'être*) had left her Norwegian base, when we were at battle stations for days at a time surviving on thick cocoa and slabs of corned-beef sandwiches. I left *Berwick* in Plymouth, had a week's leave and was told to report to the CO of 816 Squadron at Machrihanish.

My joy on meeting my new colleagues was immense. The CO was a Captain of Marines, Olly Patch no less, DSO DSC and all, a flight Commander at Taranto and the only man ever to sink three ships (two Italian submarines were refuelling from a tanker at the same time) with one torpedo. The Senior Observer was a two-ringed, RN (A), heavily bearded extrovert called Charles Simpson, who had been a London copper before the war and was last heard of as the vicar of a remote parish in the far west of Ireland. There was one other RN (A) officer, Sub-Lieutenant 'Dook' Norfolk, wearing a DSC that he had been awarded flying Swordfish in the Western Desert (very sadly, he was lost on our first minelaying operation). All the other officers were RNVR (A) boys, including three or four Kiwis.

816 had been one of the squadrons aboard *Ark Royal* when she was torpedoed the previous November and was now being re-formed to be purpose-trained for use on the new escort carriers that were due to come into service in the year. I think that the Squadron was one of the first to be equipped with armour-piercing rockets for anti-U-boat work; previously Swordfish had carried depth-charges similar to those used on destroyers etc., but slightly modified to be slung under the lower plane.

The use of rockets meant a different mode of attack and during July and August we flew many hours practising this new art, attacking smoke floats with rockets. A frequent diversion on these trips was to attack basking sharks—of which there were hundreds lying just below the surface of the Scottish sea lochs—with smoke floats. The sharks invariably ignored our efforts.

The other innovation was the introduction of ASV sets to Swordfish. Officially and for security reasons not acknowledged at that time, the Air to Surface Vessel equipment was in fact an elementary form of radar. The set sent out a signal directly ahead of the aircraft and rebounded back to the aircraft if it hit a solid object; the echo was picked up by antennæ fixed on the port and starboard wings. The returned signal was transmitted to a vertical cathode ray tube in the observer's cockpit, where it was seen as a 'blip' of light, of equal size to right and left if the object was dead ahead of the aircraft or as a larger 'blip' to the right if the object was to starboard (or to the left if port), when the precise bearing could be determined by turning the aircraft to get 'blip's of equal size each side of the centre line. The range of the object from the aircraft was measured by the time it took the signal to return, and this was indicated by the position of the 'blip' on the vertical line of the tube from the baseline. From memory, I think that the set could be adjusted to maximum ranges of five, ten or fifteen miles. From the observer's point of view, the ASV set was a marvellous invention: it was the first real aid to navigation, which had hitherto been entirely dependent on dead-reckoning.

It appeared to be the norm in most naval squadrons that the CO flew with the Senior Observer (in a very few cases the CO was an observer, in which case he flew with the Senior Pilot), but otherwise it seemed to be a matter of chance as to which pilot teamed up with which observer and air gunner. My first Swordfish pilot was Pete Pryor, at twenty-four years of age quite old by squadron standards, the average age being about twenty-one years and six months at the time (although a year later it was twenty years and six months).

We completed our working-up at the end of August, when we were sent on ten days' leave. On our return to Machrihanish we found that our Swordfish had been painted an ominous black, and we were told that, since there were still no escort carriers available, we were to fly night operations over the English Channel under Coastal Command from one of their major bases at Thorney Island. At this time the Squadron had six Swordfish and a complement of eight crews (i.e., eight each of pilots, observers and TAGs) but only the CO and the two RN (A) observers had any operational experience of any kind, and few of us had more than a dozen hours of night-flying experience, which was to be our operational preoccupation for the next four months. It was probably inevitable that we should experience significant losses during this period, so that, of the original twenty-four aircrew, nine were lost, and of the nine replacements a further three were lost. Sadly, a further seven of the remaining aircrew were to be lost when *Dasher* blew up in March 1943 (see pages 114–115). Some of the crews had been shot down during minelaying operations but others were lost as a result of navigational errors returning to a blacked-out Britain.

Dead-reckoning navigation is only successful if the observer can keep a regular check on the wind speed and direction, particularly in aircraft cruising at only 82 knots. The conventional method of determining wind speed and direction(see right) assumed daylight conditions, when the procedure was that, simultaneously with dropping a smoke float and the observer starting a stopwatch, the pilot executed a 180-degree turn to starboard and then flew straight on a reciprocal course until the observer told him that 90 seconds had passed, whereupon the pilot executed another 180-degree starboard turn and then reverted to his original course. The observer noted the times when the smoke float was on the aircraft's beam and quarter and then, by means of a formula and some relatively simple calculations, he could determine the wind speed and direction to quite a reasonable degree of accuracy. When flying from a carrier at sea, it was quite usual to repeat this performance every forty or so minutes, or in particularly

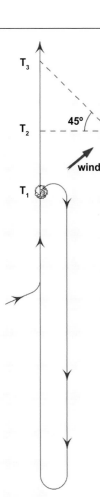

A. WIND-FINDING: FOUR POINT METHOD (left and below)

1. Datum point is selected, and when over this point, at a steady altitude and airspeed (AS), a smoke float is dropped and the stopwatch started (T).
2. Aircraft performs Rate 1 turn (180 degrees) and flies on reciprocal course.
3. After exactly 90 seconds, aircraft carries out a second Rate 1 turn and steers original course.
4. Times when smoke float is directly abeam (T_2) and when directly on the quarter (T_3) are noted.

Plotting (below)

1. T_1 is 3 minutes (180 seconds). The difference between T_1 and T_2 is x (say, 20), and between T_2 and T_3 is y (say, 22). Then

$$\frac{y \times T_1}{T_3} = z \quad \left(\frac{22 \times 180}{240} = 18\right)$$

2. Wind speed $= \dfrac{q \times \text{TAS}}{T_2} \quad \left(\dfrac{24 \times 100}{200} = 12\right)$

3. When T_1 and T_2 are equal, wind is directly abeam. Wind speed is then calculated thus:

$$\frac{y \times \text{TAS}}{T_3}$$

When T_2 and T_3 are equal, wind is directly head or tail. Wind speed is then calculated thus:

$$\frac{y \times \text{TAS}}{T_3}$$

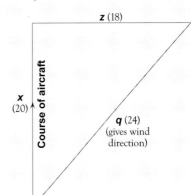

Note: Markers were of three types, smoke floats, aluminium sea markers and dust markers. There was a delay before the stopwatch was started to make allowance for altitude. By 1943 tables were available to enable calculations to be made and subsequently observers were issued with an official plastic calculator.

B. WIND-FINDING: DOUBLE DRIFT METHOD (right)

1. Take a back bearing (bb), alter course and then take another.

Plotting

1. Draw AB to represent first course, proportionate in direction and length to TAS.
2. Draw AC to represent second course, proportionate as before.
3. Draw back bearings for B and C, meeting at D.
4. DA represents wind in direction and speed. Note that time does not enter the equation.

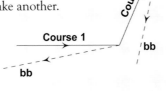

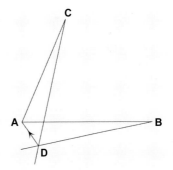

C. WIND-FINDING: DRIFT AND BEARING USING ONE DATUM (left)

1. Fly from datum (A) for a specified time (say, 5 minutes) and then take a back bearing (bb). Alter course and take another back bearing of the same datum after the same specified time.

Plotting

1. Plot AB and BD to represent first and second courses, respectively, proportionate to distance and direction.
2. Produce AB to C, making BC = BD.
3. Lay off back bearing from C and then that from D, these intersecting at E.
4. EA = wind speed and direction. Speed given is for 10 minutes, so multiply by 6.

squally conditions even more frequently. It was obviously impossible to go through this procedure at night without attracting unwelcome attention, and the best that we could hope to do on our trips over the Channel was initially to assume that the Met Officer's forecast of wind speed and direction was accurate, and on this basis calculate the departure course. However, we always took departure over Selsey Bill, a distinctive feature on the coast, and checked its bearing for as long as we could see it (often ten minutes). Though we were unable to determine the wind by this method, at least we knew the initial track of the aircraft resulting from the initial course. The only other method of calculating wind speed and direction on these night trips was when it was possible positively to identify our position on reaching the French coast and then, knowing the courses that the pilot had steered, one could calculate the wind speed and direction on the way out and hope it would remain the same for the return. The new ASV sets were very valuable for identifying positions on the coast. They did not provide a plan view of the coast, but with increasing experience of the sets and after a few trips we could identify enough characteristics of the coastline between the Seine estuary and the Cherbourg peninsula (our usual area of operations) to give a good clue of our location.

The minelaying operations to Cherbourg and Le Havre were pretty hazardous, since, to surprise the enemy, we were required to fly no higher than 100 feet over the Channel and to go down to no higher than 50 feet when dropping the mine in order to avoid damaging it. Our barometric altimeters could not be relied upon, so we had to rely on our eyes. It is not easy in near total darkness not to become almost mesmerised staring at the black sea, and we suspected that at least one of our aircraft simply flew into the water and was lost for this reason.

Our first minelaying trip to Cherbourg, which was particularly well defended with both heavy and light 'ack-ack', resulted in our losing two of our six aircraft. We had gone in to lay our mines at ten-minute intervals, which, it was agreed in retrospect, was a serious error. In all our

subsequent trips we went in individually, at irregular intervals over a period of six or seven hours, with the idea that this might provide more of an element of surprise, and at least would keep the German gunners awake all night and help to demoralise the local civilian population because of the frequent air-raid warnings. I think all of us had some fairly hairy experiences during these trips, but it seems to be generally agreed that the Germans never fully appreciated just how slowly we flew in our old 'Stringbags' since their cones of fire were always well ahead of us.

Apart from the minelaying operations and some anti-E-boat patrols, our other principal activity was armed reconnaissance along the French coast, from Dieppe in the east to Cherbourg in the west. At that time the Germans were attempting to get their armed raiders (fast, heavily armed merchant ships used for attacking poorly escorted convoys) from the Baltic to Brest by sailing fast night 'hops' from port to port along the western seaboard of Europe. These trips were always undertaken on the darkest nights, when the armed raider would be accompanied by up to half a dozen fast E-boats. The penultimate run for these convoys was from Le Havre to Cherbourg, which was the 816 Squadron's particular patch, though on one or two occasions we went as far as Dieppe and patrolled the area from Le Havre to the Somme estuary.

It was the practice that, whenever an intelligence report came from the Underground in France that an armed raider was likely to make a run, 816 or a sister-squadron (811 or 819) would patrol our patch all night, with the second squadron standing by armed with torpedoes for a night attack. The patrolling squadron would send out a single aircraft about every ninety minutes, followed by another aircraft, throughout the night. The patrols averaged about three hours, with about ninety minutes on station (i.e., actually patrolling, about five to ten miles off the French coast). Since the Germans always chose the darkest

Below: A Swordfish Mk I carrying a 1,500-pound sea mine. The weapon was interchangeable with the standard torpedo.

Above: Two photographs showing the port aerial for the early ASV Mk I radar. The starboard fitting was a mirror image.

nights for these fast runs from port to port, our searches were entirely dependent on the use of our ASV sets. We normally flew at around 1,500 feet.

My crew and I were extremely fortunate that on our first patrol, at about 2100, we located an armed raider accompanied by five E-boats about five miles off the coast and about fifteen miles out of Le Havre en route to Cherbourg. I immediately conned my pilot Pete to fly up-wind of the convoy when he released the first of our two flares. It was a huge thrill actually to see the ships sailing at full speed, and one could not but admire the discipline of the Germans, for, though they were lit up as if it were midday, not a gun fired, and when the flares were extinguished there was no sign of them. It was also very exciting to send off a real enemy sighting report with the ship's position, course and speed. We expected to be required to shadow the convoy, but base acknowledged our report and ordered us to return forthwith since the weather was fast closing in. We were horrified on our return to Thorney Island to find that our sister Swordfish squadron was still on the ground, armed with torpedoes but grounded by the weather. We went to bed deflated at what we thought was a lost opportunity, but after waking up about ten the following morning we learnt that a destroyer patrolling the Channel from Portsmouth and acting on our sighting report had led a flotilla of destroyers to intercept the German vessels and had sunk the armed merchant raider and four of the five E-boats.

This success was almost our undoing forty-eight hours later, when we were on our second patrol with instructions to start in the Seine estuary just off Le Havre and search east to Dieppe. Our first sighting had been such a piece of cake and we were very 'hyped up', so we could not believe our luck when, right at the start of the patrol I got an image on the screen of the ASV set almost identical to that of two nights previously. Pete and I later agreed that we felt at the time that if we achieved another sighting there could be a gong or two in the offing. Once again I conned Pete up-

wind and yelled to him to drop a flare. The contrast with the previous occasion could not have been greater as, the second our flares appeared, all hell let loose with tracer and heavy 'ack-ack' coming up from all quarters. Within a few seconds three powerful searchlights had locked on to us, and since we were flying only at 1,500 feet we were blinded by the lights. We could just make out that we were right over the River Seine and that the 'convoy' that I had located was a mixture of jetties jutting out from the Le Havre docks and numerous small ships at anchor in the river! In retrospect, I thanked God that Pete was a keen tennis player and had wrists of steel as he yanked the old Stringbag into as nearly vertical a climb as was possible without stalling the engine and reached the cloud base at about 3,000 feet. The searchlights were locked on to us all the time, but somehow the German gunners could not believe that a flying machine could move so slowly and make such tight turns. The whole performance probably lasted only three or four minutes but it seemed a lifetime.

Once in the clouds, Pete flew at maximum throttle to get away from the cones of tracer that we could still see coming through the clouds. The air gunner and I had really been terrified witnesses since we dropped the flares, but at last my instinct told me to check the course we were now flying. My magnetic compass told me that we were flying due east over the fields of Normandy. Pete's twists and turns, which had undoubtedly saved us, had also completely disoriented his gyro compass, and for the rest of the trip I 'steered' the plane from my magnetic compass, yelling to him when he veered off course. We re-crossed the coast to the west of Dieppe and continued our patrol to the mouth of the Somme and then returned to Le Havre. We picked up no further ASV blips. It was just as well, since we had no flares left: in the excitement, Pete had let go our two flares at the same time over the Seine.

Looking back now, virtually every operational trip from Thorney Island provided all of us with at least one unforgettable incident—though usually associated with the weather or the barrage balloons protecting Portsmouth a mere four miles to the west of the aerodrome!

Devastated *Lieutenant-Commander Brian Bennett* DSC

After about a week working up with *Dasher* we sailed for Scapa Flow in the Orkneys; it would be late January 1943. The next stop was Iceland to join the escort of a convoy to Murmansk. As I recall, the weather was foul—not unusual in those parts—and, with very little daylight at that time of the year in northerly latitudes, very little flying was done. We rendezvoused with two cruisers and several destroyers in Seydisfjord while the convoy gathered in Akureyrifjord, or *vice-versa*. Neither was the place for a run ashore—just snow-covered mountains down to the water's edge. And so we set off for Russia.

Dasher's flying complement was fragmented. There was a flight of Hurricanes (three, I think), fitted with belly hooks for deck-landing and with strengthened fuselages. Their wings did not fold so they spent most of their time parked on deck to avoid cluttering the hangar. There was a flight of Swordfish from another squadron, again three, I think, and 816's six Swordfish. There were also three lots of maintenance personnel aboard. This was a recipe for confusion and misunderstanding. *Dasher* had one lift at the aft end and a smallish hangar which did not run the full length of the ship. She was a merchant ship conversion—a 'banana boat' rather than a carrier constructed *ab initio* from a merchant hull, a 'Woolworth carrier', as were the later escort carriers.

I well remember, as Duty Officer, being called on to 'range' two of 816's Swordfish which happened to be at the back of the hangar. By the time various non-816 personnel had been persuaded to shift their aircraft around,

over half an hour had elapsed before our aircraft were ready to take off. Not at all clever. My explanations were requested in writing. I mention this only because it led, I feel sure, to the formation of composite squadrons for escort carriers with one line of command. Later, on board HMS *Tracker*, 816 comprised ten Swordfish and six Seafires and was the only squadron aboard. *Dasher* was part of a steep learning curve.

The first day out of Iceland, the weather was fair and the sea calmish and we flew anti U-boat patrols, but towards evening the barometer began to drop like a stone. By midnight, the anemometer on the bridge was showing 90 knots and then went off the clock—and so did the wooden wind dodges around the bridge. Being a sea-going type as well as an aviator, I was watchkeeping at the time and was sent below with the others.

That storm scattered the convoy. *Dasher* started taking in water below as welding fractured, and one of the cruisers,

This spread: HMS *Dasher* as completed, camouflaged, and at Boston in 1942 with two Swordfish ranged amidships. The ship's single lift has been lowered.

either *Sheffield* or *Cumberland*, was put out of action with damage to the forward turret. *Dasher* made her way back to Scapa for repairs. We hadn't exactly covered ourselves with glory, but worse was to follow.

The Squadron flew ashore to Hatston in the Orkneys, where our arrival coincided with a visit to the Home Fleet by HM King George VI. One aircraft from the Squadron was paraded for inspection along with other FAA aircraft, and for some reason I was detailed to stand by it. (Probably I was the only one with a clean shirt, or, more likely, I was the junior boy and the other pilots thought it a chore to be avoided.) Then we left for Machrihanish.

We rejoined *Dasher* about mid-March and exercised in the Firth of Clyde and the Irish Sea preparatory to escorting an outward-bound convoy to Halifax, Nova Scotia. Late in the afternoon on 27 March 1943, *Dasher* was off Arran. The aircraft had just landed-on and had been struck down for maintenance and refuelling. Some aircrews were ashore at Machrihanish, due to land-on the following day, but eight of us were in the wardroom having a 'cuppa' when there was a *thump*-like sound, the lights went out and all was eerily quiet—no engines nor other shipboard noises. We immediately went to our Action Stations in the Aircrew Ready Room just above the wardroom and donned our Mae Wests. Then my observer and I went up the ladder to the flight deck. There was smoke and signs of fire in the after lift. At that moment *Dasher* began to go down by the stern—and at an angle which increased alarmingly quickly.

We crabbed our way across the deck to the catwalk. Two Hurricanes parked forward broke loose and trundled over us. Having made the catwalk, we climbed up to the bow, which was now some sixty feet or so in the air. Those of the ship's crew who were able to were jumping into the water. There was no point in following suit: either they would jump on us or we on them. So we sat there. *Dasher* now began to sink rapidly. At some point my observer jumped; he was not seen again. I went down with the ship and floated away. The last I saw of her was the bow passing by over my left shoulder. All this had taken a mere three or four minutes. Puffs of black smoke began appearing in the water and shortly the sea was ablaze, presumably with aviation fuel from the ruptured tanks when the ship hit the bottom. I managed to swim round the fire and was picked up after about half an hour in the very cold water by a seaboat's crew from some naval vessel; I do not know which.

The Squadron was devastated. Only seven of the 'troops' survived, for the latter were at the heart of the explosion. Of the pilots and observers aboard, two pilots, including the CO, and one observer were lost. Of the total ship's company of 528 only 149 survived.

When 816 Squadron had re-formed in 1942 it consisted of just over 100 personnel made up of twenty-four aircrew and eighty 'troops'. By the time I reported to *Dasher* six months later it had been joined by twelve new aircrew to replace those lost whilst at RAF Thorney Island. After the explosion of *Dasher* we had lost a total of nineteen aircrew and seventy-two 'troops'—a grand total of 91 out of 116 chaps. Whatever success we think we might have achieved has to be measured against the loss of 91 young men whose average age would be about twenty-three.

816 would have to begin again.

115

White Knuckle Riders *Lieutenant-Commander (A) Paul Housden* VRD RNVR

In February 1943 I was a pilot in a Swordfish squadron of nine aircraft and we were all at 8,000 feet, in attacking formation, three by three, looking for a suitable target. We knew what we were all looking for—a battleship, heading towards the coast of East Africa. Our intention was to attack her with torpedoes and sink her.

Dropping torpedoes against major warships was our speciality. It was what we had been trained to do over many months. Initial training had taken place at RNAS Crail, known in the Royal Navy as HMS *Jackdaw*. Here the new boys practised torpedo dropping from the desired height of fifty feet precisely, holding an essential, straight-and-level dropping run of just ten seconds, to achieve a clean, nose-down entry of the torpedo into the sea.

In order to assist this steady launch, each torpedo was equipped with two spools of about twenty feet of wire, fixed to the aft end. As the torpedo fell away from its aircraft, these two wires had to unwind completely. In this way the descent was steady, rolling in the air was prevented and an entry into the sea in a slightly nose-down attitude was achieved. Perhaps we were good at it, perhaps we were not, but, in the fullness of time, we found ourselves over the Indian Ocean, at latitude 60 South, where it was very hot. This was the time of the Equinox in the Southern Hemisphere, and the tropical sun was directly overhead. In our open cockpits we had no shelter from its rays.

The ethos of the Fleet Air Arm is encapsulated in the dictum 'Find, Fix and Strike', and this was our Squadron's intention. A battleship was in the vicinity and we had to find it and use the opportunity to test our skills. However, this was an exercise: the Japanese were the enemy in this theatre, and no Japanese ships were nearby. We were, we hoped, already honed to a high degree of excellence and were about to try to prove it, in a full-scale rehearsal. So here we were, hanging in the tropical heat at 8,000 feet, peering down through a thick heat-haze, searching the ocean for a camouflaged target.

At last! There is our quarry! The leader has seen it too, and signalled us to move into attack formation. Three aircraft in 'vic' formation, behind them another 'vic' of three and behind them again another. The first three will go down in line abreast, then the second trio and then the third. Our quarry is a large warship, painted in disruptive camouflage, keeping a straight course, possibly unaware, as yet, of our approach.

The attack now begins in earnest. We must aim to lose 7,000 feet of height at maximum speed. Our pull-out from the dive will be delayed until the very last moment, and for this manœuvre the Swordfish's great quality is that it will flatten out from a near-vertical dive in a short distance—no more than a thousand feet.

We go down not far from the vertical. Unable to get a clear view of the target because the upper mainplane

Below: A Swordfish I of the Torpedo Training Unit, based at RNAS Gosport, engaged in 'fish-dropping' trials before the war.

COURTESY PHILIP JARRETT

partially blocks my view, I stand on the pedals. I look over the top of the mainplane with my head well out in the slipstream. The sensation of speed is hugely exhilarating: the aircraft seems almost to be dancing with the unexpected joy of a speed it can never experience in level flight.

We have to watch the first wave of three and, we hope, discover what evasive action they are causing the target ship to adopt. Once the enemy sees the tracks being taken by the three torpedoes in the first wave, it will attempt to turn on to a parallel course. The torpedoes may then miss. This is the standard tactic, called 'combing the torpedo tracks'. Here, now, is our opportunity. We have to twist and turn in our dive to come at the enemy at right angles to his new course. It needs flying skill of a high order and a good tactical appreciation of the altering situation.

This is why we have had to practise over and over again, and understand the angle of aim-off required. If the target is travelling at high speed, the angle of aim-off ahead is crucial. It has taken two hours to fly to intercept the target and to reach our cruising altitude of 8,000 feet. I am leading the second wave of three aircraft, and have to position myself and my two wingmen for the final approach. Whichever way the target turns, no matter how many alterations of course it makes, we three have to launch at right angles to his line of advance. If we fail, then the final sub-flight of three, following us in, will be making the same decisions, according to how the attack develops.

We pull out from the dive at 1,000 feet, actually levelling out at 50 feet and remembering that we will sink somewhat for a few further feet owing to the Swordfish's speed. We aim the entire aircraft at the target, making sure that we are straight, not skidding or sliding, giving a kick to the rudder one way or another, if necessary, to correct our aim. Then we press the torpedo release button and wait—wait for those endless ten seconds of straight and level flight, while the torpedo drops away and unwinds the twenty feet of steadying wire as it falls. Our torpedoes are dummies, because this whole exercise is the final demonstration of our skills, brought, we hope, to the ultimate state of perfection.

Our last, but most critical, evolution is to get away quickly. Had the target been a real enemy warship her defensive gunfire would now be at its most lethal. We would have to avoid the shells and bullets, so each aircraft turns downwind and throws itself about the sky. It jinks and dodges and gets out of range with all possible speed. With the dummy torpedo gone on its harmless way, our collaborator, the cruiser HMS *Mauritius*, breaks off the action and reverts to her normal duties. On this particular afternoon there are nine aircraft and nine happy crews able to return to base.

In late February 1943 I was Senior Pilot of 796 Naval Air Squadron, an Operational Training Unit. It was based at Tanga in East Africa under the direction of Lieutenant (A) A. J. L. Temple-West. It was with a great deal of relief that we later learned that we would be redeployed. The Japanese menace had been contained. We were to be used in a rôle for which the Swordfish was also well-suited, and most of us went to 836 Squadron on convoy escort duty, flying from MAC ships. The Tanga base was disbanded in April 1944.

Below: Arming 822 Squadron Swordfish at RNAS Hatston in the Orkneys. Aircrew stand by, ready to depart.

COURTESY PHILIP JARRETT

Closing the Gap *Lieutenant-Commander John Shoebridge MBE*

In the autumn of 1940, following the Battle of Britain, Winston Churchill observed that the only way our country could be defeated was by U-boats in the 'Battle of the Atlantic'. This was indeed true: if the German submarine force could cut the 'Atlantic lifeline', then the United Kingdom would be starved of food, weapons and supplies of all kinds. By late 1941, and carrying on into most of 1942, the situation was serious indeed. Certainly, thanks to the shipyards, more escorts (corvettes) were becoming available for convoy protection duties. Ships' crews were rapidly becoming efficient at convoy work and new equipment, especially radar, was improving all the time. Even so, merchant ships were still being sunk at an alarming rate, and of course the Merchant Navy crews were irreplaceable.

Perhaps the biggest unsolved problem at the time concerned air cover. The RAF did fine work, flying its long-range Sunderlands, Catalinas and Liberators from Northern Ireland and the West Country, as did the RCAF from its Canadian bases, but of course it was just not possible to provide air cover for long periods, and in addition there was the 'Atlantic gap'—a swathe of water some 750 miles wide in the middle of the ocean where, owing to limitations of range, it was impossible to provide shore-based air cover of any sort. The obvious solution to this problem was aircraft carriers, but at that time these were just not available. Of the big fleet carriers, probably only three or so were serviceable and in any event they would have been a prime target for the German U-boats. The smaller escort carriers, each operating some eighteen aircraft, were also too few in number. Then somebody had a very bright idea. Why not convert a number of existing merchant ships to aircraft carriers? This was much quicker method of introducing additional flight decks than building new carriers. Thus was the merchant aircraft carrier—the 'MAC ship'—born.

The two sources from which ships were drawn for conversion were the Ministry of War Transport—whose ships, operated by various companies, had their names prefixed with the word 'Empire'—and the Anglo-Saxon Petroleum Company, and, when the programme was completed, a total of six grain ships and thirteen tankers had been modified. It was understood that, even after conversion, each type of ship would still carry some eighty per cent of its original cargo.

The tankers had four arrester wires and a crash barrier, but no hangar. They carried three aircraft, which had to be shunted to and fro during flying operations. As can be imagined, problems arose with the aircraft and they were often replaced on return to base in Northern Ireland. The grain ships had a hangar but no barrier, and they embarked four aircraft. If more than one aircraft was airborne, then the first one to land had to be struck down before the second could be brought in. The deck crew got very adept at carrying out the required manoeuvres but, inevitably, delays did occur.

The MAC ships themselves were purely merchant ships with a flight deck fitted. The tonnage of the grain carriers was some 8,000–10,000 and that of the tankers some 12,000, and top speeds were between 11½ and 13 knots. The flight decks were about 400 feet long by 55 feet wide. The aircraft employed were Fairey Swordfish, frequently the Mk III. This version was fitted with the very latest air-to-surface (ASV) radar, state-of-the-art at the time if by modern standards extremely primitive. The Mk III was also fitted with a fine-pitch propeller to enable take-offs to be accomplished from the very short flight decks, although it limited the top speed to some 100 knots. The cruising speed on patrol was some 70 knots and the deck-landing approach speed 58 knots. To save weight, both front and rear machine guns were generally removed and for patrol purposes only two-thirds of the maximum fuel load was carried, giving an endurance of no more than three hours.

836 Naval Air Squadron was commissioned in March 1942 but in the spring of 1943 its rôle was redesignated so

as to provide aircraft and crews for manning the MAC ships as the latter came into service. As a matter of record, the first deck landing on a MAC ship was made on 7 May 1943 when Lieutenant-Commander Ransford W. Slater OBE DSC touched down on the converted grain ship MV *Empire MacAlpine*. An experimental flight escorted the first 'MAC convoy' from Liverpool to Halifax, Nova Scotia, and one further double crossing was undertaken, by which time the Squadron was installed at its new base at RNAS Maydown, near Londonderry.

As the MAC ships came into service, so new flights were formed to man them and the Squadron eventually comprised some twenty-five flights of three or four Swordfish each together with a Headquarters Staff at Maydown and a very small maintenance unit (perhaps no more than twelve personnel) across the Atlantic at Dartmouth, near Halifax.

A four-aircraft flight comprised four pilots, four observers and one Deck Landing Control Officer ('bats-

Above: 836 Squadron Swordfish—the nearest aircraft is NE875 and equipped with R/P rails—up from RNAS Maydown.
Left and below: Two MAC ship tanker conversions, MV Rapana (left) and MV Ancylus (below). The vessels' merchant origins are clearly evident in their lines. The device at the bows is an acoustic hammer, a defence against mines.

man'), all of whom were commissioned, and four telegraphist air gunners. Normally the nine officers comprised one lieutenant and eight sub-lieutenants, the former being CO of the flight. The DLCO was a qualified pilot and his duty was rotated after each double crossing of the Atlantic. The maintenance party consisted of a petty officer and sixteen ratings. As will be seen, a flight was self-sufficient and, except for major maintenance, was expected to look after itself.

At Maydown the HQ comprised the CO of the Squadron (a lieutenant-commander), a Senior Pilot and a Senior Observer (both senior lieutenants) and the Squadron Engineer Officer, together with maintenance personnel adequate for major overhauls and repair work. The HQ was responsible for the supply of flights to ships, overall training and discipline, store, pay and records, etc.

The ships were commanded by a Merchant Navy captain, and deck and engineer officers and crew were all from the Merchant Navy too. To make things legal (and to avoid the aircrew being classed as 'pirates' if captured), all RN officers were signed on the ships' books as deck officers and were paid the princely sum of one shilling a month (!). On a personal note, I recall that, after a year on board *Empire MacAlpine*, calculating that we were due twelve shillings (a

lot of beer in those days!) we formed a deputation and visited the captain, who stated that he would gladly pay us but that we would then owe some fifteen shillings in trade union dues. We retired, defeated.

Each MAC ship had attached to her a Royal Navy lieutenant-commander who was a qualified observer. This officer was directly in command of the Naval Flight aboard the ship, both for discipline and for control of flying operations as required by the Senior Officer (Escort). The Merchant Navy captain was in command of the ship in all respects other than those concerning aviation. In practice this arrangement worked extremely well and relations between RN and MN personnel remained most harmonious—in fact the MN crew members grew rather proud of being part of the crew of an aircraft carrier.

There is little doubt that the Battle of the Atlantic was well on the way to being won by the time the first MAC ship, *Empire MacAlpine*, came into service. However, by helping to close the 'Atlantic Gap', the vessels made a significant contribution to the successful conclusion to the battle. The very fact that the Senior Officer (Escort) had an aircraft immediately available was of prime importance.

Following the two proving voyages, the first 'routine' crossing took place in September 1943. This convoy (with *MacAlpine* and 'B' Flight 836 Squadron) was heavily attacked by U-boat wolf packs and several escort vessels and merchantmen were sunk. After this inauspicious beginning, however, only two more ships were lost in convoys escorted by MAC ships and. By the autumn of 1944 virtually every Atlantic convoy would have a MAC ship as part of the escort. Although no submarines were sunk by 836 Squadron, the primary job—keeping the enemy submarines' heads down—was most successful, thus preventing them from tracking and assembling wolfpacks around a convoy.

The MAC ship operated in a 'channel' immediately astern of the Convoy Commodore. Provided the wind was from ahead it, was normally possible for the ship to remain within the convoy when operating aircraft. Should the wind be from astern, however, then the ship invariably dropped well to the rear of the convoy and it was thus important for the aircraft to land-on with the minimum waste of time. In a 'fast' convoy (10 knots), the 'catch-up' rate was only some two knots and if the ship was two or three miles astern one felt very lonely and vulnerable.

At this point a few words concerning the actual operation of the aircraft would not come amiss. The 400-foot-long flight deck was adequate, although in light winds only just. Aircraft operations were directly controlled by the Senior Officer (Escort) and dawn and dusk patrols were the normal daily routine. These were codenamed 'Cobras' and consisted of circling round and round the convoy with the object of keeping sub-marines under water and thus unable to sight the convoy. These patrols were normally of each two hours' duration.

The other main type of sortie was codenamed 'Mamba' and this was flown when a suspected submarine had been detected by HF/DF from the escort vessels. This involved proceeding on a direct bearing to a distance of, say, 75 miles. Weapons carried by the Swordfish were either eight armour-piercing rockets or two depth charges. The MAC

ships were good sea boats and we could fly in most weathers, although, obviously, there were occasions when the sea was simply too rough and the ship was pitching and rolling far too much to permit flying. On one occasion an RN escort carrier was with the convoy and it was made very clear to us by this vessel that we were inferior and very much a junior partner. One day it was too rough for them to operate but—surprise, surprise!—we could still fly *our* aircraft. *That* put them in their place, and we felt ten feet tall!

I would add that the MN captains and officers grew highly skilled at ship handling and took a great pride in their performance. Their ships had far less manoeuvrability than their RN counterparts. Our relationship with the MN officers was superb. We were accommodated in double cabins and the flight would be in a separate section of the officers' living quarters. The ship had no ward room bar and dining room as did the RN carriers, but a separate dining room and a separate 'smoke room', this latter serving as a 'drinking area'. Bottles of spirits or beer would be ordered from the Chief Steward at the beginning of a trip and paid for at the time. Supplies kept in our cabins could be replenished! In the evenings, operations permitting, bottles would be brought into the smoke room and a party would ensue—very often joined by off-duty MN officers.

Halifax, Nova Scotia, we found great fun. The city was much derided by the Canadians but to us it was an oasis of bright lights and good food, neither of which were, of course, obtainable in Great Britain. We were all made members of the Canadian Naval Officers Club—which was as well because the city itself was 'dry'! We normally flew off the ship to the RCAF base at Dartmouth, Nova Scotia, and stayed there for eight or nine days before returning home with another convoy. The requirement was for us to complete one hour of flying for each day in port. This task was normally accomplished in the first two days and the remaining time was spent golfing, partying and accepting the (very generous) local hospitality. Life at Maydown followed a similar pattern to that at Dartmouth except that, being right under the noses of Squadron 'bigwigs', we were more circumspect. Londonderry in those days was a friendly and happy place.

I will conclude these reminiscences—because that is really what they are—by mentioning that I served with 'B' Flight 836 Squadron from June 1943 to the end of the war in May 1945, when the Squadron was disbanded. That is over sixty years ago, but I trust that my memory (assisted by flying logbooks) has served me faithfully. Just in case, though, please do not be to hard on the pianist!

Right: The motor vessel—MAC ships were never HM Ships—*Empire MacAlpine*, with four 836 Squadron Swordfish on deck. The grain conversions featured a small aircraft hangar, and the outline of the access lift can be discerned here, immediately forward of the aircraft parked at the stern. The four arrester wires are virtually amidships. There is a 4-inch HA/LA gun on the stern 'fantail', and 20mm Oerlikons in 'cut-outs' along the edge of the flight deck. The batting platform and associated safety net can be made out just forward of the second wire on the port side. The tiny island superstructure, topped by a homing beacon 'lantern', was offset from the flight deck, but even so it can readily be seen that there was little clearance for a Swordfish taking off.

With Alacrity *Lieutenant (A) Bill Penlington* RNVR

Sunday 3rd Oct. [1943]

0830: Weighed anchor Greenock. Weather: cloudy and raining, low vis., stiff W. wind. Dress: sea-going rig, i.e. battledress & jerseys.

1130: ALT [Attack Light Torpedo] by six Barracudas—not very well executed—one dive-bombed the ship & dropped a practice bomb. Three destroyers with us as escort (part of 8th Escort Group).

1200: Anticipated ALT by Beaufighters and Hampdens did not materialise—weather too bad. Speculation as to our destination & task.

1300: Address by Captain over broadcaster but he did not reveal much except that we were going to warmer climes.

1600: Rendezvous with *Franconia* (with Admiral Holt on board) and the other three destroyers of 8th EG. Ships in force: *Fencer, Franconia, Inconstant, Wrestler, Whitehall, Viscount, Burza, Garland. Burza & Garland* Polish. Sea quite rough. Sailing on westerly co., speed 9. Two convoys 2 or 3 days ahead which we are supposed to catch up and escort.

Monday 4th Oct.

Squadron Duty Officer—parade 0745. No flying, weather too bad. Lots of sick ratings. Nearly sick myself. Speed reduced to 5 knots on account of zigzagging.

Tuesday 5th Oct.

. . . Weather rough—feeling very seasick. Still no flying owing to weather conditions, speed still very slow. Two convoys ahead must be further away. Boys feeling browned off.

Wednesday 6th Oct.

0500: Got up early to fly—weather much calmer but ship still pitching a lot.

0845: Took off in 'D' with my usual crew. Take-off not bad, tho' drifted towards island. Armed with 2 DC. Patrol Viper & Crocodile 6. 2½-hour patrol, saw nothing. Very pleasant in the air after unstable existence on the ship. Jettisoned DCs. 842's first patrol on ops.

1130: Landing on a pitching deck. First attempt came in too high, missed wires, opened up and was just able to stagger off deck. The Stringbag kept flying beautifully. Landed-on OK at 2nd attempt.

Nearing U-boat patrol lines—should be busy during the next few days. Vague idea that we are going to the Azores. Slept in Ready Room. Beautiful moon. U-boats within 60 miles.

Thursday 7th Oct.

0435: Flew off three S/fish, A/S patrols. Ship fairly steady. Visibility poor. Was able to zzzz this racket going on in crew room.

0700: Address over broadcaster by Captain. Destination Azores. *Fencer* and three destroyers providing A/S screen ahead of convoy. *Fencer* remaining one week for air patrols round the islands—should be good fun if weather OK.

0900 S/fish 'H' three quarters of an hour overdue. Reason: lost its way. Crew: Merrick, Simpson, Morgan—recently joined the Squadron. Search sent off but no sign of them. Bloody shame, as the a/c was in R/T touch.

1000: Took off in 'Thunderbird' on an Alligator patrol. Lew gave me wrong course but he picked up the convoy OK and carried out patrol.

1245: Landed on. Reading A. J. Cronin's *Citadel*.

1800: For exercise, 'Action Stations'. Flying over miles & miles of ocean with no friendly points of land to show where you are is an awesome experience in poor visibility. You realise just what sort of hope you have of ever being picked up if you have to ditch . . .

Below: HMS *Fencer* with two of her Swordfish on the flight deck. Operation 'Alacrity', in which she took part, was a top-secret operation to establish air bases on the Azores, territory administered by Portugal which, although technically neutral during World War II, was nevertheless allied to Great Britain by dint of a treaty that dated back to 1373. A joint British-American venture, its objectives were to project Allied air power over the central Atlantic in the struggle against the U-boats and also to thwart any plans the enemy might have had to occupy the islands for his own purposes. It was a great success, but even to this day it is sparsely documented.

COURTESY JOHN ROBERTS

COURTESY BILL PENLINGTON/BRUCE VIBERT

Above: An 842 Squadron Swordfish making, at first glance, a clean landing on board HMS *Fencer*. Not so: the main wheels have displaced one of the arrester wires, which has thus been missed by the hook. The result is seen on page 84. Many Swordfish were still at this time equipped with their torpedo sights; indeed, during 1943 *Fencer* was still stowing torpedoes–there was always a chance that the German battleship *Tirpitz* might attempt a foray similar to that which had led to the loss of her sister-ship *Bismarck*, and every eventuality had to be covered.

Friday 8th Oct.
0500: Took off in 'J' on dawn patrol. Beautiful sight watching the dawn break from the air.
0730: Landed. Nothing to report.
0900: Destroyers DC-dropping. Saw land–Terceira 60 miles.
1245: Flew off again in 'J' on Crocodile patrol, then escorted into Angra harbour. Volcanic-looking island with small white houses. Carried out harbour patrol . . .
1630: Landed-on. Fighter patrol flown off. Sachs pranged into barrier; kite OK. Night flying stations. During the day Thomson signalled that he had discovered submerged U-boat–nothing doing though. Slept in Torpedo Office.

Saturday 9th Oct.
0330: Called
0500: Flew off in 'J' on dawn patrol–Crocodile. Got very bored in the air. Shot up a destroyer.
0800: Landed. Nothing to report. Had breakfast, then a zzzz.
1400: Took off in 'A' on search. Very boring . . .
1700: Landed-on. Now flown eighteen hours in four days. The boys are beginning to look tired, especially 'F' [Commander Flying] & 'ASO' [Air Staff Officer].
1830: Flap due to signal from Metcalfe being mis-construed. U-boat false alarm. Beautiful moon for A/S. Slept in Chart Room.

Sunday 10th Oct.
0450: Took off on dawn search. Saw Pico, 7,650 feet high.
0800: Landed-on. Nothing seen. Flying carried on until
1700: Ship anchored off Angra. Twinkling lights. Scented

Below: 842 Squadron's 'F' about to take off with depth charges for an anti-submarine patrol, October 1943; one of the Squadron's Seafire IBs is visible at far right. The Swordfish appears to be have a personal marking forward of the pilot's cockpit–'O.H.M.S.!'–and the aircraft's propeller spinner is, in common with other 842 NAS Swordfish at this time, decorated with a red star.

COURTESY BILL PENLINGTON/BRUCE VIBERT

Left: An 842 Squadron Swordfish is refuelled by hand at Lagens on the Azores. By this time, October 1942, Swordfish were routinely being delivered to the Fleet Air Arm with white-painted sides and undersurfaces, retaining disruptive camouflage on the upper surfaces only.
Below: A general view of Lagens, with the RAF camp at left and 842 Squadron's aircraft, including a Seafire, at right.

air. Everyone restless to go ashore. Aircraft released until 0900.

Monday 11th Oct.
Morning. Spent gazing at Angra in brilliant sunshine. Had photo taken on FD.
1430: Took off on search laden with water supply—bit for living two or three days on new drome. Diverted to look for U-boat.
1735: Landed-on Lagens drome. Had corned beef and dry biscuits for supper. Living under fairly primitive conditions but all of us enjoying the life. Very little water—one wash a day and no shaving. Heard that Chadwick and crew had gone into the drink on take-off. All fished out OK but their belongings were lost. Had a good sleep on a camp bed . . .

Tuesday 12th Oct.
0900: 'Angry' patrol. Beans & bread for breakfast.
1200: Landed.
1400: Raining. Beans & bread for lunch.

1530: Caught a truck into Angra. Most interesting trip thro' the villages—abject poverty—maize—hovels—rain.
1700: Arrived Angra with Lew, Curly, Tommy. Changed £1 at the port. Obtained permit from Town Commandant (town out of bounds). Mooched thro' shops — bought films. Fruit, watches, prices very reasonable.
1900: Docks to catch transport. Raining—got soaked—streets & roads just muddy tracks.

Wednesday 13th Oct.
0700: Got up, lit stove, cooked bacon for breakfast.
1200: Took off for patrol.
1400: Landed. Re-lit fire & made tea—cooked beans. We now have real plates, knives, forks, etc. Luxury. Newsreel cameras to film 'first' a/c to land on drome. Six U-boats around islands. No good looking for them during the day. We should fly at night. Gets dark at 6 o/c. Time 2 hours behind GMT. Glaser found a chicken but heaven knows who is going to cook it. Keeping these notes helps me to keep account of the days. Bubonic plague in 1941 killed off half the village here, therefore it's out of bounds. The peasants do almost anything for a cigarette.

2000: Went to hear dance band in the hangar—very good. Pansy Kelsall tells a story. RAF types in our hut drinking with some of the boys. 'Vino Velho' Muscatel (firewater). Glaser went to bed with chicken.

Thursday 14th Oct.
0620: Took off & patrolled round Terceira, San José Graciosa—very interesting, especially San José.
0835: Landed. Weather closed down. Boni cooked chicken—what a mess. Boni is Chief Cook. Listened again to band in the hangar during the evening. Pansy & his 'castanias' (chestnuts) . . .

Friday 15th Oct.
0900: 'Angry'.
1100: Landed—bad weather.
1400: Two Seafires readiness 'A'. Tan in one.
1430: Had my first shave for five days—caught a truck into Angra. Shopping. Bought another pipe. Had an excellent meal: soup, fish, meat, bananas, white wine. Girls with chaperones.
1900: Caught truck . . . We are getting a little cheesed off with life, but it's still good fun. Quite a change.

Saturday 16th Oct.
Fine day. Standby strike.
0200: Airborne—beautiful night.
0240: Landed. Saw nothing.

Sunday 17th Oct.
Did not fly. Went for walk along cliff tops in afternoon—had a splash around rock pool—lava—spray. Vibert & Wragg joined ship—Cooper & Barnes came ashore laden with beer. Early to bed.

Monday 18th Oct.
Woke up with stomach ache & general feeling of lassitude. Lew built a new stove. Have just been sick. Finished reading *Elizabeth and Essex* by Lytton Strachey—very good.
1440: Took off on photographic trip.
1515: Landed. Oil leak. Two 'Forts' arrived. Feeling better now.

Tuesday 19th Oct.
Morley & Pansy Kelsall returned to ship. Sachs & Gilbert arrived. Went into Angra in evening—hour's walk—charming old town almost untouched by modern civilisation—like scene from a ballet. Beer, liqueur chocolates, fried eggs in dirty café.
2320: Briefed for night flying—NF [night flying] cancelled.

Wednesday 20th Oct.
Visitors: Kenyon, Chadwick, Glassborrow, Bennett, Chrisford, Pay Bob & Doc. Paid 100 escudos. Life becoming tame. Discussion regarding messing with RAF. Reading short stories from de Maupassant. Had some beer and wine. Bill Jones' birthday . . .

Thursday 21st Oct
0900: Angra patrol . . .
1200: Landed. Cooked some baked beans for tea and pan-melted marg & cheese over them—not bad. Went for a stroll into the bubonic village of Lagens. Went to bed. Lew stayed up & drank too much wine. U-boat hunt at night—no joy. We are getting browned off & want to get away again.

Friday 22nd Oct.
0620: 'Angry'.
0900: Landed.
Went to Praya in afternoon with Glaser & Hutch. Had a good swim. Portuguese 'tabac'.
1900: Back in camp—standby night flying. Cooper, Barnes and Smart 'Angry' (after bucolic revelry in Praya).

Saturday 23rd Oct.
Forts & Hudsons arrived. Four S/fish crews & Seafires embarked. Cooper, Tivy, Metcalfe & myself remaining another night. Fun and games in a tent of a Fortress type. Lew bummed a ride in a Fort.
1500: I've had the Raff! A little matter of transport to aircraft & the too-fussy little 'admin' types ('wingless wonders').
1800: Landed & enjoyed some fried spuds cooked by Mr W. Smart, S/Lt (A) RNZVR—damn nice too. Ate chestnuts in F/O Hales' tent. After a while Hales looked pretty grim & was sick later.

Sunday 24th Oct.

0400: Everybody up stowing beds and blankets, tidying up generally. Breakfast in RAF Mess. Lew buys a local's umbrella. Small boys with chickens.

0600: Transport for ground party. Swiped all the 'gash' rations I could carry.

0900: We took off & paid our farewell by a box formation. 'J' is running badly since Millar gave it that caning the other day.

0930: Landed-on. Had a shave & am now sitting at the desk in dressing gown writing these few notes feeling beautifully clean—must get a haircut tonight—nice to sit down to a well cooked and served meal.

1400: Talk from 'F' about past faults & future ops. We are going to remain at sea for about ten more days in order to take part in a U-boat battle. Sounds exciting & here's hope that it may lead to a spot of leave when we finally get to our home port . . .

1630: Took part in a vigorous game of deck hockey in which Cooper nearly took a header into the 'oggin.

1800: Up hook and away again—northward bound with the destroyers *Inconstant*, *Garland*, *Burza*—no flying—clocks retarded one hour.

Monday 25th Oct.

0230: Shaken (in more ways than one!). Standby dawn patrol—breakfast coffee & toast.

0400: Took off instead of 'B'—search—nothing seen.

0710: Landed-on. 0830–1230 zzzzz—lovely!

1500: Ship refuelled Burza.

1800: Should be nearing U-pack tomorrow—fingers crossed & many prayers said. Turned in early in cabin 21.

Tuesday 26th Oct.

NF. Tommy pranged his wing tip on HF/DF mast, carried out his patrol & nearly lost himself, and finally pranged his undercart on landing. No one hurt, but kite W/O. Fortunately he was flying his own a/c. We now have only 8 S/fish. Quiet morning with no flying for me. Sea calm.

1215: Time for lunch. Hear that ratings have only 20 soup bowls between 400, that we have only enough food for 14 days & that the DDs [destroyers] are worse off than we.

1500: Ship refuelled *Inconstant* & passed keg of rum—managed to get some photos. Carried out modifications on camera so that I can get 16 snaps instead of 8 off one reel.

Wednesday 27th Oct.

0500: Dawn patrol. Sighted oil patch. Returning to carrier I am almost overcome by carbon monoxide from exhaust which was entering cockpit through loose panel. Saw U-boat in the distance but it submerged while we were still 5 miles away. By now I hardly had a clue. Landed safely but spent the rest of the day in bed under MO's watchful eye. Off flying for two days. Captain creates a stink re U-boat.

Thursday 28th Oct.

Feeling OK now but 'Old Man' (Pelly) says not for flying.

1130: There was a 'Tan Tivy' from Kenyon. U-boat submerged & Ken attacked, results unknown. He made a magnificent prang on landing & completely

---

Morocco-Bound *Chief Aircraft Artificer Bill Banham*

Nineteen forty-four. Convoy KMF.34 safely delivered by, amongst other ships, the escort carrier HMS *Nairana*, home to 835 Squadron, equipped with Hurricane fighters and Swordfish anti-submarine aircraft. With the ship lying alongside the dockyard at Gibraltar, at rest after a fairly uneventful operation, the hangar deck of *Nairana* was a hive of industry preparing the ship's aircraft for the return convoy. For various reasons—not unconnected with the

Nairana's top speed, 16 to 17 knots, and the weather—three of the six Sea Hurricanes carried by the ship needed urgent repair work.

At this stage of World War II, the Sea Hurricane was being replaced by more advanced fighter aircraft, mainly of American design and construction, and consequently, as far as the Royal Navy was concerned, spare parts had become very limited. The air station at RAF North Front, Gibraltar,

W/O kite—seven now serviceable.

1800: Boni pranged on deck—bent oleo—six kites serviceable. What price the Old Man's 100% serviceability? Throughout the day the ship has had an average pitch of 30 feet & also a hell of a roll (crash on the flight deck).

Friday 29th Oct.

0700: Dawn patrol—beautiful sunrise—sighted convoy, 31 ships which we are to escort home, we hope. Hell's slow convoy though, 7½kts. Dropped message on deck from a/c giving position of convoy.

1130: Clocks back one hour. Turning carrier into wind quite tricky when in centre of convoy. Destroyers refuelling from tankers and re-provisioning from us. Dark now at about 1700. Steaming at 7½ knots, seems as though we are barely moving.

Saturday 30th Oct.

A heavy swell running. Deck pitching too much for normal flying, though in emergency a/c will take off. Escorted by Catalina. Finished a report on being gassed in 'J'.

1800: Paid £11.3.0. Seems more than I should receive, but why worry? Tiny Admiralty trawlers escorting convoy. Gramophone record 'Alone Together', Arti Shaw.

Sunday 31st Oct.

0200: Clocks advanced one hour.

0745: SDO [Squadron Duty Officer]. Three kites airborne on search. Deck heaving 30–40 feet. All kites landed safely on throughout the day.

Monday 1st Nov.

0600: Ready to take off in 'G'. Standby patrol. Engine nearly caught fire. Finger trouble on deck—aircraft lights being switched on, etc.

0900: Sea very rough. 40-knot wind, visibility 2 miles, deck pitching 40 feet. Boniface pranged into bridge [see photographs on page 70]. Kite repairable & crew OK. Storm brewing. Flying cancelled—4 a/c lashed on deck. We should be out of U-boat zone now.

Tuesday 2nd Nov.

0400: Urgh!—had to get up to inspect lashings on the 4 kites on deck. Eee but it's blowing oop thar.

0530: We left convoy—steamed on. Now on our way back to Greenock. Wonder if we will get leave???

1630: Walked about 2 miles up & down the deck. Steaming 13 knots—good show, should be in by Friday.

Wednesday 2nd Nov.

0530: Rudely awakened.

0720: Dawn patrol ahead of ship. Pleasant trip. Sighted a large streak of oil extending about ½ mile. Flap before TO. No Very pistol, mag. drop, etc.

1030: Had a merry evening in the wardroom. Should be in Greenock 0700 Friday.

Thursday 4th Nov.

No flying. Weather too rough—45-knot gale.

Friday 5th Nov.

0730: Anchored Greenock.

1230: Boarded liberty boat for 10 days' leave.

---

was unable to offer much in the way of the parts required, although some progress was made in this respect. However, by some means, information had come to hand that, subsequent to the Germans being cleared out of North Africa in 1943, American forces had taken over a large aerodrome at Casablanca and that a small RAF contingent had been based there to clear up damaged and obsolete aircraft left over from the fighting. It was understood, furthermore, that, amongst the aircraft so collected, a number of Hurricane fighter-bombers had been salvaged—ideal, as these particular aircraft were almost identical to the Sea Hurricanes on *Nairana*. Whatever negotiations may have taken place, the writer was informed that he was to be flown, together with Lieutenant Byram, the ship's Air Engineering Officer, to Casablanca, there to obtain any spares that could be utilised for the Squadron's aircraft.

To North Front early one morning with Lieutenant Byram, and there waiting was a Bristol Beaufighter (Merlin-engined version) complete with a pilot from the Naval Air Station. We boarded and away, and for the first few minutes everything was in order. We had cleared the Rock and were on course when I was summoned up front to the

Left: HMS Nairana *at Gibraltar. One of the few British-built escort carriers in the Royal Navy, she spent most of her wartime career in the Arctic, on convoy protection work.*

pilot's cockpit. There he pointed to the starboard engine, and asked, 'Should we continue?' The reason for his query was immediately obvious—a thin stream of oil was coming from the lower engine cowling immediately behind the propeller. This suggested to me that the constant-speed unit in that location had blown a seal and that to continue may well have led to a complete engine failure—fatal with this particular aircraft. It was decided to turn back, and fortunately the decision was made just in time as the original oil leak had considerably increased by the time we landed.

The following day, again to North Front, this time accompanied by Lieutenant Mearns (later Commander Mearns DSC), Senior Pilot of *Nairana's* Hurricane flight. Waiting for us was another Beaufighter. On take-off, the aircraft left the runway and immediately swung violently to port, heading straight for the Rock. The pilot, fighting to get control, appeared to have got the nose of the aircraft down when, with a rending crash, the aircraft ploughed into a cemetery near the base of the Rock. The whole structure carried on, the front end breaking away from the rear fuselage aft of the gunner's position (occupied by the writer). Both sections eventually came to a stop amongst the wreckage of gravestones and monuments.

Meantime I had been catapulted along what was left of the front fuselage, collecting cuts and abrasions on the way. I released the gunner's canopy and quickly exited the aircraft (although it would have been quicker to get out through the back as there was a large aperture where the rear fuselage had been as the latter had broken away on impact). Both the pilot and Lieutenant Mearns had earlier exited their part of the aircraft. Accompanied by the usual bells and whistles, the fire tenders and ambulances from both the RAF and the Navy quickly appeared. Luckily, the aircraft did not catch fire and the only sign of blood on the three crew members was to be found on myself, whose back and rear end had been damaged after being thrown along the fuselage. The ambulance crews seemed quite disappointed but took pleasure in plastering my damaged parts with Sulfa powder and yards of bandages.

Back to *Nairana*, to be informed that a third attempt would be made to get to Casablanca. And so again to North Front, and again accompanied by Lieutenant Mearns. This time, however, one of the Navy's Swordfish was placed at our disposal, to be flown by my companion.

After the usual pre-flight checks and some remarks about the scruffy appearance of the aircraft—which, compared with *Nairana*'s Swordfish, had been stripped of all equipment, defensive and offensive—we climbed aboard and were off. With some apprehension on my part we were airborne, riding the sky in an unarmed aircraft in wartime,

but luck and an excellent pilot carried us along and soon the sandy coast of North Africa was in sight. Putting the nose of the aircraft down and reducing altitude, Lieutenant Mearns started to follow the coastline toward our objective.

As we neared Casablanca, it became obvious that the war had passed on: as we flew at low level over the sand dunes, families could be seen enjoying themselves in and out of the water. It passed through my mind, and probably that of my pilot, that there were no such amenities for our families back in Britain, who, after four years of hostilities, were still locked into wartime restrictions.

Beneath our wings lay the aircraft-packed runways of the American air base—lines of smart and, for the time, modern aircraft. There was no sign of biplanes of any type. The pilot, on instructions from the control tower, made the landing and waited on the runway. Out of seemingly nowhere an American jeep appeared, painted yellow and with a large board on the back of the vehicle with the words 'Follow me' painted on it. Away we went, following the jeep to the taxiway adjacent to the tower, where at the request by hand signals from American personnel, we stopped our engine and awaited instructions.

The aircraft was by now surrounded by American military, whose comments ('Which war have you Limeys

Tragedy *Lieutenant (A) Jock Bevan* RNVR

This is an unedifying story, but I feel that the passage of sixty-three years is sufficient to have cleared the way for facts to be disclosed. It culminated in a dramatic tragedy in which I was partly involved.

It was on board the MAC ship MV *Empire MacCallum*, about 5.30 p.m. local time, not far off the coast of Newfoundland, on 6 February, 1944. The Swordfish was LS299 of 'K' Flight 836 Squadron. It was being flown by Bill Gunner, with Sid Hughes as TAG and myself as observer.

The weather in the north-western Atlantic had seen a series of gales which had prevented our flying anti-U-boat patrols for about a week. This was fine by us, the aircrews, but our Commander (Flying) saw things differently. This individual was a regular RN Lieutenant who seemed to consider that Reserve officers (like ourselves) were in some way inferior to those in the Regular Service. The CO of 'K' Flight was also a Lieutenant, but a Reserve officer. This was Len Oldknow, who had recently returned from a long spell in the Egyptian desert flying Walrus amphibians in 701 (Rescue) Squadron. He was a humorous and cynical type, with no time for 'class' superiority. He was also my regular pilot.

On that day, 6 February, the Atlantic calmed down and the sun came out. Our Commander (Flying) seems to have considered this a good opportunity for trying out some air-to-sea photography (although this seemed to feature extremely rarely in anti-U-boat warfare). Len, who had just had the very unnerving experience of my getting him lost in mid-Atlantic, told Commander (F) that he did not intend to risk the lives of his crew or himself on such an unnecessary non-operational exercise; he had better find

someone else! The gallant Lieutenant thereupon ordered the photographic expedition into the air anyway and handed me a state-of-the-art, quarter-plate camera with which to show my skills.

It was a beautiful sunny evening and we had a great time 'beating up' the other ships in the convoy and taking their portraits. At the controls was Bill Gunner, whose proper place was on the port side of the ship as Deck Landing Control Officer but who presumably had been persuaded to take Len's place. The office of DLC had controversially been taken by an apparently unqualified pilot.

Eventually I used up all my film and we approached for a landing. Whether it was because of inexpert 'batting' signals or lack of experience in mid-ocean deck landings, Bill brought LS299 in too high and too far over to starboard. The result was that the upper starboard wing was

COURTESY JOCK BEVAN

come from?' etc.) were quite amusing. Having requested information as to where the RAF contingent were located (packing cases on the far side of the aerodrome), it was necessary to re-start the engine—again a source of great amusement to the admiring audience, who, witnessing the winding-up procedure of the inertia starter, again offered their observations ('Have you Limeys never heard of electric starters?', 'How long does it take to wind up the elastic?'). Luckily the good old Pegasus fired up first time and away we trundled to the RAF Unit, where their ground crew took over the refuelling of our Swordfish.

Lieutenant Mearns disappeared to report to the senior RAF officer with reference to our flight plans while I was taken by the Unit's technical warrant officer to the salvage dump, there to view an astonishing variety of parts. What a delight! A complete squadron of aircraft could have been assembled using the bits available!

To work, and, aided by several RAF technicians, a selection of items was quickly mustered. Everything that we needed to service the ship's Hurricanes was available. And so back to our aircraft, with a line of Eastern gentlemen carrying the parts, one a set of cowling panels, one festooned with tailwheels, one a bag of landing gear parts and the last carrying a generator and a hydraulic pump. The

cortège wended its way to our aircraft, where with some difficulty it was stowed on board. Handshakes all round. Within minutes of completing the stowage, Lieutenant Mearns appeared, also accompanied by Eastern gentlemen, but this time carrying boxes of eggs. It was with some difficulty that these were also fitted in, leaving just enough room the second crew member.

The intrepid aviators climbed aboard, and this time an RAF team cranked up our starter. Again the Pegasus fired up first time and settled down to an even rhythm. The pilot taxied to the end of the runway, watched by quite a crowd of US and RAF personnel, the aircraft was cleared to take off, and away we went, Lieutenant Mearns making sure that the departure was as spectacular as possible and adding a few extra tricks before settling down on our return trip to Gibraltar.

The return passed without incident. We landed back at North Front, there to be picked up complete with spares and eggs and transported back to *Nairana*. We arrived back on board the ship just in time for an evening meal.

It had been an interesting and productive exercise. The result, two or three days later, was that HMS *Nairana* cleared Gibraltar for the return trip with a homebound convoy, her six Hurricanes fully operational.

---

demolished by contact with the carrier's island and the Swordfish spun into the sea, landing the right way up and facing astern.

The aircraft's inflatable dinghy was automatically deployed, but unfortunately there was insufficient compressed air in its cylinder fully to inflate it. We pulled it clear of the aircraft. Normally, the fully inflated dinghy would be secured by an easily shearing lanyard to prevent it from drifting away too soon, but ours, only half-inflated, did not have enough buoyancy to shear the lanyard and was therefore pulled down as the Swordfish headed for Davy Jones. By mischance the lanyard had fouled my right leg and so I, too, was heading in that direction. I managed to free myself just as I became aware that the Atlantic's blue water was becoming rapidly darker. It seemed to take ages to regain the surface. Bill and Sid were still there, and the

former had obviously followed the correct procedure and inflated his Mae West to the proportions of its namesake. However, neither Sid nor I had had much luck with ours. We then realised that Sid was a non-swimmer and in great distress.

Bill was doing his best to keep Sid afloat when, suddenly, a ship's lifeboat appeared alongside. Captain Hawken of the *Empire MacCallum* had seen the situation and had hove-to, immediately ordering away a boat manned by four engineer officers. These gentlemen managed to drag all three of us from the water, where we had by now been swimming for twenty minutes and which was just one degree above freezing. One of them, Mr Gurney, dived in three times. I do not remember much more until I found myself lying in *MacCallum*'s Sick Bay. Next to me was Sid. He was grey and completely still. Later, back in our own cabin, Captain Hawken came to tell us that Sid had died. I recalled that it was Sid who had broken radio silence for a compass bearing when I had got us lost a few days earlier . . .

Below: A series of poignant images capturing the final moments of Swordfish LS299, 6 February 1944.

No Upper Charlies *Lieutenant (A) Tommy Thomson* DSC RNVR

After SFTS in Canada, we were brought together at Hullavington and the few weeks we spent there were very hectic. At first, the Swordfish seemed huge with its wingspan of around forty-five feet and the way it sat up—like riding a Clydesdale after being used to a nimble pony—but the greatest difficulty of all was ensuring that one did not get lost. In Canada it could only be *that* road, *that* railway, *that* village, or *that* town: here there were scores of roads, villages and railway lines within a radius of a few miles. Of course, there were also a very large number of aerodromes, and members of the group quite often landed away from home. One pilot became so disorientated that he ended up at an airstrip almost one hundred miles to the north.

Some of the course were frightening themselves to sleeplessness on teased-out Hurricanes that popped and banged and leaked but nevertheless managed to remain airborne. These men were the chosen *élite*, the future fighter plots, and I was envious for I was one of the majority who would fly at a sedate speed throughout the rest of the war. On reflection, I was in fact one of the lucky ones, flying many more hours than the fighter pilots and not writing myself off by doing Upper Charlies too close to the ground. I managed to get used to the new environment without becoming lost, and found that the Swordfish was a forgiving—if seemingly clumsy—aircraft.

The real training began at RNAS Crail and RNAS Arbroath, and we flew both Swordfish and Albacores, discovering all the things that one can do against U-boats and shipping and trying to do them with efficiency. When we thought that we were ready for operations, I was asked for my preferred posting and said Malta, because the idea of carrier work did not appeal to me. I discovered that I had to get through a period of 'stooging' at Worthy Down before I joined a new Swordfish Squadron, 842, and it was then more training, mainly at Machrihanish. This seemed to go on for ever, and we felt that we would never become operational—although the quality of our flying sharpened up considerably and I, for one, became a part of the Stringbag (or it became part of me).

I never went to Malta. Instead, 842 flew from the escort carrier HMS *Fencer* and worked mainly with the Atlantic and Russian convoys in all weathers, with much movement on board the ship—which was about the same length as the great ocean swells and as a result got her nose into many a trough. On one occasion I was trundling along the deck in darkness for a pre-dawn take-off when the ship dipped to starboard and the HF/DF mast ripped off several feet of my wing. We staggered off into blackness and carried on with the patrol. The Swordfish really was a tough aircraft.

In one Atlantic convoy a U-boat suddenly appeared on the surface among the ships and dived before a shot could be fired. I was on deck on standby and was flown off with no instructions, although I guessed that the U-boat was in trouble and would go rapidly astern and then surface for repairs. This indeed happened, and I found her as she began to surface. Three depth charges were laid across her just aft of the conning tower and she lurched up before disappearing. An escort vessel rushed to the spot and picked up breaking-up noises at depth. My old Stringbag brought me a DSC for this.

'He's Diving! He's Diving!' *Lieutenant-Commander Bill Henley* DSC*

On 13 December 1944 convoy RA.62 was three days out of Murmansk and had reached a position about 350 miles north-west of the Lofoten Islands, still within the Arctic Circle. The convoy consisted of twenty-nine merchant ships; the surface escort included HM Ships *Campania* and *Nairana*, two of the few British-built escort carriers. Together with the similar *Vindex*, these vessels provided close air cover for the Russian convoys throughout the winter of 1944/45 as their riveted hulls were considered more able to meet the rigours of Arctic operations than the welded hulls of other escort carriers. Embarked in each carrier were between four and six Wildcat fighters and between twelve and fourteen Swordfish Mk IIIs.

Campania and *Nairana* split the day between them. *Campania* had taken over as duty carrier at noon and was launching two Swordfish on 'Cobra 20s' (patrols around the convoy at twenty miles' radius) on a 2½-hour cycle. In addition, two aircraft were at readiness on deck. As it was too cold to keep the crews in the cockpits, they remained, fully kitted up, in the Ready Room, venturing forth at intervals to warm up the engines and electronics. All the aircraft were armed with three 250-pound depth charges, two on inboard carriers under the port wing and one on an outboard carrier under the starboard wing. This asymmetric loading was necessary as the centre-line carrier had been displaced by the Mk III's radome. It took account of torque and slipstream effects, reducing the out-of-balance lateral trim to an acceptable level.

Some time about 1525, when what passed for daylight was long gone, one of the patrolling aircraft reported homing on to a contact on the port quarter of the convoy. Flares were dropped, illuminating a U-boat, which, instead of diving (the usual response at night), appeared to be ready to fight on the surface. All Swordfish crews had strict orders that in such an event they were not to attack but, to use modern parlance, to 'call for back-up'.

Right: The aircrew stations of a brand new, pre-delivery Swordfish Mk III. The ring of the pilot's ring-and-bead gun sight is evident, and the flexible machine gun, now operable by the observer, is stowed in its customary position within the rear fuselage top decking. The starboard ASV radar aerial is also prominent, and the small, semi-circular handholds to aid crew entry to each cockpit can be seen. The observer's instrumentation has yet to be installed or has been removed—doubtless for reasons of security.

Above: The courtesy visit: the Swordfish flown by Tommy Thomson takes off from the Schipol–The Hague highway to cheering crowds, 9 September 1945.

The convoys to Russia were not too pleasant, mainly because the open cockpit at low temperatures caused the lips to dry out, crack and bleed. Aircrew could not conduct a useful look-out crouched down out of the slipstream, and I remember that the goggles were not too wonderful: anything modern went to the RAF. I also did several trips on fleet carriers while the Squadron worked on anti-submarine patrols, and on these occasions I was finding myself airborne before I reached the bridge—a strange experience.

All through the winter of 1943/44 and through to October 1944 , 842 Squadron worked its anti-U-boat patrols and during that time only one ship was sunk. It was a terrible sight as the black column of smoke turned to red and the vessel broke her back and slipped under the sea. Some of the crew members were picked up by one of the escorts.

After the end of the European War a Naval Exhibition was sent to Holland to say 'thank you' to the Dutch for their courage during the Occupation, and I was in charge of the FAA section—a Swordfish, a Seafire and a Firefly. I had a meeting with Rotterdam's Chief of Police and Mayor, who stopped all the traffic on the main road for thirty minutes while the three aircraft were flown off to Amsterdam.

Altogether I flew my beloved Stringbag for about a thousand hours, and one of my most interesting experiences was to complete a loop off the island of Jura near Machrihanish.

It took some time for the Command to decide whether, in view of the position of the U-boat, it was worthwhile sending back-up, but eventually the decision was made to launch the standby aircraft. These were 'L'/813, manned by 'Hutch' Hutchison (pilot) and Ian Farningham (observer) and 'Q'/813 with 'Sam' Chapman (observer) and myself (pilot). We were senior and would lead, but shortly after take-off Sam reported our radar unserviceable and so we handed over the lead to Hutch and Ian. The night was dark but clear and I had no problem in maintaining a loose echelon starboard, being able to see our companion's white-painted fuselage in addition to the small, blue, rearward-facing formation lights, one in each wing tip and one on the tail. We flew at around 1,000 feet.

Approaching the vicinity of the sighting, Ian picked up a contact; he homed in and Hutch dropped flares, but there was nothing to be seen—it seemed as though the U-boat had dived at the last minute. Hutch dropped his depth charges to act as a deterrent to surfacing; the longer the U-boat remained submerged, the less chance it had of catching up with the convoy. Then the ship recalled us.

We were now about fifty miles away. The effect of head-wind and convoy speed on the Mark III's cruising speed of 80 knots meant that it would take a good hour to reach the convoy. It was looking as though we were in for a long but fruitless sortie, but suddenly, after we had been going for 15–20 minutes, Ian came up with 'Contact sixty degrees to port at twelve miles.' He said afterwards that the convoy was just coming on to his radar at 35 miles when this new contact appeared, and it was so strong that he had to adjust his radar to avoid being blinded by it.

We immediately turned towards the contact. During training we had always acted singly at night, but a brief chat on the radio confirmed that Ian and Hutch would home in, drop flares and remain at altitude. Sam and I would take it from there. During the run-in I turned the cockpit lights up bright for a moment or two to make sure I had selected the right switches and set the distributor which determined the distance apart that the depth charges would drop—sixty feet, based on twice the weapons' lethal radius (nineteen feet) plus the diameter of the U-boat's pressure hull (twenty-two) What I forgot, however, was that, because of recent modifications to the circuit, it was necessary to set double the distance: I set the customary sixty feet, and thus the charges would drop thirty feet apart. This later earned a mild rebuke from a member of the Naval Staff!

Eventually Ian said 'Stand by' and then I saw his flares fall away. Following the established drill, I turned forty-five degrees to starboard, commenced a fifteen-degree dive and increased speed to 130 knots. The loom of the flares came up astern. Almost immediately Sam coolly and clearly reported, 'U-boat bearing Red 160 degrees.' After losing about 400 feet of height, I commenced a turn to port, maintaining the dive. As soon as I could I looked out to port and saw the U-boat. It was larger than any other sub-marine I had ever seen, and was going flat out, butting into a head sea, leaving a broad wake that extended beyond the light of the flares. Then Sam shouted, 'He's diving! He's diving!' I replied, 'It's all right. We'll get him!'

I completed the turn and, still in the dive, headed towards the U-boat from about fifty degrees on its port bow and aiming to cross its track just forward of the conning tower. At a height of about eighty feet, and with the tower beginning to disappear under the nose of my aircraft and with the upper casing of the U-boat just awash, I pressed the release button and felt the effect on the aircraft as the charges fell away. Easing out of the dive, I started a climbing turn to port.

There was then a great shout from Ian: 'A beautiful shot!' He had seen the splashes of the first and third depth charges entering the water, accurately straddling the U-boat. There was no splash in the middle, but Sam, who had a close-up view, maintained that there had been three explosions. The middle charge must have fallen into the disturbed water alongside the U-boat or actually hit its hull and bounced off.

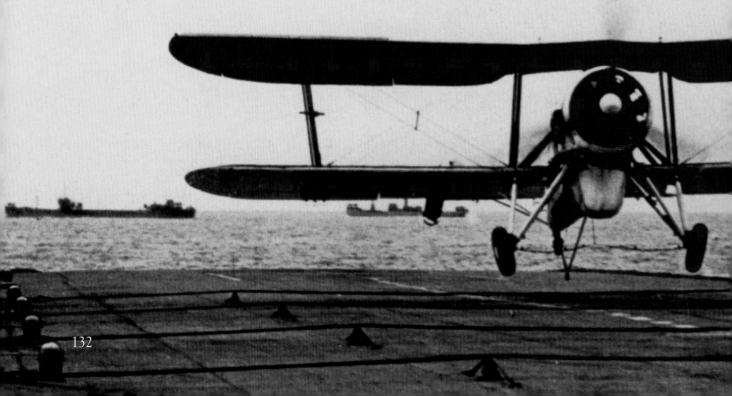

COURTESY ROB GARDINER

Above: The Swordfish's prey in the Battle of the Atlantic—German U-boats. The menace of these submarines was constant from the day war broke out until VE-Day in 1945. While, as is pointed out in these pages, the number of 'kills' achieved by Swordfish was small, the mere presence of these aircraft right across the Atlantic ensured that the enemy submarines were unable to operate to anything like their potential.

Below: 'Landing-on, I blotted my copybook somewhat . . . but the undercarriage held up.'

I turned through about 150 degrees and looked out to starboard, seeing a single broad column of water with the wake going into the middle of it. A few seconds later the column subsided and there was the rear one-third of the hull of the U-boat projecting from the water at about 45 degrees. It hung there for a moment or two before plunging quite rapidly beneath the surface. Then the flares went out.

Levelling off at 600–700 feet, I dropped a couple of flares and, descending to 200 feet, flew over an oil slick about 300–400 yards across and with a lot of debris floating in it although nothing that we could identify. There was no more we could do, so we returned to *Campania*.

Landing-on, I blotted my copybook somewhat. When the radome replaced the centre-line carrier on a Swordfish, a stainless-steel wire cable with a breaking strain of two tons was strung between the two wheels and adjusted to become bar-taut just before the undercarriage reached full compression. My landing broke the cable but the undercarriage held up. That was it, save for debriefing and report-writing.

The Admiralty were very conservative when assessing the results of attacks on U-boats. As we could not produce any physical evidence of the sinking it was classified Class B— 'Probably sunk'. In the summer of 1946, however, presumably after access to German records, an Admiralty Fleet Order was published giving brief details of all U-boat sinkings. Swordfish 'L'/813 and 'Q'/813 were credited with having sunk U 365!

COURTESY PHILIP JARRETT

CARE AND MAINTENANCE

Chief Aircraft Artificer Bill Banham

MAINTAINING an aircraft of any shape and style is one of the most responsible jobs that exists, since the safety of the aircrew is paramount. The Fairey Swordfish, specifically in terms of its airframe and engine technology, was a comparatively easy aircraft to maintain and up to certain limits could be effectively repaired also.

Maintenance procedures could be defined in various categories, as follows:

(a) Replenishment, i.e. maintaining the correct levels of fuel and oil;

(b) Routine inspection, whereby the whole of the aircraft and engine installation was subjected to scrutiny, and which comprised four sub-categories—Between Flight, After Flight, Daily and Periodic Inspections (for example, after thirty flying hours);

(c) Rectification, where such activities were carried out as to correct any shortcomings revealed by inspection; and

(d) Repair and Replace, for example replacing a damaged landing strut and carrying out a repair of the latter in the workshop.

A Between Flight Inspection involved an overall external check immediately after a flight had been completed and had to be pronounced satisfactory before another could be authorised. It was definitely *not* a 'Kick the tyres, light the fire and go!' operation.

In a Daily Inspection, the entire engine installation—engine, propeller, exhaust system, fuel and oil pipe runs, auxiliary engine-driven components and engine controls—was scrutinised for its serviceability,

Below: A stripped-down Swordfish, with the oil cooler prominent. Keeping the oil fluid was a constant problem in the freezing Arctic conditions and extemporary shrouds were frequently fitted to forestall engine seizure.

the examination of the systems for external oil leaks, and their rectification if necessary, being of particular importance. Any report from the pilot of inconsistent engine behaviour was investigated and rectified; indeed, the aircraft was not permitted to fly again until this had been resolved satisfactorily. An external examination of the entire airframe was carried out, to identify signs of damage, special attention being paid to the stowage of the dinghy and its release mechanism. In addition, the following components and systems were examined:

  — all movable control surfaces—elevators, rudder, ailerons—to ensure proper freedom of movement;

Below: Panelling around the forward fuselage could be readily removed by unscrewing their securing bolts—although there were a great many of them! The Pegasus engine was enclosed by a simple circular cowling.

  — surface trimmers, for satisfactory operation;
  — arrester hook, including its release mechanism and stowage facility;
  — air pressure in the braking system, for correct operation without leakages (the rudder bar would then be operated with the brake lever 'on' and the differential of the braking system checked);
  — tyre pressure, with rectification as required;
  — tyre surfaces, for signs of wear or damage (a heavy landing would of course call for a more intensive investigation involving the entire landing gear, particularly in the vicinity of the main attachments and hinge points);
  — cockpit area, involving the security of the seats and the serviceability of the seat belts, parachute stowages, etc;
  — Foreign Object Detection (FOD), a most

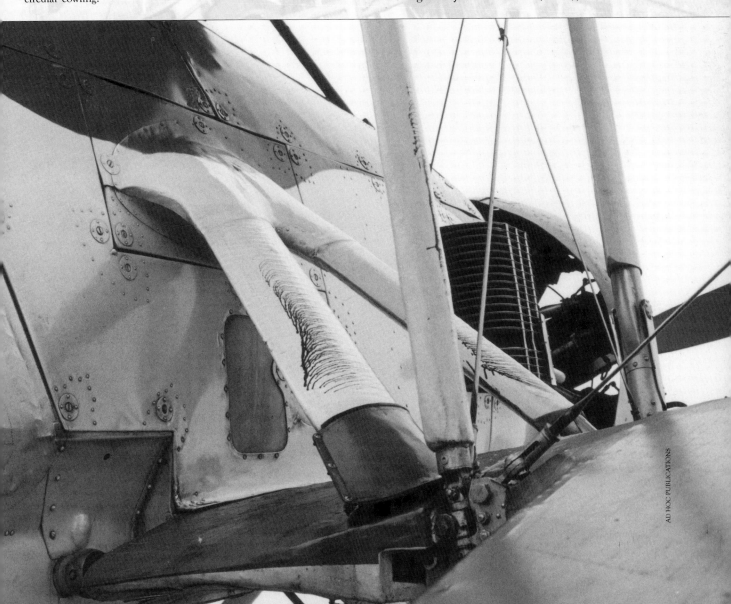

AD HOC PUBLICATIONS

AD HOC PUBLICATIONS

essential procedure, carried out to ensure that all areas of the structure, particularly the interior of the cockpit, were free from loose articles such as tools, nuts, bolts and even personal possessions. Loose objects could cause catastrophic accidents if caught up in the aircraft's control system.

The Periodic Inspection was a regular and extensive check and was immediately followed by the carrying out of any remedial work arising. In addition to the procedures followed for the Daily Inspection, it would typically include changing all eighteen sparking plugs, adjusting valve settings, examining each cylinder for signs of overheating and checking the security of the cylinder attachments. A feature of the thirty-hour inspection in particular

involved taking a sample of the petrol lying static in the carburettor and checking it for contamination—any sign of which required the aircraft's entire fuel system to be drained and replenished. The Periodic Inspection would also call for the removal of all panelling enclosing the structure so that the accessible areas could be checked for damage etc—particularly corrosion. This last, since the Swordfish was primarily a maritime aircraft, required continuous surveillance, with immediate rectification if required. Attention was also always paid to the security of the fuel tanks so that any evidence of fuel leaks could be uncovered. Similarly, the landing gear received close scrutiny during the thirty-hour 'down time', entailing the removal of wheels so that brake blocks and wheel bearings could be assessed for wear

AD HOC PUBLICATIONS

Above: Periodic Inspection required the removal of all panels to reveal the inner workings of the aircraft, including cabling, piping and control wires. In this photograph, the sprung footholds to assist the crew climb on board their Swordfish are clearly evident; they are angled so as to present approximately horizontal surfaces when the aircraft is on the ground.

Left: The Swordfish's sturdy starting handle. Two men, plus the pilot, were needed to fire up the Pegasus. The engine itself was generally very reliable, performing well in both the dusty heat of North Africa and the below-zero temperatures of the Arctic environment.

Right: Members of the Royal Navy Historic Flight at RNAS Yeovilton prepare to start the Pegasus engine of LS326.

or damage. The oleo legs or shock absorbers were serviced as required, again with particular attention paid to the attachment points.

Generally speaking, the thirty-hour inspection was the highest category in the maintenance programme that was carried out during an operational cycle; the more extensive work (at, say, 120 flying hours) was conducted when the parent ship was in harbour or the aircraft were otherwise shore-based.

For various reasons—not least the lack of storage space on board ship—only one spare engine for each aircraft type was available to the sea-going Chief Aircraft Artificer. A complete engine change could be carried out, but the restricted space and the motion of the ship meant that this was a hazardous operation (although it could be, and was, achieved when needed).

A unique feature of the Swordfish was the procedure that had to be followed for starting the engine, and of all the maintenance and day-to-day tasks that entailed a degree of risk, this was one of the most hazardous. The engine installation embodied what was generally known as inertia starting, wherein a large handle was inserted in an aperture in the fairing behind the Pegasus in the port side. This engaged a chain-and-sprocket drive which in turn rotated a balanced flywheel, and this, upon rotation, would be clutched into the engine to turn the crankshaft assembly.

To start the engine, the handle was inserted and turning commenced until, at a predetermined speed (gauged by experience), the pilot, having switched on his fuel system, primed the engine and set his throttle and mixture control, would shout 'Contact!', activate the ignition and pull a selector linkage to engage the starter. The energy generated by the flywheel would, it was hoped (!), be sufficient to turn the engine over enough revolutions for it to fire and then settle down to controllable running. On the whole, this rather archaic procedure worked very well, seldom failing to achieve 'start-up', but if indeed the Pegasus refused to start it was usually because of incorrect priming. A failed start-up, with all its attendant delays, required the entire procedure to begin again. This in turn entailed switching off the engine's ignition system, manually rotating the propeller for several revolutions and then turning the starting handle as before.

Engine starting placed one or both ground crewmen in considerable danger. In order to operate the starting handle, one crewman stood facing the port side of the aircraft, his left foot on a foothold located in the forward bracing strut of the main landing gear and the other on the lower centre-section. The second crewman stood with both feet on the lower centre-section, similarly facing the port side of the aircraft. In this fashion the maximum rotational movement of the handle could be achieved. However, the second man had the aircraft's propeller immediately to his left side, and if he were to slip from his foot rest as the engine fired the possible consequences can be imagined—and if extreme cold,

a slippery flight deck and a howling wind, not to speak of the movement of the ship, are thrown into the equation . . .

Immediately a successful start had been accomplished the groundcrew were required to remove the starting handle and replace it into the special stowage compartment on board the aircraft. There was no provision in the Swordfish for any alternative means of starting the engine, so the handle was not an item to be misplaced.

Operating aircraft from on board carriers under wartime conditions is a specialised discipline, and the routine followed in HMS *Nairana* is illustrative. Where possible, each aircraft was allocated a dedicated crew of one airframe and one engine mechanic, these, with the pilot, forming an effective team with the aircraft in question their particular responsibility. In order to achieve optimum availability, all repair and routine servicing was brought up to date. Thus, for example, even if a thirty-hour service was not quite due, the work was advanced so that the maximum allowable flying time became available from the start of the operation. To assist the work of the mechanics looking after each aircraft, a support team was formed to 'fill in' for individual crew members who might be indisposed or otherwise unavailable. Finally, all technical personnel were expected to help with refuelling, re-arming, repositioning and securing aircraft on the flight deck or within the hangar.

The Swordfish received very little in the way of modification throughout its period of service. The

Applied Mathematics Applied *Sub-Lieutenant (A) Stanley Brand RNVR*

Our convoy was in 'U-Boat Alley', the central 600 miles of the North Atlantic where land-based aircraft could not provide air protection for ships bringing food, oil, men and munitions from the United States to Great Britain in the build-up for the invasion of 'Fortress Europe'. We had been hit by a series of overwhelming storms which made our Merchant Navy oil tanker roll and pitch like a bucking bronco because of the 1,000 tons of steel deck which she carried 30 feet above the waterline. Operating our three Swordfish aircraft from the tiny deck was difficult enough in still water, but with violent pitch and roll accidents just had to happen. Once we were airborne there was no choice but to face whatever hazards were presented to land back on the ship, for the nearest alternative haven was 1,000 miles away. All three aircraft were wrecked, and each in turn had been hastily cleared from the landing area to offer our other airborne colleagues a chance, if needed, to reach safety.

We worked until dusk to clear the deck in case we might pass a convoy going in the opposite direction, from whom we might borrow a serviceable Swordfish. By Aldis lamp the Senior Officer of the Escort was enthusiastic but, because of the need to maintain radio and radar silence, not hopeful. And so to bed, at the end of an eventful day—but not to dream. I was too occupied with a problem. There seemed to be enough 'bits' to be assembled into one complete Swordfish. But how to get them together with only a couple of trolley jacks for lifting? Sharing a cabin with Bill Thomson, my observer, made it possible to build and discard ideas with sensible discussion.

Dawn broke and in the Saloon we got into a huddle with the Merchant Navy Chief Engineer and First Officer, all the aircrew, the Senior Naval Officer and the Chief Petty Officer in charge of groundcrew. We had one engine with a propeller which was bent backwards when it had hit the deck, showing that it was not under power and so the bearings were probably unshocked. The other two propellers were bent forward, being powered, so were useless to us, and their engines would be of doubtful value. The usable engine was in a fuselage with collapsed undercarriage and damaged fin, rudder and tailplane caused by hitching ropes by which the thing had been heaved up and down the deck using MN volunteers. We had one pair of port wings and one pair of starboard wings in need of minor patching, and two sets of fin, rudder and tailplane assemblies which were salvageable. In stores we had three propellers and two complete sets of undercarriage, plus several serviceable wheels and bits.

From this collection we could assemble one Swordfish—if only we could bring the pieces together and lift them into position long enough to bolt them home. The mast was strong enough to support the three-ton weight of a complete aircraft, but as it was above the island we could not position anything directly beneath it. The solution lay in Bill's and my applied maths background: we put a strop around the mast and used an existing pulley to get the strop, plus a block and tackle, as high as possible up the mast, to offer the lifting power necessary for our purpose.

The fuselage with the 'good' engine was placed athwartships on deck with the prop shaft, padded with old sacks, almost touching the steel side of the bridgework. The block-and-tackle from the mast was hitched to the lifting shackle fitted to the centre section of the upper wing, put there by design for lifting Swordfish floatplanes out of the water. Another block-and-tackle was installed between the aircraft's tailwheel and the strong mounting of an Oerlikon cannon in a sponson on the port side of the ship. With the fuselage resting on jacks forward and aft, it was levelled into its flying attitude relative to the deck and then the port and starboard wings were manhandled into position (thanks to a massive

Right: Blackburn employees raising the tail of a Swordfish by trolley jack. Beneath the tailplane can be seen, stowed, the 'vee'-shaped locking struts employed when the aircraft's wings were folded.

type was to have been superseded by the Fairey Albacore—also a biplane, albeit one that incorporated a number of refinements—but although the latter was built and entered front-line service it did not offer much by way of improvement in terms of performance or general operational capability. However, the very fact that it existed may have encouraged the Powers That Be not to bother about improving the Swordfish.

The headwinds inherent in the Swordfish's design precluded any real advance in top speed, irrespective of the type of powerplant that may have been fitted, although, in my opinion, a more efficient engine such as the Pratt & Whitney R-1860—in service in the United States in certain Sikorsky flying boats, and available—merited consideration. This particular engine, although only marginally more powerful than the Bristol Pegasus, was years ahead in terms of its technology and would have offered an effective means of absorbing the Swordfish's ever-increasing load-carrying demands, and, with an injector replacing carburation, better fuel consumption.

I and many of my contemporaries never understood why a canopy could not have been provided to protect the aircrew. A number of Swordfish operating in Canada were so equipped, together with a quite comfortable heating system. Finally, although reliable in an archaic way, the physical effort demanded of the groundcrew, and the danger to which they were subjected, when starting the engine could and should have been resolved by the fitting of a combustion starter such as a Coffman.

---

turn-out of MN personnel) and bolted into position. By pulling on the block and tackle fastened to the tail wheel, the prop shaft was kept clear of the bridge structure whilst the aircraft was lifted by the mast tackle until it was high enough to mount the undercarriage. After sighs of relief all round, the fin, rudder and tailplane could now be fitted, and servicing in preparation for flight got under way. It was at this point that I began to realise the enormity of my commitment.

Limp and weary after days of continuous stress, I went to my bunk, restless at the thought of what I had let myself in for: without exception, it was assumed that I was going to test-fly the bastard that I had fathered. It crossed my mind that, had I joined the RAF, there would be a runway with yards to spare, to allow me to get the feel of any deficiency so that I could abort in safety before getting airborne (or, better still, get on the blower to the Maintenance Unit and sign a chit for three replacements, then go

out to the pub with my girl whilst awaiting their delivery). On the other hand, if I was polite I might ask the Skipper if he would be so kind as to prepare the motor launch for a speedy recovery in the event that I went into the drink far enough ahead to avoid being run over by a 10,000-ton ship with a huge built-in meat-slicer at its rear. If, however, it flew, and there was never yet a Swordfish which didn't, our convoy might sail into the Clyde intact and me with it.

I was up and dressed before I was called in the dark next morning, and so was Bill, who insisted that he was going to fly with me, jokingly exercising his fortnight's seniority to overcome my insistence that it was stupid to risk his neck. In our briefing room it was agreed that I would do a circuit of the convoy about four miles outside the escorting corvettes and then come in to land.

The team had already warmed up our creation and checked and double-checked everything possible. To consolidate our relationship I gave a nonchalant 'thumbs up' to the Deck Landing Control Officer, who then signalled for 'chocks away' and sent me off. As I reached the bridge my tail came up and my nose went down and I had difficulty in forcing the stick back to prevent the propeller carving up the steel deck. Quickly winding the tail-trim back to its fullest extent, I put on total bias to hold the nose up, but to little effect. By this time I was over the bow and had dropped to a level where my wheels bounced on the crest of a wave, so I shouted to Bill over the intercom, 'Ditch! Ditch! Ditch!' He shouted back, 'No—I am going aft!' By this time I had my feet braced against the dash to hold the stick right back and was keeping straight with ailerons.

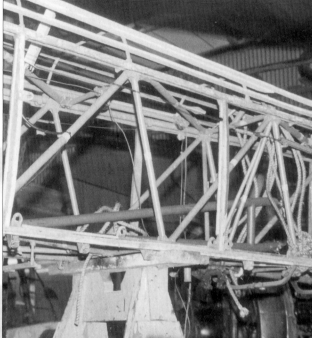

Almost imperceptibly the pressure on my arms and legs reduced and I very slowly gained a few feet in height. Shouting to Bill failed to get an answer, and eventually, at about thirty feet, I plucked up courage enough to take my eyes off the horizon and glance over my shoulder. There was Bill, sitting astride the fuselage right aft at the tailfin, holding on to the fin, where (I found out later) he had cut hand-holes in the fabric by the leading edge. The combined effect of the drag his body caused above the line of flight, and the shift aft in the centre of gravity, were enough to get us up to deck height, where, after a very gentle 360-degree turn I was able to make a deck-height, horizontal and full-throttle approach to land. I knew that if I made a mess of things it would cost Bill his life as he would be catapulted from his perch. With the tail up so high, the arrester hook would probably miss the wires, so I would have to close the throttle and brake immediately my wheels touched. I saw that the crash barrier had been left in the 'down' position so that I could go round again if necessary, showing that, on board, they were aware of a dilemma.

Opposite, upper left: A portion of the upper wing structure, showing the stowage recess for the vital dinghy.
Opposite, upper right: The rear fuselage structure, viewed from the port side.
Opposite, lower: The structure of the starboard lower mainplane. Notice the grab handles along the edge of the wing tip.
Below: Recovering an 813 Squadron Swordfish by sheerlegs on board HMS *Eagle*, August 1939. The aircraft is carrying the new style of coding introduced just before the war; unusually, however, *Eagle*'s aircraft retained their 'silver' finish well into 1940 (because the necessary camouflage paint stocks were not available at the time in the Far East, the theatre in which she was operating).

But all went well, and after mugs of very sweet tea laced with rum, and several cigarettes, the whole incident was analysed to get to the cause. The Chief Petty Officer in charge of maintenance went off in a hurry and came back less than an hour later to say that the rack-and-pinion system which controlled the angle of attack of the tailplane was engaged several teeth beyond those in the tails of the one remaining wreck with an undisturbed tail, and thus the leading edge of the tailplane was higher than it should have been and could not be brought down to the correct position. The correction was made, but the Flight Commander refused to let anyone pilot the aircraft but himself. However, he insisted that he should be accompanied only by a volunteer mechanic (who, by Bill's example, would know exactly what to do in the event of the problem repeating itself). I felt very humble when there were two.

The alteration was carried out and a successful test flight proved that the diagnosis was correct. We were back in business and could flaunt our presence again, shouting 'Boo' and hoping that Jerry wouldn't risk getting a hole punched in his U-boat and would submerge rapidly—though, knowing that we were so slow, not before he took his washing off the jackstay. That day I carried out a dusk patrol around the convoy fifteen miles out beyond the escorts, and I confess to having a heart bursting with the pride of being the one and only airborne defender of such a huge collection of powerful and invaluable resources, pitted against such a ruthless, intelligent, well-equipped enemy. No time to dream. I had to get back to land-on before dark as I would not be popular if the carrier had to light up like a Christmas tree. In any case, night landings on a merchant aircraft carrier were not my idea of fun.

COURTESY PHILIP JARRETT

Recyclable Stringbag *Sub-Lieutenant (A) Jack Thomas* RNVR

On 17 November 1943, Swordfish W5863 was damaged in a taxying accident at Machrihanish (Category X—'Can be made serviceable by local resources'). On 19 December that year it was damaged by being flown into during formation flying (again, Category X). On 10 March 1944, at Inskip, I set out in W5863 with my observer, Sub-Lieutenant Lippard, and TAG, Leading Airman Hawkesworth, on a night anti-submarine bombing exercise against a target on Cockerham Sands in Morecambe Bay. It was a clear, starlit night with no moon, and we crossed the coast at 1,000 feet. Suddenly, without warning, the reliable Pegasus engine cut out. Somewhat unnecessarily I shouted, 'The engine's stopped!'

'That's your department,' retorted my observer coolly.

'There are too many obstructions on the land,' I said, 'so I'll try to ditch as close to the shore as possible. Hang over the side and let me know when we get close to the water.'

He started to say, 'You've got about a couple of hundred feet to . . .' when we ditched in about an eighth of an inch of liquid. The tide was out, and in the starlight the wet sand had appeared to be smooth water.

There were a lot of expensive crashing sounds as the undercarriage broke off, the wings tore away and the remains of the fuselage skidded to a halt. All went silent except for the whirring sound of the gyro compass. I started to giggle, and then so did the other two, and for a few minutes we were absolutely helpless with laughter. Then we decided that we'd better make for the land, and, carrying our parachutes, we struggled the few hundred yards to the shoreline.

On the land everything was in darkness. Then, in the distance, we could see a faint glimmer of light. We made for this, and it turned out to be a farmhouse. Knocking on the door, we asked if they had a telephone. Unusually for those days they had, so I was able to phone the airfield. I had a somewhat bizarre conversation with Commander (Flying), who couldn't understand how I was talking to him on a landline when I was supposed to be airborne. After I had explained the situation he brusquely said, 'Just stay where you are and I'll send a lorry to pick you up and you can repeat the exercise—only do it properly next time!'

As it turned out, the lorry driver lost his way and it was about two hours later that we got back to base, only to find that night flying for the night was finished. I was told that the cause of the prang would be probably put down to pilot error—not a happy thought.

The next day an Air Engineer Officer was sent to the crash site to ascertain what had gone wrong. I was informed later that the problem had been caused during the previous engine inspection. The fuel leads had been incorrectly

connected up and the main tank and reserve tank had 'swapped places'. This meant that, although, according to normal procedure, I had taken off using the reserve (gravity feed) tank and on being airborne I'd switched over to the main tank, in fact the opposite had occurred, and when the small reserve tank was empty the engine stopped.

My good name was cleared, and the accident was written down as a Category Y2 (next to total write-off).

Above: Thoroughly bent and therefore Category ZZ, one might have thought, but no—824 Squadron's HS 316, seriously damaged after an engine failure on take-off from RNAS Hatston on 28 May 1943, was repaired and went on to serve on board MAC ships with 836 Squadron.

Below: Mk III NR894 (notice the serial number chalked on the propeller) and other Swordfish during final assembly at Sherburn-in-Elmet in early May 1944. The radar has yet to be fitted although the light stores racks are already in place.

The Errant Swordfish *Chief Aircraft Artificer Bill Banham*

The story begins in the early part of 1944, by which time the Royal Navy, having got to grips with the menace of German U-boats and to a certain degree the efforts of the *Luftwaffe*, was at last on the offensive. Much of this success, apart from new advances in technology, could be accounted for by the availability of increasing numbers of small aircraft carriers, which, together with their mixture of anti-submarine and fighter aircraft, were able to 'find, fix and strike' as necessary.

HMS *Nairana*, one of the small aircraft carriers on which the following incident took place, was one of the few ships of this type built within the United Kingdom, the majority being of American construction and supply; it should be noted that, limited by their size, the carrying capacity of these ships was very much determined by the type of aircraft embarked. Whilst I was serving, *Nairana*'s complement was six Hurricane fighters and ten Swordfish anti-submarine aircraft. The Hurricane, lacking a wing-fold facility, took up a large amount of hangar space, and consequently the anti-submarine element had been reduced from the normal twelve aircraft to ten. With the increased availability of these aircraft carriers, however, it became possible to operate them in pairs. In this case *Nairana*'s working partner was HMS *Activity*, similarly British-built. *Activity*, however, had particularly restricted hangar space and carried only half the number of aircraft compared to *Nairana*.

So it was that *Nairana* and *Activity*, together with their escort, had completed an anti-submarine sweep in the North Atlantic and were returning to harbour. It was normal practice that when two carriers were operating together they would, when circumstances permitted, take it in turns to carry out anti-submarine sweeps, leaving one ship with a clear flight deck to cover emergency landings. In the event, this is what was needed. One of the *Activity*'s Swordfish crash-landed on her flight deck, tearing out the safety barrier and rendering her arrester wires inoperative. As a result, *Nairana* became the operational carrier, launching search aircraft to take over the patrol. Meanwhile one of *Activity*'s Swordfish was still airborne, and, as it was

impossible for her to land on her parent ship owing to the complete disorganisation that reigned on that ship's flight deck, it was taken on board *Nairana*.

As night fell and both ships had moved out of the operational area, flying was curtailed, leaving *Nairana* with an extra Swordfish without hangar space in which to strike the aircraft down. It was decided to position the aircraft on the lift and secure it with wings folded, the lift being taken down to Hangar Deck level and the hangar fire curtain lowered, thus leaving the aircraft contained, as it were, in a lidless box. The night passed without incident, although the sea became very rough, accompanied by strong winds.

Dawn Action Stations sent the hangar crews to work, part of which entailed raising the fire curtain, and there, revealed to all and sundry, was the Swordfish still on the lift but looking like a partially plucked chicken, with fabric hanging off in all directions.

Here it should be noted that, although the main structure of Swordfish aircraft consisted of metallic tubing and alloy pressings, the overall shape of the wings, the fuselage and the empennage was maintained by a skin of coarse linen fabric, tightly contained by stringing and finally doped so as to maintain a stiff, smooth cover.

What had happened? Examination revealed that (a) the aircraft had been correctly secured to the lift with its wings folded and (b) the struts that secured the wings in the folded position had fractured, leaving the wing assemblies free to swing back and forth on their hinges. *Nairana* had been rolling during the night; this class of ship could set up a really vicious series of rolls in even comparatively quiet seas, and the sea had certainly not been quiet overnight. The conclusion, therefore, was that both port and starboard wing-fold retaining struts had, over time, became fatigued and at some stage the rolling of the ship had finally caused the breakage, leaving both wing assemblies free to swing backwards and forwards against the fuselage, tearing the fabric covering of both the lower mainplane, the tailplane and parts of the fuselage.

At first appearance the strips of fabric hanging from the aircraft seemed to have suffered such damage that there was

little chance of restoring the aircraft into an acceptable flying state. However, a proper inspection revealed that, apart from the broken wing-fold struts and the loss of fabric, the main structure of the aircraft was undamaged. The struts could be replaced as the ships carried these items as spares, but what about the loss of fabric? This was not too important for the fuselage, but fabric was essential for wing and tailplane integrity.

Again, the ship's aviation store had the answer: several bolts of fabric and a supply of the necessary dopes were available. Had we the necessary skills to carry out the repairs? Few of our mechanics had achieved any skill in the art of fabric work and in this case the requirements were quite extensive. It was decided to have a good attempt, and two young mechanics volunteered. In the meantime, a trawl of the ship's seamen revealed that, amongst the various trades that wartime conscription had embraced, there was a professional sailmaker. This very valuable person was quickly co-opted into helping our two air mechanics with the job of recovering the damaged areas of the aircraft.

It was obvious that, with no available hangar space to enable work to proceed uninterrupted, drastic measures were required, and after some discussion it was decided to range one of the Hurricanes and locate it on the flight deck, well secured and as far out of the way as possible, leaving the flight deck clear by placing it broadside-on. The resiting of this one aircraft created enough space in the hanger to enable the damaged Swordfish to be worked on in comparative comfort.

The whole arrangement worked well and by 2000 hours on that day the dedicated work of the sailmaker and the

two air mechanics, helped by a sewing machine that had been unearthed, resulted in the damaged areas being completely restored. The tired workers were sent off to their hammocks and a relief crew carried out the required doping, also, of course, replacing the damaged wing-fold struts. At Dawn Action Stations the following day a detailed inspection was carried out. The remedial work that had been done was absolutely perfect—an excellent job all round.

Now, of course, it was time to restore the aircraft to its parent ship, and therefore, during the forenoon, the aircraft received its pre-flight inspection, was ranged for take off and was started up. *Nairana* swung into wind with *Activity* steaming on a parallel course, both ships rolling quite heavily and matching speeds. Along the sides of the *Nairana*, an audience of off-duty crewmen, including our fabric experts, watched the operations. Then came 'fly off', and away went the newly repaired aircraft, carrying out a preliminary pass over, *Activity* then positioning in line astern for it to land on. The Swordfish flew straight and level down *Activity*'s flight deck, but then, unbelievably, and to the horror of the spectators on both ships, it smashed straight into the ship's safety barrier! So much for the dedicated work that had been carried out by *Nairana*'s crewmen! Fortunately, the aircrew were uninjured,

Finally, to add to the débâcle, it was observed that *Activity*'s mobile crane, advancing along the flight deck to give aid to the crashed aircraft, was suddenly caught by particularly vicious rolls of that ship and disappeared over the side, the driver leaping out just before it dropped into the sea!

Above: An 824 Squadron Swordfish comes to grief 'doing the splits' on board the escort carrier HMS *Striker*, April 1944. The aircraft cannot, unfortunately, be positively identified, but it carries an interesting emblem, apparently depicting a mouse jumping over the nose of a cat, on the engine panelling.
Left: In extreme cases aircraft were so damaged as to be irreparable, and rather than consume space on board ship they were unceremoniously consigned to the ' 'oggin'— after having been stripped of all useful components for spares. This 'burial at sea' was conducted from on board the escort carrier HMS *Striker*.
Right: A close look at the fabric covering of the starboard lower mainplane. Notice the aerodynamic cross-section of the flying wires.

FRONT-LINE SQUADRONS

AS has been remarked elsewhere, the Fairey Swordfish was the only aircraft of any of the combatants during World War II to have been in service in greater numbers at the end of the conflict than at the beginning. In September 1939 thirteen front-line squadrons were equipped with the type, and by the end of hostilities in Europe there were still four, and some twenty of the well over fifty second-line units that had operated Swordfish—several of them virtually throughout the conflict—were still active on type.

The aircraft's colour schemes evolved with remarkable rapidity to reflect the changing environments in which the Swordfish was serving.

Fairey Swordfish Mk Is of 820 Naval Air Squadron prepare to take off from HMS *Ark Royal*, spring 1939.

The colourful and distinctive prewar liveries were quickly displaced by sombre camouflage colours on the outbreak of war, greys and greens being more suited to maritime operations in the face of a determined enemy. Night operations saw those squadrons affected introducing black finishes, while, at the other extreme, the employment of the aircraft on Arctic convoy duties encouraged the introduction of white paint on all but the uppersurfaces.

The pages that follow demonstrate the wide usage of the Swordfish, and the squadrons are considered, not in order of any importance or distinction, but, within their 'front line' and 'second line' categories, strictly numerically.

810 NAVAL AIR SQUADRON

Located at RNAS Gosport *et alibi* and on board HM Ships *Courageous, Ark Royal, Illustrious* and *Queen*

Commission: 03/04/33–22/08/45 (Swordfish Mk Is 00/09/37–00/03/43, Mk IIs 00/03/42–00/03/43)
Commanding Officers: Sqn Ldr H. M. Mellor RAF, Capt N. R. M. Skene RM (16/06/40), Capt. A. C. Newsom (16/06/40), Lt-Cdr M. Johnstone DSC (16/07/40), Lt J. V. Hartley (11/09/41), Lt-Cdr R. N. Everett (29/12/41), Lt-Cdr W. E. Waters (31/01/43),   Lt-Cdr A. J. B. Forde (18/03/43), Lt-Cdr A. G. McWilliam RNVR (27/02/44), Lt-Cdr P. C. Heath (16/12/44)
Senior Pilots/Senior Observers: Not known

Left and right: 810 Squadron, previously flying Blackburn Sharks, re-equipped with Swordfish soon after the Coronation Review in 1937 and were assigned to the fleet carrier *Courageous*, whose ship's colour, blue, was sported as a diagonal band across the rear fuselage. In the photograph at right, L2743 carries a flight leader's emblem on its fin.

COURTESY PHILIP JARRETT

Left: In early 1939 the Squadron re-embarked *in Ark Royal*, one of three Swordfish units allocated to the brand new carrier. The wings bands, were, accordingly, changed to red/blue/red striping. Nine of the twelve aircraft are seen here, with the parent ship in the distance.

Right, upper: An apparent deck landing accident involving Mk I P4131/'2A' on board *Ark Royal*, probably early 1940. The handsome prewar *décor* has given way to disruptive camouflage: survival is now the priority. The 'Royal Navy' legend is, unusually, positioned between the fuselage roundel and the call-sign.

Right, lower: Swordfish K8375/ '2Q' in freshly applied camouflage in 1940; the aircraft's previous call-sign had been 'A2Q'. The use of orthochromatic film for this photograph has resulted in the yellow surround to the fuselage roundel appearing as a dark shade and the red areas virtually black.

COURTESY RICHARD L. WARD

COURTESY RICHARD L. WARD

811 NAVAL AIR SQUADRON

Located at RNAS Gosport, Lee-on-Solent, Arbroath, Machrihanish, Hatston *et alibi* and on board HM Ships *Furious, Courageous, Biter* and *Vindex*

Commissions: 03/04/33–24/05/39, 15/07/41–09/12/44 (Swordfish Mk Is 00/10/36–24/05/39), Mk IIs from 00/11/41, Mk IIIs from 00/07/44)

Commanding Officers: Lt-Cdr L. I. G. Richardson, Sqn Ldr J. A. S. Brown RAF (12/12/37), Lt-Cdr E. O. F. Price (21/01/38), Lt-Cdr S. Borrett (01/07/39), Lt-Cdr R. D. Wall (15/07/41), Lt-Cdr W. J. Lucas (29/10/41), Lt-Cdr H. S. Hayes DSC (27/02/42), Lt J. G. Baldwin (28/01/43), Lt A. S. Kennard DSC (12/04/43), Lt-Cdr E. B. Morgan RANVR (29/11/43), Lt-Cdr E. E. G. Emsley RNVR (27/07/44)

Senior Pilots/Senior Observers: Not known

Left, top: Swordfish were issued to 811 Squadron late in 1936, replacing Blackburn Baffins on board HMS *Furious*. Their distinctive marking was red, although this did not invariably take the form of a diagonal band, as can be seen in this photograph dating from about mid-1937; those aircraft that do feature the band, however, also have their fin leading edges trimmed in red. It has been suggested that the cowling colour was also red, although this cannot be confirmed. Notice the strongly marked dinghy compartment on the upper wing of K8437.

Left, centre: The Coronation Review at Spithead on 20 May 1937 involved huge numbers of military aircraft—and the participation of several Swordfish squadrons. Included amongst the latter were 811, six of whose aircraft are seen here.

Left, bottom: 811 Squadron personnel at RNAS Donibristle in 1938, with the CO, Lt-Cdr Price, seated third from the right. Despite the Royal Navy having been given back control of its aviation-related organisation in July 1937 under the Inskip Award, RAF uniforms still outnumber RN uniforms by a considerable margin.

Opposite, top: Swordfish K8440 about to touch down on HMS *Furious*. The painting of call-signs beneath the upper wing was common practice on FAA Swordfish during this period and into 1941.

Right: 812 Squadron's K8867 ashore in late 1939 in the heat of RNAS Dekheila, its camouflage paint very recently applied.

COURTESY RICHARD L. WARD

812 NAVAL AIR SQUADRON

Located at RNAS Gosport and Hal Far, at various RAF East Coast airfields, *et alibi*, and on board HM Ships *Glorious, Furious, Ark Royal* and *Argus*

Commission: 03/04/33–18/12/42 (Swordfish Mk Is from 00/12/36, Mk IIs from 00/10/42)
Commanding Officers: Sqn Ldr N. A. P. Pritchett RAF, Sqn Ldr J. H. Hutchinson RAF (26/04/37), Lt-Cdr J. D. C. Little (01/11/38), Lt-Cdr A. S. Bolt (16/06/39), Lt-Cdr N. G. R. Crawford (22/04/40), Lt-Cdr W. E. Waters DFC (06/09/40), Lt-Cdr J. A. L. Woods (16/11/41), Lt-Cdr B. J. Prendergast (30/05/42)
Senior Pilots/Senior Observers: Not known

COURTESY RICHARD L. WARD

Above: 812's L9724 was a victim of either mishap or enemy action over occupied France on 15 November 1940 while working with RAF Coastal Command on minelaying and bombing operations. The crew, Lieutenant Bentley and observer Sub-Lieutenant Davis, were captured by the Germans and interned as prisoners of war. For this sortie the observer had been accommodated in the TAG's cockpit, the former's normal position taken, as can be seen, by a Long Range Tank. The aircraft has had its disruptive camouflage taken down the fuselage sides and wears the tail code 'G3L'.

---

813 NAVAL AIR SQUADRON

Located at RNAS Seletar and Kai Tak, RAF North Front, RNAS Donibristle *et alibi*, and on board HM Ships *Eagle*, *Illustrious* (detachment), *Campania* and *Vindex*

Commissions: 18/01/37–18/10/43, 01/11/43–15/05/45 (Swordfish Mk Is until 00/03/43, Mk IIs 00/11/42–18/10/43 and 01/11/43–00/07/44, Mk IIIs from 00/06/44)
Commanding Officers: Lt-Cdr C. R. V. Pugh, Lt-Cdr N. Kennedy DSC (01/09/38), Lt-Cdr D. H. Elles (09/01/41), Lt-Cdr A. V. Lyle (25/22/41), Lt-Cdr C. Hutchinson (25/03/42), Lt-Cdr J. H. Ree (27/06/43), Lt-Cdr D. A. P. Weatherall (01/08/43), Lt-Cdr J. R. Parish DSC RNVR (01/11/43), Lt-Cdr C. A. Allen RNVR (02/09/44), Lt-Cdr S. G. Cooke RNVR (12/10/44)
Senior Pilots/Senior Observers: Not known

Below: The prewar markings of 813 Squadron's Swordfish featured black diagonal bands across the fuselage; flight leaders' aircraft were for a period identified further by means of black fin markings, as here. During the war the Squadron was engaged primarily in the Far East, Indian Ocean and Mediterranean theatres (some of its aircraft were detached to take part in the Taranto attack); its second wartime commission saw it over in the North Atlantic on convoy protection duty.

152

814 NAVAL AIR SQUADRON

Located at Southampton, RAF China Bay and Colombo Racecourse *et alibi*, and on board HM Ships *Ark Royal* and *Hermes*

Commission: 01/12/38–31/12/42 (Swordfish Mk Is throughout)
Commanding Officers: Lt-Cdr N. S. Luard DSC, Maj W. H. N. Martin RM (27/12/40), Lt A. F. Paterson (25/09/42)
Senior Pilots/Senior Observers: Not known

AD HOC COLLECTION

Above: 814 Squadron spent the first months of its commission with Swordfish assigned to the new prestige carrier *Ark Royal* but when war broke out it was reallocated to the diminutive *Hermes*. Its aircraft survived the loss of that ship by dint of being ashore when she succumbed to Japanese air attack. The nine Swordfish of the Squadron are seen here just prior to the outbreak of war, wearing very fetching chevron-type fuselage markings in the red and blue colours of *Ark Royal*. The three flight leaders are toting torpedoes.

815 NAVAL AIR SQUADRON

Located at RNAS Hatston, RAF Bircham Newton, RNAS Dekheila *et alibi* and on board HMS *Illustrious*

Commissions: 09/10/39–10/11/39, 23/11/39–24/07/43 (Swordfish Mk Is 09/10/39–10/11/39 and 23/11/39–00/02/43, Mk IIs from 00/02/43)
Commanding Officers: Lt-Cdr S. Borrett, Lt-Cdr R. A. Kilroy DSC (17/04/40), Lt-Cdr K. Williamson (03/08/40), Lt-Cdr J. de F. Jago (16/11/40), Lt-Cdr F. M. A. Torrens-Spence (15/03/41), Lt-Cdr T. P. Coode (27/10/41), Lt-Cdr P. D. Gick (14/12/41), Lt-Cdr J. W. G. Wellham DSC (29/09/42)
Senior Pilots/Senior Observers: Not known

Right: Swordfish P4225/'U3A' of 815 Squadron in her original colour scheme in late 1939 or early 1940. This aircraft is understood to have been one of the participants in the Taranto raid (Operation 'Judgement') in November 1940, although by that time it would have been re-marked and re-coded for service on board HMS *Illustrious*.

COURTESY BILL BANHAM

153

816 NAVAL AIR SQUADRON

Located at RNAS Ford and on board HM Ships *Furious*, *Ark Royal*, *Avenger*, *Dasher*, *Tracker* and *Chaser*

Commissions: 12/10/39–13/11/41, 01/02/42–01/08/44 (Swordfish Mk Is 12/10/39–13/11/41, 01/02/42–00/10/42, Mk IIs 00/06/42–01/08/44)

Commanding Officers: Lt-Cdr Lt J. Dalyell-Stead, Lt-Cdr H. H. Gardner (19/10/39), Lt-Cdr T. G. C. Jameson (06/05/40), Capt O. Patch RM (01/02/42), Lt R. C. B. Stallard-Penoyre (15/10/42), Lt P. F. Pryor (22/04/43), Lt-Cdr F. C. Nottingham DSC RNVR (12/07/43), Lt-Cdr P. Snow (03/05/44)

Senior Pilots/Senior Observers: Not known

Right: 816 Squadron spent its war years on Swordfish around home waters and on Atlantic convoy protection duties, also working for a period under the authority of RAF Coastal Command. Here, on board HMS *Tracker*, HS674 is seen following an accident in October 1943; the wartime censor is clearly nervous about the underwing stores it is carrying. The details of the unofficial artwork near the pilot's cockpit are unknown.
Below: Three R/P-toting Swordfish IIs up from St Merryn in summer 1944, adorned with D-Day 'invasion markings'.

818 NAVAL AIR SQUADRON   *Believed no crest sanctioned*

Located at RNAS Evanton, Hatston and Campbeltown, RAF Ratmalana, RNAS Lee-on-Solent, RAF China Bay *et alibi* and on board HM Ships *Ark Royal, Furious, Formidable, Unicorn* and *Atheling*

Commissions: 30/08/39–24/06/42, 22/10/42–14/10/44 (Swordfish Mk Is until 00/11/41, Mk IIs from 22/10/42)
Commanding Officers: Lt-Cdr J. E. Fenton, Lt-Cdr P. G. O. Sydney-Turner (19/03/40), Lt-Cdr T. P. Coode (24/10/40), Lt-Cdr T. W. B. Shaw DSC (28/07/41), Lt-Cdr A. H. Abrams (22/10/42), Lt-Cdr W. H. Lloyd RNVR (07/07/43)
Senior Pilots/Senior Observers: Not known

Right: Like 814 Squadron, 818 was commissioned for service on board *Ark Royal*. It flew also from HMS *Furious*, taking part in the defence of Norway before re-joining 'The Ark' for service with Force 'H' in the Mediterranean. It was whilst in that theatre that the ship was detached to help in the hunt for the battleship *Bismarck*, in which operation the Squadron served with distinction. This photograph shows L7636, appearing to be crewed only by the pilot, about to depart from *Ark Royal*'s starboard accelerator, winter 1940/41.

FLEET AIR ARM MUSEUM

819 NAVAL AIR SQUADRON

Located at RNAS Ford, Dekheila, Hal Far and Lee-on-Solent, RAF Bircham Newton *et alibi* and on board HM Ships *Illustrious, Avenger, Archer* and *Activity*

Commissions: 12/02/40–13/01/41, 25/10/41–10/03/45 (Swordfish Mk Is 12/02/40–13/01/41 and until 00/06/43, Mk IIs from 00/04/42, Mk IIIs from 00/08/44)
Commanding Officers: Lt-Cdr J. W. Hale DSO, Lt-Cdr D. G. Goodwin DSC (25/10/41), Lt H. S. McN. Davenport (10/04/42), Lt O. A. G. Oxley (23/01/43), Lt-Cdr P. D. T. Stevens RNVR (20/04/44)
Senior Pilots/Senior Observers: Not known

Right: 819 was another of the units participating in 'Judgement' in November 1940 as one of HMS *Illustrious*'s 'own' squadrons, but as a result of that carrier's crippling by Axis bombers in January 1941 the unit lost many personnel and was disbanded. It re-formed nine months later primarily for work on board escort carriers in the anti-submarine rôle. This view of P4221 was probably taken in the summer of 1940, before the identifying legend 'Royal Navy' began to appear above the serial numbers on Fleet Air Arm aircraft.

COURTESY PHILIP JARRETT

COURTESY BRIAN LOWE

Above: Swordfish 'A', assigned to 819 Squadron at RAF Manston, in the summer of 1944, the *raison d'être* of its all-black finish—hiding from the enemy at night—somewhat defeated by the application of D-Day 'invasion' stripes. A 'fix' from the unit's months spent in extreme temperatures amongst the Russian convoys is apparent—a duct leading from the rear of the Pegasus engine to the oil cooler, added to help prevent the engine oil solidifying. The prominent line running along the fuselage is a recently installed external dinghy release cable—a welcome aid to an aircrew unfortunate enough to have to ditch.

COURTESY BRIAN LOWE

LES SAYER COLLECTION

Above: Swordfish NF119/'X', of 819 Squadron and nicknamed 'Black Mischief', at rest following a take-off accident at the Belgian airfield of Knocke-le-Zoute in the early months of 1945. The Squadron operated as, in effect, a component of RAF Coastal Command for the final twelve months of the war in Europe, engaged principally in North Sea patrols.

Left: 819 Squadron personnel at Swingfield, Kent, in September 1944. The CO, Lieutenant-Commander Stevens, and several of his officers are 'Wavy Navy' (i.e., Royal Naval Volunteer Reserve), as can be seen from the rank insignia. The Squadron TAGs are in the front row.

820 NAVAL AIR SQUADRON

Located at RNAS Gosport, Eastleigh, Ford et *alibi* and on board HM Ships *Courageous*, *Ark Royal* and *Victorious*

Commission: 02/05/33–13/11/43 (Swordfish Mk Is 00/09/37–00/06/41)
Commanding Officers: Lt-Cdr A. C. G. Ermen, Lt-Cdr G. H. Hodgkinson (07/01/39), Lt-Cdr A. Yeoman (29/08/40), Lt-Cdr J. A. Stewart-Moore (27/10/40)
Senior Pilots/Senior Observers: Not known

AD HOC COLLECTION

Above: A much-published photograph—and the subject of a popular contemporary picture postcard—showing 820 Squadron's Swordfish over *Ark Royal* before the war. The bands across the rear fuselage were red (inner) and blue (both outer).
Right: 820 Squadron's telegraphist air gunners pose for a photograph with the CO, Lieutenant-Commander Ermen (seated second from left) and Senior Observer Lieutenant-Commander Palarait (to his left). The TAGs are (back row, left to right) Tommy Goodman, 'Geordie' Watson, Jock McColl, Dickie Rolphe, 'Lofty' Stanton, 'Queenie' Taylor, Viv Cordwell and 'Guts' Shelverton. To the CO's right are Jock East and to the SObs's left Hughie Hann.

LES SAYER COLLECTION

FLEET AIR ARM MUSEUM

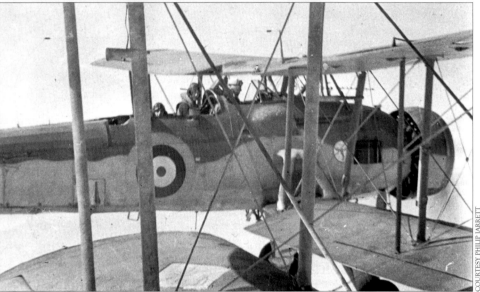

COURTESY PHILIP JARRETT

COURTESY BRIAN LOWE

Above: The splendid finishes of 820's Swordfish inevitably, and in common with those of most other front-line FAA aircraft, gave way to sombre hues on the outbreak of war. This aircraft has a shiny black 'fish' under its belly, and the roundel, though modified, is in the prewar position well aft of the cockpits. The use of a bold serif face for the serial number, whilst hardly widespread, was not uncommon within the FAA during the war.

Left, upper: The three photographs on this page were taken during the early months of 1941, and this image may depict one of the aircraft from 820 Squadron that took part in the *Bismarck* operation in May that year. An individual interpretation of the Squadron's flying fish emblem—the creature is posed on its tail—appears just abaft the oil cooler.

Left, lower: Like the Swordfish depicted above, 820's P4024 is sporting an unofficial flying fish insignia on its forward fuselage—though here the style is less *avant garde*.

Right: Eight of 821 Squadron's Swordfish ranged on board *Ark Royal* in early 1939; parked further forward are the Hawker Osprey fighters of 800 Squadron. It is instructive to compare this photograph with that on page 121.

821 NAVAL AIR SQUADRON

Located at RNAS Gosport, Lee-on-Solent, Hatston, Dekheila *et alibi* and on board HMS *Courageous*, *Ark Royal* and ('X' Flight) *Argus*

Commissions: 03/04/33–21/01/41, 15/07/41–10/10/43 (Swordfish Mk Is 00/09/37–21/01/41, 15/07/41–12/03/42)
Commanding Officers: Sqn Ldr G. R. M. Clifford RAF, Lt-Cdr J. A. D. Wroughton (29/03/39 and 14/09/39), Lt-Cdr G. M. Duncan (24/05/39), Maj. W. H. N. Martin RM (29/05/40), Lt-Cdr R. R. Wood (27/12/40), Lt C. W. B. Smith (15/07/41)
Senior Pilots/Senior Observers: Not known

Left: 821 Squadron Swordfish prepare to depart from HMS *Ark Royal*, early 1939. The fuselage bands, although presented in the same manner as 820 Squadron's at that time, bore call-signs in the '670' and '680' series whereas 820's were in the '640' and '650' range. Later that year, the call-signs were changed, to be prefixed 'A4' and 'A5', respectively, the individual aircraft identified by a different letter suffix (for example, 'A4B', 'A5K'). During the war, the Squadron operated in the Atlantic and Indian Oceans and in the Norwegian campaign in its first commission; in its second, it operated a few Swordfish briefly in North Africa until it re-equipped with Fairey Albacores.

AD HOC COLLECTION

822 NAVAL AIR SQUADRON

Located at RNAS Gosport, Donibristle, Hatston, Crail *et alibi* and on board HM Ships *Furious* and *Courageous*

Commissions: 03/04/33–24/05/39, 01/07/39–17/09/39, 15/10/41–19/02/46 (Swordfish Mk Is 00/08/37–24/05/39, 01/07/39–17/09/39, Mk IIs 15/10/41–00/03/42) (822A Flt 15/05/39– 01/07/39 with Mk Is)
Commanding Officers: Lt-Cdr A. M. Rundle, Lt-Cdr J. B. Buckley (21/04/38), Lt-Cdr K. Williamson (28/07/38), Lt-Cdr W. H. G. Saunt (822A Flt, 15/05/39), Lt-Cdr H. L. McCulloch (822A Flt, 01/06/39), Lt-Cdr P. W. Humphreys (01/07/39), Maj. A. R. Burch RM (14/10/41)
Senior Pilots/Senior Observers: Not known

Left: The most highly decorated Swordfish in the prewar Fleet Air Arm were arguably those assigned to 822 Squadron, since, as well as red waist bands (trimmed in white and with the angle reversed compared to those of other units), black fuselage top-decking was also favoured. K6011/'901', seen here under recovery following an accident in 1938, also sported a broad red band across the upper wing and a black fin adorned with the Squadron crest.

COURTESY PHILIP JARRETT

Right, upper: Also dating from 1938, this image shows another exotic paint scheme on an 822 NAS Swordfish, with wing tips and fin finished in what is usually described as a black and white 'chequerboard' pattern but was in fact rather more complex since the black rectangles were interlinked to form a 'honeycomb' matrix. The design on the tailfin was aligned with the rudder post rather than the aircraft's true fore-and-aft datum, producing a somewhat odd visual effect when the aircraft was flying. The fuselage band is again red (for HMS *Furious*).

Right, lower: Their gaudy finishes swept away with the onset of hostilities, 822's Swordfish slipped into relative anonymity. Seen here in typical first-generation World War II camouflage, which included fuselage roundels coloured red and blue only and call-signs presented in triangular fashion on the tailfin, (P401[?])/ 'U5Q' was one of the Swordfish to be lost on board HMS *Courageous* when the carrier was sunk in the Western Approaches by U 29 on 17 September 1939.

Below: It was two years before 822 NAS re-formed, but the unit flew Swordfish again only for a few short months. It is seen here at RNAS Hatston on the occasion of a visit by HM King George VI in February 1943.

823 NAVAL AIR SQUADRON

Located at RNAS Hal Far, Dekheila, Hatston, Crail, Machrihanish *et alibi* and on board HMS *Glorious*

Commissions: 18/08/33–03/12/40, 01/11/41–00/07/44 (Swordfish Mk Is 00/11/36–03/12/40, 01/11/41–00/04/42)
Commanding Officers: Lt-Cdr G. C. Dickens, Lt-Cdr D. W. MacKendrick (21/05/37), Lt-Cdr R. A. Kilroy (01/02/38), Lt-Cdr R. D. Watkins (24/05/39), Lt-Cdr C. J. T. Stephens (27/05/40), Lt-Cdr D. H. Elles (03/07/40), Lt-Cdr A. J. D. Harding DSC (01/11/41)
Senior Pilots/Senior Observers: Not known

Background image: Swordfish from 823 Squadron, from HMS *Glorious*, practise for the 1937 Coronation Fly Past. The waist bands denoting that carrier were yellow, and, like 822 NAS, the unit chose to paint the fuselage top decking of their aircraft in black; the cowling rings were usually (though not invariably) to be seen painted black also, whilst flight leaders' aircraft had their tailfins further emblazoned with black paint for easy recognition by the remainder of the aircrews.

Left: Varied applications of black paint characterised 824 Squadron's Swordfish prewar, though all had the black-for-*Eagle* waist band.

Bottom: K5972 with a plain cowling but with, apparently, its wheel hubs picked out in yellow. Despite appearances, the band is also yellow.

824 NAVAL AIR SQUADRON

Located at RNAS Kai Tak, RAF Seletar, RNAS Dekheila, RAF North Front and RNAS Lee-on-Solent, Machrihanish and Donibristle *et alibi* and on board HM Ships *Eagle*, *Unicorn* and *Striker*

Commissions: 28/10/34–11/08/42, 01/10/42–16/10/44 (Swordfish Mk Is 00/04/37–11/08/42, 01/10/42–00/01/43, Mk IIs 00/11/42–16/10/44)

Commanding Officers: Sqn Ldr A. B. Woodhall RAF, Sqn Ldr R. G. Forbes RAF (27/04/38), Lt-Cdr H. Gardner (24/05/39), Lt-Cdr A. J. Debenham DSC (15/06/39), Capt F. W. Brown RM (11/08/41), Lt J. A. Ievers (01/10/42), Lt-Cdr E. L. Russell DSC RNVR (12/03/43), Lt-Cdr G. C. Edwards RCNVR (02/03/44)

Senior Pilots/Senior Observers: Not known

Right: 824 Squadron's P4206 in drab early-wartime hues. The Squadron was decommissioned in August 1942 with the loss of HMS *Eagle* but was re-formed speedily to tackle the U-boat threat in the North Atlantic.
Bottom right: 824's sea-going home for the remainder of its days flying Swordfish was the escort carrier HMS *Striker*, on board which this 'prang' occurred in August 1944.

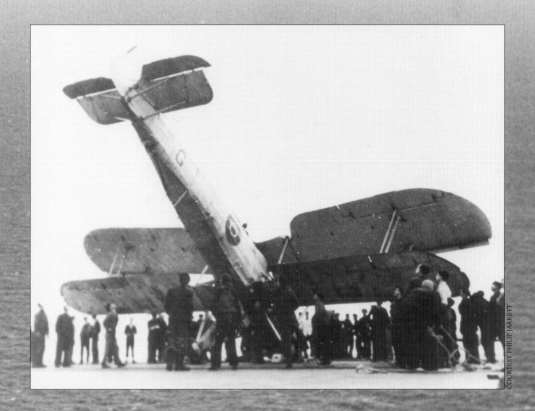

COURTESY PHILIP JARRETT

COURTESY PHILIP JARRETT

163

825 NAVAL AIR SQUADRON

Located at RNAS Hal Far, Gosport, Dekheila, Hatston, Lee-on-Solent, Donibristle and Campbeltown, RAF
Manston and RNAS Machrihanish and Yeovilton *et alibi* and on board HM Ships *Glorious, Furious, Victorious, Ark
Royal, Avenger, Vindex* and *Campania*

Commissions: 08/10/34–13/11/41, 01/01/42–12/04/45 (Swordfish Mk Is 00/07/36–13/11/41, 01/01/42–00/06/44, Mk IIs
00/03/42–00/06/44, Mk IIIs 00/06/44–12/04/45)
Commanding Officers: Lt-Cdr H. A. Traill, Lt-Cdr J. I. Robertson (17/03/37), Lt-Cdr A. Brock (11/09/37), Lt-Cdr A. J. Hale
(19/08/38), Lt-Cdr E. Esmonde DSO (31/05/40 and 01/01/42), Lt-Cdr S. Keane (23/02/42), Lt-Cdr S. G. Cooper (15/12/42),
Lt-Cdr A. H. D. Gough (29/02/44), Lt-Cdr F. G. B. Sheffield DSC RNVR (05/05/44), Lt-Cdr P. Snow (25/02/45)
Senior Pilots/Senior Observers: Lt P. Gick (SP in 1941), Lt C. C. Ennever (SObs in 1941)

Above: Supervised by an RAF officer, Royal Navy maintenance personnel inspect 825 Squadron's K5942, damaged following a rather heavy landing at RNAS Gosport in the summer of 1937. Below: K8869 of 825 NAS roasts in the heat of the Mediterranean sun in the summer of 1939, disembarked from HMS *Glorious*, whose yellow identification band shows dark owing to the orthochromatic film used for the photograph. The call-sign is again '968', leading to the suspicion that this aircraft may have been the replacement for that depicted above. The Squadron crest is displayed very prominently on the tailfin.

Right: 825 was one of the FAA squadrons to take part in the pursuit of the *Bismarck* in May 1941, its aircraft flying from HMS *Victorious*. This photograph is understood to have been taken during that operation, and depicts a mishap involving one of its Swordfish, V43[??], returning from a routine patrol after the attack. A scrutiny of the original image suggests that the call-sign '5F' is present beneath the wing tip.

Left: Following the serious losses suffered by the Squadron in February 1942 (see pages 106–107), 825–'Nihil Obstat' (Nothing Will Stop Us)—regrouped and worked up for maritime patrol and convoy protection duties, its principal quarry switching from the enemy's large surface warships to his patrol boats and submarines. At the end of 1943 its aircraft and crews embarked in the escort carrier HMS *Vindex*, on board which this photograph was taken a couple of months later. The CO, Lieutenant-Commander Cooper, is in the front standing row fifth from the left and his successor, Lieutenant-Commander Gough, is standing behind his left shoulder.

Above: Personnel of 825 Squadron, with the Squadron crest proudly displayed; the CO appears to be Lieutenant-Commander Cooper once more. Very noticeably, the vast majority of the officers are RNVR. The Swordfish is displaying its call-sign, 'F', beneath each wing tip, and matelots are judiciously posed so as to shield the ASV aerials. Wisely, the aircraft's lower wings have been trestled!

826 NAVAL AIR SQUADRON

Located at RAF Bircham Newton, RNAS Dekheila, RAF Nicosia *et alibi* and on board HMS *Formidable*

Commission: 15/03/40–25/08/43 (Swordfish Mk Is 00/07/40–00/08/40, 00/03/41–00/09/41)
Commanding Officers: Lt-Cdr W. H. G. Saunt DSC, Lt-Cdr J. W. S. Corbett (24/06/41)
Senior Pilots/Senior Observers: Not known

828 NAVAL AIR SQUADRON   *Believed no crest sanctioned*

Located at RNAS Ford and on board HMS *Eagle*

Commission: 15/09/40–01/09/43 (Swordfish Mk Is 00/10/41–01/09/43)
Commanding Officer: Lt-Cdr D. E. Langmore DSC, Lt-Cdr G. M. Haynes RAN (19/12/41), Lt-Cdr M. E. Lashmore DSC (30/11/42)
Senior Pilot(s)/Senior Observer(s): Lt Maund (SP in 1942)

Main image: 826 and 828 Squadrons were theoretically Albacore units, including Swordfish on establishment principally as insurance owing to the problems afflicting their would-be successor aircraft (see pages 94–95). In 829 Squadron, Swordfish managed to see the Albacores off completely. Here '3B', with attractive, star-decorated wheel covers, has just landed on board HMS *Illustrious*, *circa* March 1942.

LES SAYER COLLECTION

COURTESY PHILIP JARRETT

829 NAVAL AIR SQUADRON

Located at RNAS Ford, Campbeltown, St Merryn, Dekheila, Lee-on-Solent, Machrihanish *et alibi* and on board HM Ships *Formidable* and *Illustrious*

Commission: 15/06/40–07/10/42 (Swordfish Mk Is 00/07/40–00/09/40, 00/03/41–00/12/41, Mk IIs 00/12/41–07/10/42)
Commanding Officers: Lt-Cdr O. S. Stevenson, Lt-Cdr J. Dalyell-Stead (12/10/40), Lt-Cdr L. C. B. Ashburner (29/03/41), Lt-Cdr F. M. Griffiths (24/12/41)
Senior Pilots/Senior Observers: Not known

830 NAVAL AIR SQUADRON

Located at RNAS Hal Far

Commission: 01/07/40–31/03/43 (Swordfish Mk Is throughout)
Commanding Officers: Lt-Cdr F. D. Horne DSO, Capt. K. L. Ford RM (01/08/40), Lt-Cdr J. G. Hunt (01/09/41), Lt-Cdr F. H. E. Hopkins (06/12/41), Lt-Cdr A. J. T. Roe (07/06/42), Lt A. Gregory (23/02/43)
Senior Pilots/Senior Observers: Not known

Left and right: In no campaign were Swordfish crews put under greater strain, nor suffer greater losses, than in the defence of Malta. It fell to 830 Squadron—which had started life as 767 NAS, a deck landing training unit—in conjunction with, later, 828's Albacores to help clear the waters of enemy activity around the vital Mediterranean island. At left is one of the casualties, Mk I L2833/'N', whilst at right is an all-black, torpedo-armed Mk I. Both these 830 NAS aircraft are fitted with a Long Range Tank.

COURTESY RICHARD L. WARD

833 NAVAL AIR SQUADRON   *Believed no crest sanctioned*

Located at RNAS Lee-on-Solent, RAF North Front and Thorney Island, RNAS Machrihanish and Maydown *et alibi* and on board HM Ships *Biter* and *Activity*

Commissions: 08/12/41–07/01/44, 26/04/44–13/09/44 (Swordfish Mk Is until 00/11/42, Mk IIs 00/00/42–07/01/44 and from 26/04/44)
Commanding Officers: Lt-Cdr R. J. H. Stephens, Capt. W. G. S. Aston RM (14/01/43), Lt-Cdr J. R. C. Callander (17/05/43), Lt-Cdr J. G. Large RNVR (26/04/44)
Senior Pilots/Senior Observers: Not known

COURTESY RICHARD L. WARD

Left: 833 Squadron was allocated a variety of duties during World War II, from participation in the Allied 'Torch' landings in North Africa to anti-submarine patrols in the freezing wastes of the Arctic— with, for good measure, a spell with RAF Coastal Command in between. Here W5864/'F' is seen fulfilling the Squadron's initial rôle of TBR aircraft, scheduled to embark on HMS *Dasher* (see pages 114–115) in early 1942.
Below: W5862 photographed at about the same time and carrying light underwing ordnance.

COURTESY BILL PENLINGTON

834 NAVAL AIR SQUADRON

Located at RNAS Palisadoes, RNAS Crail, RAF Exeter, RNAS Machrihanish, RAF North Front, RAF Khormaksar, SAAF Durban (Stamford Hill), RAF Vavuniya *et alibi* and on board HM Ships *Archer*, *Hunter* and *Battler*

Commission: 10/12/41–06/12/44 (Swordfish Mk Is until 00/04/43, Mk IIs from 00/09/42)
Commanding Officers: Lt-Cdr L. C. B. Ashburner, Lt L. G. Wilson (20/11/41), Lt-Cdr E. D. Child (21/01/43), Lt-Cdr D. W. Phillips DSC (12/08/44)
Senior Pilots/Senior Observers: Not known

Right: The reach of the Swordfish was worldwide, and 834 Squadron, having previously seen service on board escort carriers and with RAF Coastal Command, ended its commission patrolling the northern shores of the Indian Ocean. Neither the serial number nor the call-sign of this particular rocket-armed Mk II is known, but the location is RNAS Katukurunda in Ceylon, and the date July or August 1944.

835 NAVAL AIR SQUADRON *Unofficial crest depicted*

Located at RNAS Palisadoes, Lee-on-Solent, Hatston, Stretton, Machrihanish, Eglinton, Burscough *et alibi* and on board HM Ships *Battler*, *Ravager*, *Chaser* and *Nairana*

Commission: 15/02/42–31/03/45 (Mk Is 15/02/42–00/02/43, Mk IIs 00/10/42–00/07/44, Mk IIIs from 00/07/44)
Commanding Officers: Lt-Cdr M. Johnstone DSC, Lt-Cdr J. R. Lang (28/04/42), Lt-Cdr W. N. Waller (15/09/43), Lt-Cdr T. T. Miller (02/12/43), Lt-Cdr E. E. Barringer RNVR (17/02/44), Lt-Cdr F. V. Jones RNVR (12/08/44), Lt-Cdr J. R. Godley RNVR (15/01/45)
Senior Pilots/Senior Observers: Lt A. R. Selley (SP in 1944)

Below: A Swordfish Mk II of 835 Squadron serving on board HMS *Battler* in the torpedo-bomber rôle in 1943 is manhandled to its spotting position for take-off. The variety of helmets being worn include American styles: US-built escort carriers were delivered to the customer fully equipped! As usual, the wartime censor has blanked out the aircraft's strut-mounted radar antennæ.

836 NAVAL AIR SQUADRON

Located at RNAS Palisadoes, Machrihanish, Crail, St Merryn *et alibi* and on board HMS *Biter*; from spring 1943 at RNAS Maydown and on board merchant aircraft carriers

Commission: 01/03/42–29/07/45 (Swordfish Mk Is until 00/03/43, Mk IIs 00/03/43–00/06/45, Mk IIIs from 00/12/44)
Commanding Officers: Lt-Cdr J. A. Crawford, Lt-Cdr R. W. Slater DSC (09/07/42), Lt-Cdr J. R. C. Callander (29/06/44), Lt-Cdr F. G. B. Sheffield DSC RNVR (05/03/45)
Senior Pilots/Senior Observers: Lt-Cdr Dawson (SP in 1945), Lt-Cdr Rutley (SObs in 1945)

AD HOC COLLECTION

COURTESY RICHARD L. WARD

Left, upper: The squadron that formed the complements of the legendary MAC ships, 836 was, from the summer of 1943, organised into a number of flights, each assigned to a particular vessel. LS219, a Mk II, served with 'E' Flight (hence the call-sign) on board MV *Amastra* for a period in late 1943 and early 1944.

Left, lower: LS225 was another Mk II and is seen here in service with 'B' Flight (MV *Empire MacAlpine*) at the same time. The baker's head was the Flight's unofficial emblem.

Below: Personnel of 836 Squadron—not all of them!—at Maydown in early 1945; the CO here, seated centre, is Lieutenant-Commander Callander. The Swordfish forming the backdrop wears D-Day 'invasion markings' but this is no great surprise; aircraft issued from centralised maintenance units following overhaul rarely found their way back to their previous 'owners', and this example probably saw service in earlier months with 816 Squadron, which was well known for its 'stripes'.

LES SAYER COLLECTION

837 NAVAL AIR SQUADRON

Located at RNAS Palisadoes, Lee-on-Solent, St Merryn, Hatston, Crail, Machrihanish *et alibi* and on board HM Ships *Dasher* and *Argus*

Commission: 01/05/42–15/06/43 (Swordfish Mk Is throughout, Mk IIs from 00/06/42)
Commanding Officer: Lt-Cdr A. S. Whitworth DSC
Senior Pilots/Senior Observers: Not known

Left: 837 Squadron was equipped with Swordfish for just over a year, its destiny rudely shattered with the loss of HMS *Dasher*, the escort carrier for which it was originally earmarked. It performed valuable work in deck-landing training but did not become a fully fledged front-line squadron until it had dispensed with its Swordfish and taken delivery of Barracudas. The Swordfish from which this photograph of W5858 was taken has a very poorly looking old-model pitot tube!

COURTESY RICHARD L. WARD

838 NAVAL AIR SQUADRON   *Believed no crest sanctioned*

Located at RCAF Dartmouth, USNAS Almeda Island, RNAS Machrihanish, Maydown, Belfast and Inskip, RAF Thorney Island *et alibi* and on board HM Ships *Attacker*, *Argus*, *Activity* and *Nairana* and MV *Rapana*

Commissions: 15/05/42–13/08/43, 01/11/43–03/02/45 (Mk Is until 00/04/43, Mk IIs 00/04/43–13/08/43 and 01/11/43–03/02/45, Mk IIIs 00/05/44–03/02/45)
Commanding Officers: Lt-Cdr J. R. C. Callander, Lt R. G. Large RNVR (07/06/43), Lt-Cdr J. M. Brown DSC RNVR (01/11/43), Lt-Cdr P. Snow (19/08/44)
Senior Pilots/Senior Observers: Not known

Below: 838 Squadron was another of the FAA units established in the mid-war years for service in board escort carriers, charged with convoy protection. In the event, following brief service in this capacity on board HMS *Attacker*, it was absorbed into 836

Squadron for service with MAC ships. It was re-formed a few weeks later and resumed its A/S work, both afloat and ashore with Coastal Command. This photograph shows Squadron personnel at Dartmouth, Nova Scotia, on first commissioning in 1942.

LES SAYER COLLECTION

840 NAVAL AIR SQUADRON   *Believed no crest sanctioned*

Located at RNAS, Stretton, Hatston, Machrihanish and Maydown and on board HM Ships *Attacker* and *Activity* and MV *Empire MacAndrew*

Commission: 01/06/42–13/08/43 (Swordfish Mk Is until 00/03/43, Mk IIs from 00/09/42)
Commanding Officers: Lt L. R. Tivy, Lt C. M. T. Hallewell (21/04/43)
Senior Pilots/Senior Observers: Not known

841 NAVAL AIR SQUADRON

Swordfish detachments located at RAF Coltishall, Tangmere and Exeter

Commission: 01/07/42–01/12/43 (Swordfish Mk Is and IIs 00/01/43–00/04/43)
Commanding Officers: Lt R. L. Williamson DSC, Lt L. J. Kiggell DSC (15/10/42), Lt-Cdr W. F. C. Garthwaite DSC RNVR (28/12/42)
Senior Pilots/Senior Observers: Not known

842 NAVAL AIR SQUADRON

Located at RNAS Lee-on-Solent, Machrihanish, Hatston and Maydown, RAF Thorney Island *et alibi* and on board HM Ships *Fencer*, *Furious* and *Indefatigable*

Commission: 01/03/43–19/01/45 (Mk Is throughout)
Commanding Officers: Lt-Cdr C. B. Lamb DSO DSC, Lt-Cdr L. R. Tivy (21/04/43), Lt-Cdr G. F. S. Hodson RNVR (27/03/44), Lt-Cdr L. A. Edwards (02/08/44)
Senior Pilots/Senior Observers: Not known

COURTESY BILL PENLINGTON/BRUCE VIBERT

COURTESY BILL PENLINGTON/BRUCE VIBERT

Both 840 and 841 Squadrons had Swordfish on strength for relatively short spells. 840, only ever equipped with Swordfish, was another unit originally commissioned with a view to serving on board MAC ships, but in August 1943, when all MAC ship aircraft were pooled into 836 NAS, it was disbanded. 841 had a handful of Swordfish on strength for about a year when it was flying primarily Albacores, and these were engaged mainly in Channel patrols.

Left, upper: 842 Squadron, in contrast, was one of the hard-worked composite units engaged principally in convoy escort work (but see pages 122–127), spending virtually all of its time afloat embarked in the escort carrier HMS *Fencer*. This photograph shows three of its aircraft, well chocked and with their vitals covered against the Atlantic weather, on board that ship.

Left, lower: Another view from the flight deck on board *Fencer*, with 842's Swordfish in the background. The ship's company are practising laying a smokescreen.

860 NAVAL AIR SQUADRON

Located at RNAS Donibristle, Machrihanish and Maydown, RAF Thorney Island *et alibi* and on board MV *Acavus*, *Gadila* and *Macoma*

Commission: 15/06/43–18/03/50 (Swordfish Mk Is until 00/11/43, Mk IIs 00/11/43–00/06/45, Mk IIIs 00/03/45–00/06/45)
Commanding Officer: Lt J. van der Tooren RNethN
Senior Pilots/Senior Observers: Not known

Right: 860 was a MAC-ship unit manned by the Royal Netherlands Navy charged, as 836 Squadron, with convoy escort duties. It trained alongside 836 and, as with that unit, was divided into ships' flights. The photograph depicts a scene on board MV *Gadila*. The DLCO is signalling 'Steady' to the incoming Swordfish.

ROYAL NETHERLANDS NAVY

886 NAVAL AIR SQUADRON

Located at RNAS Donibristle and Machrihanish and RAF North Front and on board HMS *Attacker*

Commission: 15/03/42–19/07/44 (Swordfish Mk IIs 00/06/43–00/10/43)
Commanding Officers: Lt J. C. M. Harman, Lt-Cdr R. H. H. L. Oliphant (27/07/42), Lt-Cdr P. E. I. Bailey (28/10/43)
Senior Pilots/Senior Observers: Not known

Right: A small number of Swordfish were assigned 886 Squadron—which was primarily a fighter unit—for some six months in the Mediterranean theatre on board the escort carrier *Attacker* and ashore in order to provide an anti-submarine search capability during the Allied offensive against Italy. This July 1943 photograph shows Swordfish Mk II HS547 powering away, having for some reason abandoned an attempt to land-on; the safety barrier is raised and flight deck personnel are keeping their heads well down. After the war, Swordfish were flown on general duties for a few months out of Sembawang by 1700 NAS, a Sea Otter/ Walrus air-sea rescue unit.

COURTESY PHILIP JARRETT

1700 NAVAL AIR SQUADRON ('C' FLIGHT)

Located at RNAS Sembawang

Commission: 01/11/44–03/06/46 (Flight formed 08/11/45, Swordfish Mk IIs throughout)
Commanding Officers: Lt A. B. Edgar RNVR, Lt J. A. Gossett RNVR (25/01/46)
Senior Pilots/Senior Observers: Not known

CATAPULT FLIGHTS

AIRCRAFT carriers were not the only types of naval vessels from which the Fairey Swordfish was flown: from the earliest days of aviation the value of reconnaissance and 'spotting' for the benefit of conventional gun-armed warships was fully recognised, and it had proved possible to fly-off aircraft from short platforms fitted in the larger ships for this purpose. The widespread introduction of the accelerator (or 'catapult', as it was frequently if somewhat misleadingly called) did much to facilitate these operations. Recovery of the aircraft was more problematic—hence the preference for float-equipped machines, which could both take off from and land on the water close to the parent ship and be hoisted back on board to be serviced and re-armed.

In the 1930s the installation of accelerators on capital ships was general, and by 1936–37 the existing Fairey Seals and Blackburn Sharks were being supplanted by two new types, the Supermarine Walrus and the Swordfish. The aircraft were organised into flights rather than squadrons, numbered in the '700' series. Within a couple of years, however, the flights had been granted squadron status (see pages 178–179) and in January 1940, in a further reorganisation, all the catapult units were amalgamated into one establishment, 700 Squadron.

701 FLIGHT
Located at RAF Kalafrana and on board HM capital ships and cruisers
Commission: 15/07/36–21/01/40 (Swordfish Mk Is from 00/09/36)
Commanding Officers: Lt-Cdr A. G. C. Ermen, Lt M. C. Hoskin (29/03/38), Lt-Cdr J. C. M. Harman (12/08/38), Lt-Cdr
   W. L. M. Brown (24/05/39)
Senior Pilots/Senior Observers: Not known

702 FLIGHT
Located at RNAS Mount Batten and on board HM Ships *Nelson*, *Rodney* and *Resolution*
Commission: 15/07/36–21/01/40 (Swordfish Mk Is from 00/00/39)
Commanding Officers: Lt P. E. O'Brien, Lt-Cdr R. A. B. Phillimore (24/05/39)
Senior Pilots/Senior Observers: Not known

705 FLIGHT
Located at RNAS Kalafrana and on board HM battlecruisers
Commissions: 15/07/36–21/01/40 (Swordfish Mk Is 15/07/36–21/01/40)
Commanding Officers: Lt-Cdr D. W. MacKendrick, Lt P. E. O'Brien (14/11/38)
Senior Pilots/Senior Observers: Not known

Main image: The Swordfish was designed to be equally effective as landplane or floatplane, and indeed the two undercarriage systems were interchangeable. In practice, however, conversion was carried out infrequently, at least following the onset of hostilities in 1939, and with the demise of the traditional battle fleet and of the capital ship herself as an arbiter of sea power, the concept of the floatplane fell from favour. This view is of an early Swordfish floatplane, armed with a torpedo, conducting trials. Readily evident, incidentally, is the 1930s FAA practice of outlining serial numbers in white. Opposite page: L2742 in the floatplane configuration in early 1938, wearing the blue sash of HMS *Courageous* and from 810 Squadron but temporarily assigned to the battlecruiser HMS *Hood* (alongside which ship it is taxying). The destroyer visible in the photograph is HMS *Glowworm*.

Above: K8364 served as a floatplane with 701 Flight on board the battleships *Warspite* and, later, *Malaya*. It is seen here while operating from the latter; the tail emblem is the coat of arms of the Federated Malay States. The classic floatplane action took place on 13 April 1940 in Ofotfjord, Narvik, when one of *Warspite*'s two Swordfish, L9767, not only spotted for the battleship's big guns, resulting in the sinking or scuttling of seven German destroyers, but also itself bombed and sank U 64.

ROYAL AIR FORCE FRONT-LINE UNITS

THE first officer to command a front-line Swordfish squadron was an RAF officer— Squadron Leader H. A. Traill (Acting Lieutenant-Commander, Royal Navy) of 825 Squadron—and the record shows that one of the last commanders of a front-line Swordfish unit was also an RAF officer. His name was Squadron Leader Norman Wilkinson and his charge was that of No 119 Squadron RAF. Thanks to its excellent ASV radar, the Swordfish III was an ideal mount from which to conduct the Squadron's duties—seeking out and destroying, generally at night, the German miniature submarines that were known to be deployed around the coastal waters of the Low Countries—and from the end of 1944 No 119 began to supplant its existing Albacores in this way. The aircraft were well up to the task, and a small number of 'kills' were made. In later weeks Squadron detachments operated from the muddy terrain of Knocke-le-Zoute, so becoming the only Coastal Command unit to be physically based on mainland Europe during the war.

Two other front-line Royal Air Force units were equipped with Swordfish, albeit in very restricted numbers. No 8 Squadron is known to have had six and possibly seven aircraft on 'loan' from the Fleet Air Arm for a few months and that they were from time to time called upon to help police the Aden Protectorate and carry out general duties. In the central and western Mediterranean, No 3 Anti-Aircraft Co-operation Unit was equipped with Swordfish floatplanes before the war, and when the unit disbanded in October 1940 its three aircraft were taken on to establishment by No 202 Squadron as 'B' Flight (OC Flt Lt Garlick), continuing with their search-and rescue and patrol sorties. The aircraft were finally withdrawn in June 1941.

Unit	Location(s)	Commanding Officer	Period of usage	Remarks
No 8 Squadron	RAF Khormaksar	Sqn Ldr D. S. Radford	00/08/40–00/01/41	Small number of landplanes employed in general duties and maritime patrol
No 119 Squadron	RAF Bircham Newton (detachments in Belgium)	Sqn Ldr N. Wilkinson	15/09/44–25/05/45	Mk IIIs flown mainly on coastal patrol duties
No 202 Squadron	RAF North Front	Sqn Ldr T. Q. Horner	00/10/40–00/06/41	Small number of floatplanes tasked with maritime patrol

This spread: Perhaps because it was something of a curiosity amongst home-based squadrons in 1944–45, No 119 was a much-photographed unit, the dark paint finishes of its Swordfish also, no doubt, lending an air of sinister mystery to its operations. Biplanes fitted with radomes were not, moreover, an everyday sight. The paintwork is frequently described as 'all black', or 'black overall', but in fact most of 119's Swordfish had standard dark grey and dark green camouflage on their uppersurfaces. These three photographs were probably taken on a single sortie—and the aircraft had likely been spruced up for the occasion!

FLEET AIR ARM SECOND-LINE UNITS

WITHOUT the unsung but essential work of the Fleet Air Arm's second-line squadrons there would be no front-line units to go to sea, and Fairey Swordfish were amongst the most widely utilised of all naval aircraft in this respect, not only for training personnel in combat rôles but for a plethora of general-purpose activities as well. The numbered squadrons are considered in this section.

The types of training for which the Swordfish was used included not only pilot, observer and tele-graphist air gunner aircrew training, but also deck-landing, radar and instrument and refresher training, whilst other tasks to which the aircraft was assigned embraced target-towing, communications duties and general fleet requirements.

Vast indeed was the number of Swordfish squadrons engaged in this work. Some of the aircraft issued to the units were brand new, others had many flying hours; and wide was the variety of colour schemes and markings in which they appeared.

COURTESY BRIAN LOWE

Left: A few Swordfish were sent to Ceylon towards the end of the war, issued to 733 Squadron for general fleet duties. This is Mk II LS454, wearing the dark blue and white (or very pale blue) roundels standard for that theatre.
Right: HMS *Malaya*'s floatplane V4367 (700 Squadron) in full camouflage dress. Engines had to be started before the aircraft were hoisted out!

Unit	Location(s)	Commission(s)
700 NAS	RNAS Hatston and on board HM capital ships and cruisers and ('W' Flight) at RNAS Sandbanks, Lee-on-Solent, Machrihanish *et alibi* and on board HMS *Fencer*	29/01/40–24/03/44 (Swordfish Mk Is until 00/01/42; 'W' Flight Mk Is 00/07/43–00/12/43)
701 NAS	RAF Kalafrana and on board HM capital ships and cruisers	15/07/36–21/01/40 (Swordfish Mk Is from 00/09/36)
702 NAS	RNAS Mount Batten and on board HM Ships *Nelson*, *Rodney* and *Resolution*	5/07/36–21/01/40 (Swordfish Mk Is from 00/00/39)
703 NAS	RNAS Lee-on-Solent	03/06/42–01/05/44 (Swordfish Mk I 00/10/42–00/11/42)
705 NAS	RNAS Kalafrana and Ronaldsway and on board HM battlecruisers	15/07/36–21/01/40, 07/03/45–24/06/45 (Swordfish Mk Is 15/07/36–21/01/40, Mk IIIs 07/03/45–24/06/45)
707 NAS	RNAS Burscough and Gosport	20/02/45–01/10/45 (Swordfish Mk IIs and IIIs throughout)
710 NAS	RNAS Ronaldsway	07/10/44–20/12/45 (Swordfish Mk Is 07/10/44–00/06/45, Mk IIs 00/04/45–00/12/45)
722 NAS	RNAS Tambaram, RAF Cochin *et alibi*	01/09/44–24/10/45 (Swordfish Mk ?s from 00/05/45)
726 NAS	SAAF Durban (Stamford Hill)	07/07/43–03/11/45 (Swordfish Mk Is 00/08/43–00/12/43, Mk IIs from 00/09/44)
727 NAS	RAF North Front *et alibi*	26/05/43–01/12/44 (Mk ?s until 00/09/44)
728 NAS	RAF North Front, RNAS Dekheila, RAF Ta Kali *et alibi*	08/05/43–04/07/43, 14/08/43–31/05/67 (Swordfish Mk ?s 08/05/43–04/07/43, 14/08/43–00/09/44)
730 NAS	RNAS Ayr and Machrihanish	17/04/44–01/08/45 (Swordfish Mk IIs from 00/01/45)
731 NAS	RNAS East Haven	05/12/43–01/11/45 (Swordfish Mk Is until 00/06/45, Mk IIs throughout, Mk IIIs from 00/11/44)
733 NAS	RAF Minneriya and RNAS Trincomalee	01/01/44–31/12/47 (Swordfish Mk Is until 00/12/44, Mk IIs 00/09/44–00/11/45)

COURTESY RICHARD L. WARD

Commanding Officer(s)	Remarks
Lt-Cdr A. H. T. Fleming, Lt-Cdr N. S. Luard DSC (17/05/41), Lt-Cdr G. W. R. Nicholl (04/02/42), Lt-Cdr C. G. Hide RNVR (10/10/43)	Formed 21/01/40 by amalgamation of Catapult Flights (see pages 174–175)
Lt-Cdr A. G. C. Ermen, Lt M. C. Hoskin (29/03/38), Lt-Cdr J. C. M. Harman (12/08/38), Lt-Cdr W. L. M. Brown (24/05/39)	Redesignation of 701 Flight (q.v.)
Lt P. E. O'Brien, Lt-Cdr R. A. B. Phillimore (24/05/39)	Redesignation of 702 Flight (q.v.)
Not known	Service on armed merchant cruisers; one Swordfish floatplane issued for trials autumn 1942
Lt-Cdr D. W. MacKendrick, Lt P. E. O'Brien (14/11/38), Lt-Cdr G. Bennett DSC (07/03/45)	Redesignation of 705 Flight (q.v.); revived briefly in spring 1945 as Mk III training unit
Lt-Cdr S. S. Laurie RNVR	Naval School of Airborne Radar
Lt-Cdr D. R. Connor RNVR, Lt-Cdr J. F. Arnold (01/08/45)	Torpedo training squadron (TBR Course, Part III)
Lt-Cdr A. F. E. Payen RNVR, Lt-Cdr K. C. Johnson SANF(V) (23/10/44), Lt-Cdr L. G. Morris (24/10/45)	Fleet requirements unit
Lt-Cdr F. G. Hood SANF(V), Lt W. A. McElroy RNVR (04/01/45), Lt D. C. Langley SANF(V) (04/06/45)	Fleet requirements unit
Lt E. L. Meiklejohn RNVR, Lt-Cdr M. V. Dyas RNVR (01/10/43)	Fleet requirements unit
Lt-Cdr E. H. Horn RNVR, Lt P. Snow (14/08/43), Lt-Cdr P. B. Pratt RNVR (08/01/44)	Fleet requirements unit
Lt-Cdr C. White RNVR, Lt J. C. Kennedy (24/05/45)	Fleet requirements unit
Lt-Cdr K. Stilliard RNVR, Lt-Cdr R. Pridham-Wippel	DLCO ('batsman') training
Lt-Cdr R. A. Beard RNVR, Lt-Cdr L. Gilbert RNVR (01/04/44), Lt-Cdr J. Ansell RNVR (06/10/44). Lt-Cdr I. O. Robertson RNVR (09/08/45)	Fleet requirements unit

continued . . .

Unit	Location(s)	Commission(s)
735 NAS	RNAS Inskip and Burscough	01/08/43–30/04/46 (Swordfish Mk Is until 00/03/44, Mk IIs until 00/06/44)
737 NAS	RNAS Inskip, Arbroath and Burscough	15/03/44–12/11/45 (Swordfish Mk IIs until 00/07/45)
739 NAS	RNAS Lee-on-Solent and Worthy Down	15/12/42–07/03/45 (Swordfish Mk Is until 00/11/43)
740 NAS	RNAS Arbroath, Machrihanish and Ayr	04/05/43–05/08/43, 00/09/44–01/09/45 (Swordfish Mk Is until 05/08/54, Mk IIs from 00/09/44)
741 NAS	RNAS Arbroath	01/03/43–19/03/45 (Swordfish Mk Is and IIs throughout)
742 NAS	RNAS Colombo Racecourse and Coimbatore	06/12/43–31/08/46 (Swordfish Mk ?s until 00/10/45)
743 NAS	RCAF Yarmouth and Dartmouth	01/03/43–30/03/45, 18/09/46–01/05/54 (Swordfish Mk IIs 01/03/43–30/03/45 and 18/09/46–30/11/48)
744 NAS	RNAS Maydown	06/03/44–01/12/47 (Swordfish Mk Is and IIs until 00/04/44, Mk IIIs 00/02/45–00/05/45)
745 NAS	RCAF Yarmouth	01/03/43–30/03/45 (Swordfish Mk IIs until 00/02/44)
747 NAS	RNAS Fearn and Inskip	22/03/43–20/12/45 (Swordfish Mk Is until 00/02/44, Mk IIs 00/06/43–00/07/43)
753 NAS	RNAS Lee-on-Solent and Arbroath	24/05/39–09/08/46 (Mk Is 00/12/39–00/06/45)
756 NAS	RNAS Katukurunda and Colombo Racecourse	01/10/43–24/11/45 (Swordfish Mk IIs 00/03/44–00/02/45)
759 NAS School	RNAS Eastleigh and Yeovilton	01/11/39–05/02/46 (Swordfish Mk Is 01/11/39–00/06/41, Mk IIs 00/05/43–00/05/43)
763 NAS	RNAS Worthy Down, Jersey Airport and Lee-on-Solent	18/12/39–08/07/40 (Swordfish Mk Is throughout)
764 NAS	RNAS Lee-on-Solent and Pembroke Dock	08/04/40–07/11/43 (Swordfish Mk Is until 00/09/41)

Below: HS234, a Swordfish Mk II of 745 Squadron. Based in Canada, this unit was one of two (the other was 743 NAS) that undertook the training of telegraphist air gunners.

Right: The aftermath of a barrier encounter on board HMS *Battler* involving LS422 of 744 Squadron, the unit that provided training facilities for the aircrews embarking on merchant aircraft carriers.

COURTESY PHILIP JARRETT

Commanding Officer(s)	Remarks
Lt-Cdr E. S. Carver DSC, Lt-Cdr R. T. Hayes RNVR (15/03/44)	Radar training unit
Lt-Cdr L. P. Dunne RNVR, Lt-Cdr G. J. Staveley RNVR (09/11/44), Lt-Cdr F. V. Jones RNVR (05/03/45)	Radar training unit
Lt G. Smith	Blind Approach Development Unit
Lt-Cdr D. H. Angel, Lt-Cdr L. F. Diggens RNVR (05/08/43), Lt-Cdr L. T. Summerfield RNVR (23/04/45)	Observer training (No 2 Observers' School) until 05/08/42; torpedo training 30/12/43–01/09/45 (detached to RNAS Ayr from 26/01/44)
Lt-Cdr O. H. Cantrill RNVR, Lt-Cdr R. McA. Stratton RNVR (17/03/44)	Observer training (No 2 Observers' School)
Lt T. N. Stack RNR, Lt-Cdr R. MacDermott RNVR (08/01/44), Lt-Cdr T. N. Stack RNR (29/09/44)	Communications and air transport unit
Lt-Cdr R. Gillett RNVR, Lt J. N. Donaldson RCN (18/09/46), Lt-Cdr W. E. Widdows RCN (30/08/47)	TAG training (No 2 Telegraphist Air Gunners' School)
Lt-Cdr C. M. T. Hallewell, Lt-Cdr D. W. Phillips DSC (27/02/45)	Training unit for 836 NAS (merchant aircraft carriers)
Lt-Cdr R. H. Ovey RNVR	TAG training (No 2 Telegraphist Air Gunners' School)
Lt-Cdr J. A. Ievers, Lt-Cdr F. A. Swanton DSC (13/09/43)	Torpedo bomber reconnaissance pool, operational training (No 1 Operational Training Unit)
Lt-Cdr G. N. P Stringer DFC, Capt. A. Newson RM (22/10/40), Lt-Cdr L. A. Cubitt (06/05/41), Lt-Cdr A. C. Mills RNVR (30/09/41), Lt-Cdr F. R. Steggall RNVR (15/07/42), Lt-Cdr R. E. Stewart RNVR (31/03/44)	Observer training (No 2 Observers' School)
Lt W. E. Widdows RNVR (01/02/44), Lt-Cdr S. M. de L. Longsden (27/02/44), Lt-Cdr T. T. Miller (28/10/44)	Deck-landing and refresher training
Lt-Cdr B. H. M. Kendall, Lt-Cdr H. P. Bramwell DSO DSC (18/11/40), Capt F. D. G. Bird RM (01/08/41), Lt-Cdr J. N. Garnett (13/10/41), Lt-Cdr E. W. T. Taylour DSC (08/12/41), Lt E. D. G. Lewin DSO DSC (12/11/42), Lt-Cdr J. M. Bruen DSO DSC (07/12/42)	Fleet Fighter School; from 00/04/43 Advanced Flying (No 1 Naval Air Fighter School)
Lt-Cdr P. L. Mortimer	Aircrew training (No 1 Torpedo Spotter Reconnaissance Pool)
Lt-Cdr F. E. C. Judd, Lt-Cdr H. L. McCulloch (16/07/40)	Seaplane aircrew conversion training

continued . . .

COURTESY BRIAN LOWE

Unit	Location(s)	Commission(s)
765 NAS	RNAS Lee-on-Solent and Sandbanks	24/05/39–25/10/43 (Swordfish Mk Is until 00/06/41)
766 NAS	RNAS Machrihanish and Inskip	15/04/42–25/11/54 (Swordfish Mk Is and IIs until 00/11/44, Mk IIIs 00/03/44–00/11/44)
767 NAS	RNAS Donibristle, Hyères and Hal Far, RAF North Front and RNAS Arbroath and East Haven	24/05/39–01/07/40, 08/07/40–31/05/55 (Swordfish Mk Is 24/05/39–01/07/40 and 08/07/40–00/05/44, Mk IIs 00/01/43–00/05/44)
768 NAS	RNAS Arbroath, Machrihanish, Ayr, Abbotsinch and Ballyhalbert	13/01/41–16/04/46 (Swordfish Mk Is until 00/12/44, Mk IIs 00/07/43–00/10/45, Mk IIIs 00/10/44–00/10/44)
769 NAS	RNAS Arbroath and East Haven	29/11/41–29/10/45 Swordfish (Mk Is until 00/02/44, Mk IIs 00/10/43–00/02/44)
770 NAS	Located at RNAS Lee-on-Solent and Hyères	07/11/39–01/05/40 (Swordfish Mk Is from 00/01/40)

COURTESY PHILIP JARRETT

Above: Suitably kitted out with R/Ps underwing and flares beneath the fuselage, a Swordfish II of 766 Squadron flies a training mission. Except for the area of fabric carrying the call-sign, the white-finished surfaces of the airframe appear to have been darkened somewhat.

Commanding Officer(s)	Remarks
Lt-Cdr H. C. Ranald, Lt-Cdr H. L. McCulloch (08/04/40), Lt-Cdr L. B. Wilson (12/07/40), Lt-Cdr G. R. Brown DSC (21/04/41)	Seaplane aircrew basic training and conversion (Seaplane Training Course Part I from 00/09/40)
Lt-Cdr R. E. Bibby DSO RNVR, Lt-Cdr. F. C. Garthwaite DSO RNVR (24/07/43), Lt-Cdr E. B. Morgan RANVR (03/08/44)	Night torpedo attack and photographic training (component of No 1 Naval Operational Training Unit)
Lt-Cdr E. O. F. Price, Lt-Cdr J. A. L Drummond (24/08/39 and 25/07/40), Lt-Cdr P. L. Mortimer (08/07/40), Lt-Cdr A. G. Leatham (29/11/41), Lt-Cdr R. L. Williamson DSC (17/06/42), Lt-Cdr R. S. Baker-Falkner (01/07/42), Lt-Cdr C. H. C. O'Rorke (10/10/42), Lt-Cdr W. J. Mainprice (25/03/43), Lt-Cdr T. T. Miller (03/11/43), Lt-Cdr J. L. Fisher RNVR (07/11/43), Lt-Cdr B. W. Vigrass RNVR (06/05/44)	Component unit of Deck Landing Training School
Lt-Cdr V. C. Grenfell, Lt-Cdr F. D. G. Jennings (26/06/41), Lt-Cdr N. G. Hallett (28/09/41), Lt J. C. M. Harman (01/11/41), Lt P. B. Jackson (14/03/42), Lt-Cdr D. M. Brown RNVR (29/12/42), Lt-Cdr D. J. W. Williams (01/03/43), Lt-Cdr J. S. Bailey (08/07/43), Lt-Cdr J. M. Brown DSC RNVR (29/10/44)	Component unit of Deck Landing Training School
Lt W. H. Crawford, Lt-Cdr W. H. Nowell (01/01/43), Lt-Cdr S. P. Luke (07/05/43), Lt-Cdr P. N. Medd (24/01/43)	Component unit of Deck Landing Training School
Not known	Fleet requirements unit

continued . . .

COURTESY RICHARD L WARD

Above and below: 765 Squadron's duties during its 1939–43 commission were concerned exclusively with the training of aircrew to operate seaplanes, and Swordfish were among a number of types on establishment. The photograph above, with a dual-control seaplane in the centre and a pair of Walruses to the left, was taken at Lee-on-Solent; that below is understood to have been taken at Felixstowe.

COURTESY PHILIP JARRETT

Unit	Location(s)	Commission(s)
771 NAS	RNAS Portland, Lee-on-Solent, Hatston, Donibristle, Abbotsinch, Twatt *et alibi*	24/05/39–17/08/55 (Swordfish Mk Is until 00/04/45)
772 NAS	RNAS Lee-on-Solent, Portland, Campbeltown, Machrihanish, Ayr *et alibi*	28/09/39–13/10/48 (Swordfish Mk Is until 00/07/41, Mk IIs 00/10/42–00/08/45)
773 NAS	RNAS Bermuda	03/06/40–25/04/44 (Swordfish Mk Is throughout)
774 NAS	RNAS Worthy Down, Aldergrove, Evanton and St Merryn	16/11/39–01/08/45 (Swordfish Mk Is until 00/08/44)
775 NAS	RNAS Dekheila and RAF North Front	00/11/40–00/03/46 (Swordfish Mk Is 00/05/41–00/01/45)
776 NAS	RAF Speke	01/01/41–30/10/45 (Swordfish Mk IIs 00/06/44–00/12/44)

COURTESY RICHARD L. WARD

Commanding Officer(s)	Remarks
Lt-Cdr J. W. Beard, Lt-Cdr F. E. C. Judd (13/09/40), Maj. A. R. Burch RM (15/01/41), Lt-Cdr N. E. Goddard DSC RNVR (15/10/41), Lt-Cdr H. T. Molyneaux RNVR (04/05/42), Lt-Cdr W. Dobson (13/02/44)	Fleet requirements unit
Lt-Cdr M. A. Everett, Lt-Cdr R. E. P. Miers (16/21/39), Lt-Cdr K. W. Beard (06/09/40), Lt-Cdr C. L. Hill (25/05/42), Lt-Cdr A. C. Mills RNVR (04/08/42), Lt-Cdr P. J. Connolly (25/08/43), Lt-Cdr C. R. Holman RNR (11/09/44), Lt-Cdr P. Snow (16/06/45)	Fleet requirements unit
Lt-Cdr H. Wright, Lt-Cdr G. C. W. Fowler (00/09/41), Lt-Cdr K. W. Beard (06/08/43)	Fleet requirements unit
Lt-Cdr S. Borrett, Lt-Cdr W. G. C. Stokes (24/11/39), Lt-Cdr P. L. Mortimer (30/08/40), Lt-Cdr J. H. Gibbons (15/03/41), Lt-Cdr P. P. Pardoe-Matthews RNR (16/08/43), Lt-Cdr J. O. Sparke RNVR (07/10/44)	Armament training unit for observers and TAGs
Lt A. H. Abrams, Lt-Cdr H. L. McCulloch (27/10/41), Lt-Cdr J. W. G. Welham DSO (29/11/42), Lt-Cdr J. M. Waddell RNVR (08/12/42)	Fleet requirements unit
Lt-Cdr R. M. B. Ward RNVR	Fleet requirements unit

continued . . .

Opposite, top: Deck-landing practice was undertaken towards the end of a student pilot's training and, unsurprisingly perhaps, accidents were not infrequent occurrences. This Swordfish, V4571 of 766 Squadron, has had an unwanted meeting with the safety barrier on board HMS *Argus*, spring 1944.
Left: A 774 Squadron Swordfish up from RNAS St Merryn, the TAG engaged in firing practice against a sleeve target.

This page, top: 771 Squadron was a long-serving fleet requirements unit and had Swordfish on strength for the duration of the war. This is a prewar photograph of one of its floatplanes.
Below: HS550 of 771 Squadron, winter 1943/44. The censor has meticulously scratched out the individual dipoles of the port ASV radar aerial whilst managing to preserve the precise shape of the equipment!

COURTESY PHILIP JARRETT

185

Unit	Location(s)	Commission(s)
777 NAS	RNAS Hastings (Sierra Leone)	01/08/41–25/12/44 (Swordfish Mk Is 00/08/41–00/02/44, Mk IIs 00/08/42–00/02/44)
778 NAS	RNAS Lee-on-Solent, Arbroath and Crail and on board HMS *Pretoria Castle*	28/09/39–16/08/48 (Swordfish Mk Is 28/09/39–00/01/44, Mk IIs 00/09/42–00/02/45)
779 NAS	RAF North Front	01/10/41–04/08/45 (Swordfish Mk 00/10/41–00/08/42, Mk IIs 00/10/41–00/01/45)
780 NAS	RNAS Eastleigh, Lee-on-Solent and Charlton Horethorne	02/10/39–02/01/45 (Swordfish Mk Is 00/06/40–00/07/43), Mk IIs (00/07/43–00/00/44)
781 NAS	RNAS Lee-on-Solent	20/03/40–31/07/45, 27/06/46–31/03/81 (Swordfish Mk Is 00/09/40–00/12/41, Mk IIs 00/03/42–00/02/43)
782 NAS	RNAS Donibristle	01/12/40–09/10/53 (Swordfish Mk Is 01/12/40–21/03/41)
783 NAS	RNAS Arbroath	09/01/41–18/11/49 (Swordfish Mk Is 15/06/42–00/10/43, Mk IIs 15/06/42–00/07/45)
785 NAS	RNAS Crail	04/11/40–01/03/46 (Swordfish Mk Is 04/11/40–00/05/44, Mk IIs 00/04/42–00/02/44)
786 NAS	RNAS Crail	21/11/40–21/12/45 (Swordfish Mk Is 00/05/41–00/12/42, Mk IIs 00/06/42–00/00/43)
787Z Flt	RNAS St Merryn and Inskip (Sqn HQ at RAF Wittering)	15/01/43–01/07/44 (Swordfish Mk Is from 00/03/43, Mk IIs throughout)
788 NAS	RAF China Bay, RNAS Tanga and Mombasa	16/02/42–11/06/45 (Swordfish Mk Is and IIs 16/02/42–00/06/44)
789 NAS	RNAS Wingfield (South Africa)	01/07/42–25/11/45 (Swordfish Mk Is 01/07/42–00/06/43, Mk IIs 00/10/42–25/11/45)
791 NAS	RNAS Arbroath	15/10/40–10/12/44 (Swordfish Mk Is 00/04/42–10/12/44), Mk IIs 00/12/43–00/01/44)
794 NAS	RNAS Yeovilton, Angle, Dale, Henstridge and Charlton Horethorne	03/08/40–30/06/44, 02/01/45–26/02/47 (Swordfish Mk Is until 30/06/44, Mk IIs 00/04/44–30/06/44 and 02/01/45–00/06/45)
796 NAS	Port Reitz and RNAS Tanga	25/07/42–28/04/44 (Swordfish Mk Is 25/07/42–00/12/43, Mk IIs 00/09/43–28/04/44)
797 NAS	RNAS Colombo Racecourse	00/07/42–24/10/45 (Swordfish Mk Is 00/11/43–00/08/45)

BERT HOLT/LES SAYER COLLECTION

Left: The 775 Squadron air gunners' 'hotel' at RNAS Dekheila. This base, situated near the coast of Egypt, was the civil airport for Alexandria before the war, which no doubt explains the origin of the impressive placard above the entrance.

Right: One of the very few Swordfish to survive long enough to wear postwar 'D' type roundels, NF389 had an active service career in the late 1940s, being used for numerous torpedo trials prior to its transfer in 1953 to 781 Squadron, in whose care it was retained for displays and other events. The aircraft survives to this day, and current indications are that it will be restored to flying condition as a radome-equipped Mk III, possibly finished in the colours of No 119 Squadron RAF.

Commanding Officer(s)	Remarks
Lt-Cdr H. J. Gibbs RNVR, Lt-Cdr F. C. Muir RNVR (22/07/42), Lt-Cdr C. Draper RNVR (27/09/43)	Fleet requirements and local defence unit
Lt-Cdr R. A. Kilroy, Lt-Cdr J. P. G. Bryant (22/04/40), Lt-Cdr A. J. Tillard (06/01/41), Lt-Cdr H. P. Bramwell DSO DSC (21/07/41), Lt-Cdr H. J. F. Lane (01/03/43), Lt-Cdr P. B. Schofield (25/04/44)	Service trials unit (inc. deck trials)
Lt-Cdr B. F. Cox RNVR, Lt-Cdr L. Gilbert RNVR (17/01/42), Lt-Cdr J. M. Keene-Miller RNVR (22/06/42), Lt-Cdr C. R. Holman RNR (01/05/43), Lt-Cdr E. L. Meiklejohn RNVR (14/09/43)	Fleet requirements unit
Lt-Cdr H. S. Cooper, Lt-Cdr J. Goodyear RNVR (07/10/40), Lt-Cdr T. G. Stubley RNVR (17/08/42)	Conversion and pilot training unit
Lt-Cdr A. C. S. Irwin RNVR, Lt-Cdr J. M. Keene-Miller RNVR (15/02/41), Lt-Cdr Sir George J. E. Lewis Bt RNVR (04/11/41)	Communications unit and (postwar) instrument examining and adverse weather flying training. One Mk III (NF389) retained 11/03/53–00/11/63–the last Swordfish to be, technically at least, on RN establishment.
Lt-Cdr A. Goodfellow RNVR	Northern Communications Squadron
Lt-Cdr D. M. Browne RNVR, Lt-Cdr R. P. Mason RNVR (29/12/42), Lt-Cdr T. B. Horsley RNVR (30/08/44)	ASV radar training unit
Lt-Cdr P. G. O. Sydney-Turner, Capt. O. Patch DSO DSC RM (22/08/41), Lt-Cdr R. W. Thorne (01/01/42), Lt-Cdr A. H. Abrams DSC (07/09/42), Lt-Cdr J. H. Stenning (22/10/42), Lt-Cdr K. G. Sharp (02/12/42), Lt-Cdr M. Thorpe (01/07/43), Lt-Cdr R. B. Lunberg (31/12/44)	TBR training unit
Capt. F. W. Brown RM, Lt S. Keane (28/07/41), Lt R. C. B. Stallard-Penoyre (23/02/42), Lt-Cdr B. E. Boulding DSC (15/10/42), Lt-Cdr D. Norcock (10/08/43)	TBR training unit
Lt-Cdr G. H. Bates RNVR, Lt T. G. Davison RNVR (06/06/44)	Naval Air Fighting Development Unit
Lt-Cdr C. A. Kingsley-Rowe, Maj. V. B. G. Cheesman RM (01/05/42), Lt E. M. Britton (07/08/43), Lt W. N. Waller (25/08/42), Lt-Cdr E. H. Horn RNVR (12/08/43), Lt-Cdr J. A. Ansell RNVR (25/10/43)	TBR pool and (from 00/05/42) fleet requirements unit
Lt-Cdr K. C. Johnston RNVR, Lt-Cdr W. T. E. White SANF(V) (11/06/43), Lt B. Sinclair MBE (10/09/43), Lt-Cdr W. T. E. White SANF(V) (20/06/44)	Fleet requirements unit
Lt-Cdr K. B. Brotchie RNVR, Lt J. C. M. Harman (10/09/42), Lt-Cdr C. A. Crighton RNVR (12/05/43), Lt-Cdr A. P. T. Pierssene RNVR (07/04/44)	Air target towing unit
Lt R. W. H. Everett RNVR, Lt-Cdr F. C. Muir RNVR (22/07/42), Lt W. H. Stevens (16/11/42), Lt-Cdr A. L. Hill RNVR (10/04/43), Lt-Cdr T. L. Crookston (06/01/44), Lt-Cdr J. L. Appleby (02/01/45)	Air target towing unit, (from 01/07 43) Naval Air Firing Unit and (from 00/10/44) No 1 Naval Air Firing Unit
Lt H. E. Shilbach RNVR, Lt N. T. O'Neill (19/08/42), Lt A. J. L. Temple-West (12/01/43), Lt-Cdr M. W. Rudorf DSC (14/07/43)	Eastern Fleet Torpedo Bomber Reconnaissance Pool
Lt F. L. Page RNVR, Lt K. C. Winstanley RNVR (09/12/43)	Fleet requirements unit

COURTESY BRIAN LOWE

MODIFICATION 408

An important aspect of the Swordfish story is the aircraft's career in Canada. In 1942 it was agreed with the Canadian authorities that a supplementary training establishment for TAGs would come into being at the air station at Yarmouth, Nova Scotia, on the south-western tip of the territory. Known as No 2 Telegraphist Air Gunners' School (No 1 being that already established at RNAS Worthy Down)—though referred to by the Canadians as No 1 Naval Air Gunners' School—it took delivery of Swordfish from Dartmouth some 150 miles away on the Atlantic coast, which was not only the receiving station for the disassembled aircraft sent across from Britain but also the 'turn-round' depôt for 836 Squadron Swordfish operating from MAC ships.

The harsh Canadian winters inspired alterations to the aircraft that have come to be closely associated with Swordfish that operated in Canada. Whilst the extreme conditions were no more severe than those being experienced every week by aircrews assigned to protect the Russian convoys, they were hardly conducive to efficient training. As a result, Fairey Aviation designed and built a set of kits comprising a transparent canopy covering all three aircrew stations, special de-icing systems for the propeller, carburettor and pilot's windshield, and attachment points for electrically heated flying suits (although these last were never produced). The transformation was referred to officially as Modification 408.

Production difficulties and delays in delivering the kits meant that relatively few of the Swordfish Mk IIs with which the School had been supplied were modified in this way—probably no more than a couple of dozen out of the one hundred or so aircraft that were taken on strength in total. The new installations gave rise to the revamped Swordfish being referred to as 'Mk IVs', but this designation never received official sanction, probably because the changes were considered to be field modifications rather than assembly-line modifications.

Left: The cockpit canopy of the Swordfish 'Mk IV'. The rear glazing pivoted upwards to allow the trainee TAG to operate his machine gun (the weapon is not fitted here).

AD HOC COLLECTION

Above and below: Swordfish HS553 in pristine finish and toting four
250-pound bombs. These modified aircraft had neither the fixed,
forward-firing .303 gun nor an R/P capability.

OTHER SWORDFISH UNITS

Unit	Remarks
No 3 Anti-Aircraft Co-operation Unit	RAF unit 1937–41, based at RAF Kalafrana, Malta, with floatplane detachment at Gibraltar. Target-towing, air–sea rescue, etc. Absorbed into 830 Squadron (q.v.) and No 202 Squadron RAF (q.v.) in 1940.
No 4 Anti-Aircraft Co-operation Unit	RAF unit 1941–42, based at RAF Seletar and Tengah, Singapore. Spotting duties and, following Japanese advance, extemporary bombing rôle. Ceased to exist 1942.
No 273 Squadron	RAF composite unit based at RAF China Bay. At least one Swordfish on loan from FAA 1942.
No 25 Squadron	RAAF unit based at Pearce, Western Australia. Five aircraft on strength March–April 1942. Used principally in anti-submarine rôle.
No 9 Advanced Flying Unit	RAF training unit based at RAF Errol. Some Swordfish on strength 1942–45.
Aeroplane and Armament Experimental Establishment	At Martlesham Heath and (from 00/09/39) at Boscombe Down.
Marine Aircraft Experimental Establishment	At Felixstowe.
Royal Aircraft Establishment	At Farnborough.
Fleet Requirements Unit	At RNAS Lee-on-Solent and on board HMS *Argus* 1938–39. Absorbed by 770 NAS.
Seaplane Training Flight	At Calshot 1938.
Aircraft Torpedo Development Unit	At RNAS Gosport.
Torpedo Training Squadron	At RNAS Gosport. Administered by RAF. Redesignated Torpedo Training Unit 1940 and relocated RNAS Abbotsinch.
Station Flights	Various RN air stations, including RNAS Anthorn, Arbroath, Burscough, Donibristle Gosport and Hal Far.
Ships' Flights	Known to have been flown by Flights on board HMS *Indomitable* and on escort carriers of the British Eastern Fleet.
Ferry Pools	At RNAS Worthy Down and RNAS Donibristle.
Aircraft Holding/Storage Units	Storage and preparation of aircraft for issue to squadron service. At RNAS Sealand, Shawbury *et alibi*.
Repair/Maintenance Yards	RNARY Donibristle, RNARY Nairobi, RNAMY Coimbatore, RNAMY Colombo *et alibi*.
Maintenance Units	At Sealand, Shawbury, Kirkbride, Cosford *et alibi*.
Royal Navy Historic Flight	Based at RNAS Yeovilton. Maintains and displays Swordfish W5856 and LS326.
No 1 Wireless School	At Mount Hope, Ontario.
No 1 Bombing & Gunnery School	At Mountain View, Saskatoon.

Below: K8348 of the Torpedo Training Squadron at RNAS Gosport, summer 1937. In the left distance is a Blackburn Shark. Drops were routinely conducted over nearby Stokes Bay.

Opposite, top: A camouflaged Swordfish Mk I of the same establishment, now redesignated the Torpedo Training Unit, in 1940. A torpedo camera is carried beneath the port wing.

THE LAST WORD

Lieutenant-Commander (A) John Moffat RNVR

MOST of my Swordfish flying was done from the carriers *Ark Royal*, *Argus* and *Furious* in 1940–42, generally on tedious anti-submarine patrols and convoy duties in the Mediterranean and the Atlantic.

The Swordfish could carry bombs, or depth charges, or a torpedo, and still remain manœuvrable. What I did not like about it was the open cockpit in freezing conditions and the single machine gun on your right in the cockpit, with the ammunition between your legs. It had a pitiful rate of fire.

I still say today, however, that I know of no other aircraft that would have survived the taking off and landing in the Force 8 gale, and with the deck pitching sixty feet, that was necessary during the attack on the *Bismarck*—and which I did twice, on 26 and 27 May 1941. I have experienced flying the aircraft with most of the lower-wing and underfuselage canvas in tatters, and with a self-sealing tank that had a large piece of shrapnel embedded in it.

I have a lot to thank this aircraft for, having flown it for over 400 hours surrounded by nothing but sea and sky.

Below: Six decades after the end of World War II, bonds amongst Swordfish aircrew remain strong, though of course, sadly, the numbers are fast dwindling now. This photograph was taken at the TAGs' 1971 reunion at HMS *Dædalus* (RNAS Lee-on-Solent), with Swordfish NF389 taking centre stage. Pilots, observers, TAGs, handlers, armourers, maintainers—brave men of distinction every one, and men to whom we all owe a tremendous debt.

LES SAYER COLLECTION

SWORDFISH COLOURS

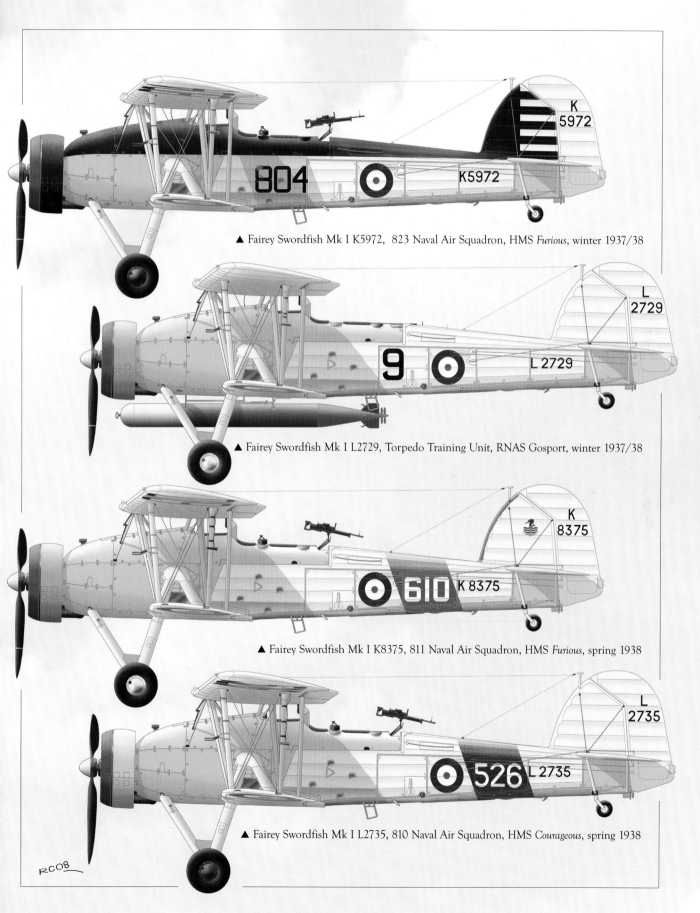

▲ Fairey Swordfish Mk I K5972, 823 Naval Air Squadron, HMS *Furious*, winter 1937/38

▲ Fairey Swordfish Mk I L2729, Torpedo Training Unit, RNAS Gosport, winter 1937/38

▲ Fairey Swordfish Mk I K8375, 811 Naval Air Squadron, HMS *Furious*, spring 1938

▲ Fairey Swordfish Mk I L2735, 810 Naval Air Squadron, HMS *Courageous*, spring 1938

RCO8

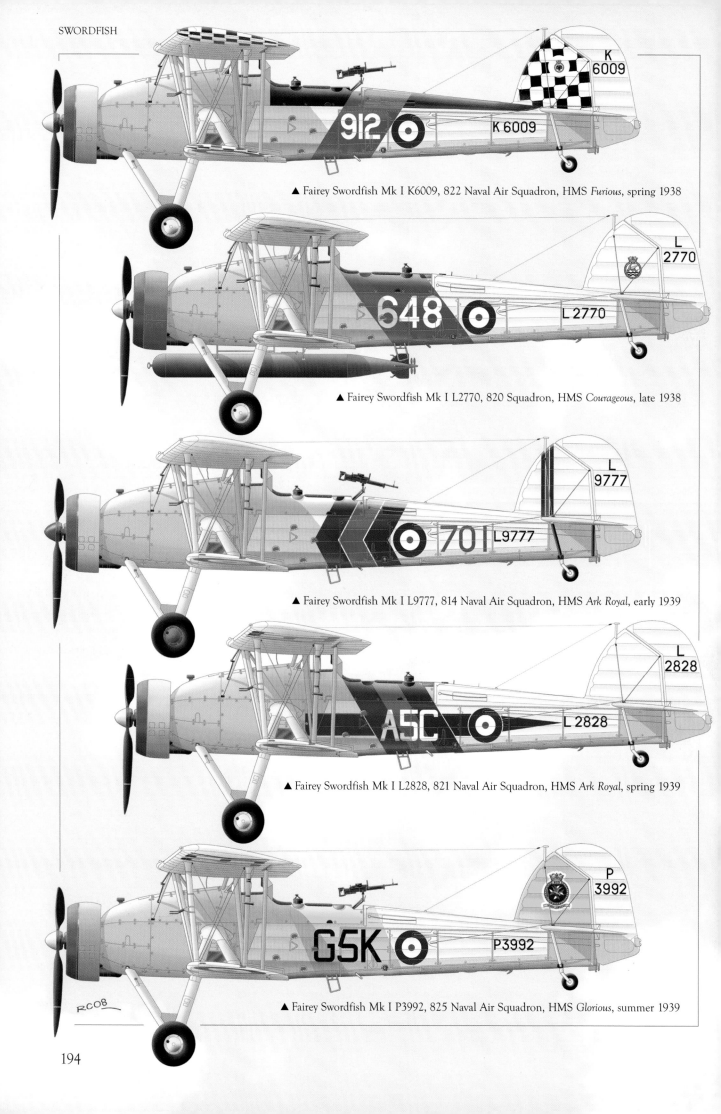

▲ Fairey Swordfish Mk I K6009, 822 Naval Air Squadron, HMS *Furious*, spring 1938

▲ Fairey Swordfish Mk I L2770, 820 Squadron, HMS *Courageous*, late 1938

▲ Fairey Swordfish Mk I L9777, 814 Naval Air Squadron, HMS *Ark Royal*, early 1939

▲ Fairey Swordfish Mk I L2828, 821 Naval Air Squadron, HMS *Ark Royal*, spring 1939

▲ Fairey Swordfish Mk I P3992, 825 Naval Air Squadron, HMS *Glorious*, summer 1939

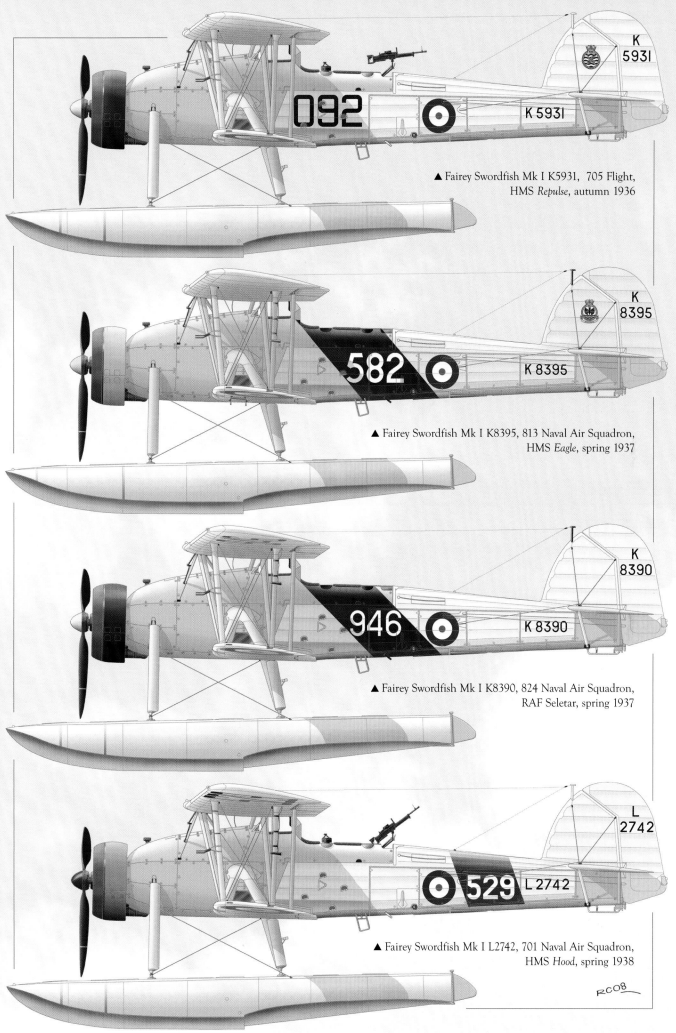

▲ Fairey Swordfish Mk I K5931, 705 Flight, HMS *Repulse*, autumn 1936

▲ Fairey Swordfish Mk I K8395, 813 Naval Air Squadron, HMS *Eagle*, spring 1937

▲ Fairey Swordfish Mk I K8390, 824 Naval Air Squadron, RAF Seletar, spring 1937

▲ Fairey Swordfish Mk I L2742, 701 Naval Air Squadron, HMS *Hood*, spring 1938

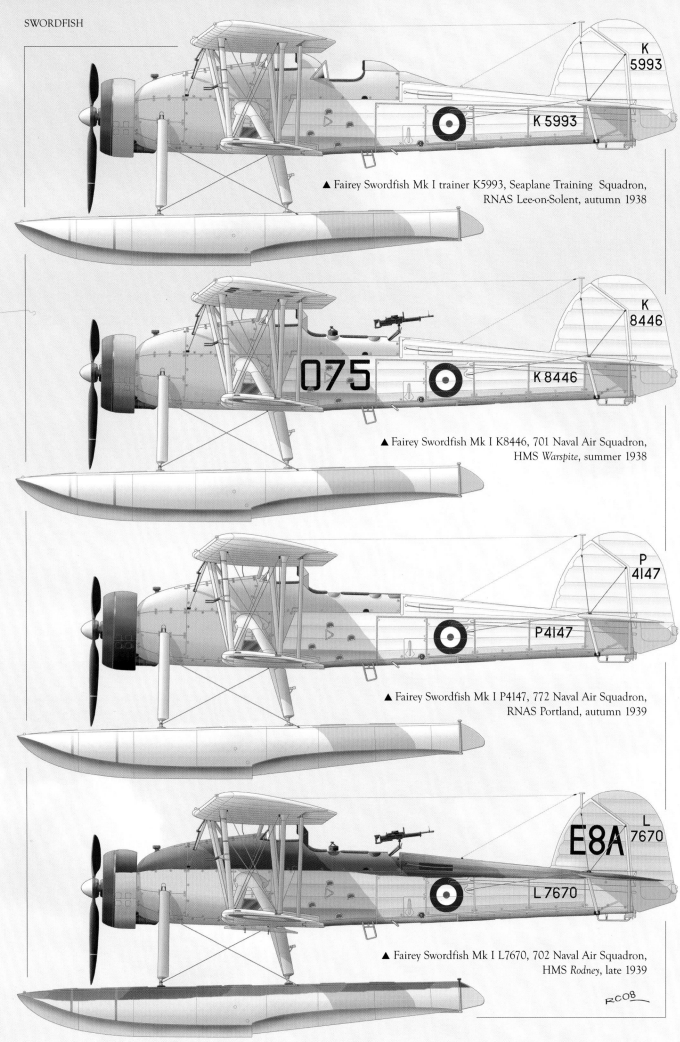

▲ Fairey Swordfish Mk I trainer K5993, Seaplane Training Squadron, RNAS Lee-on-Solent, autumn 1938

▲ Fairey Swordfish Mk I K8446, 701 Naval Air Squadron, HMS *Warspite*, summer 1938

▲ Fairey Swordfish Mk I P4147, 772 Naval Air Squadron, RNAS Portland, autumn 1939

▲ Fairey Swordfish Mk I L7670, 702 Naval Air Squadron, HMS *Rodney*, late 1939

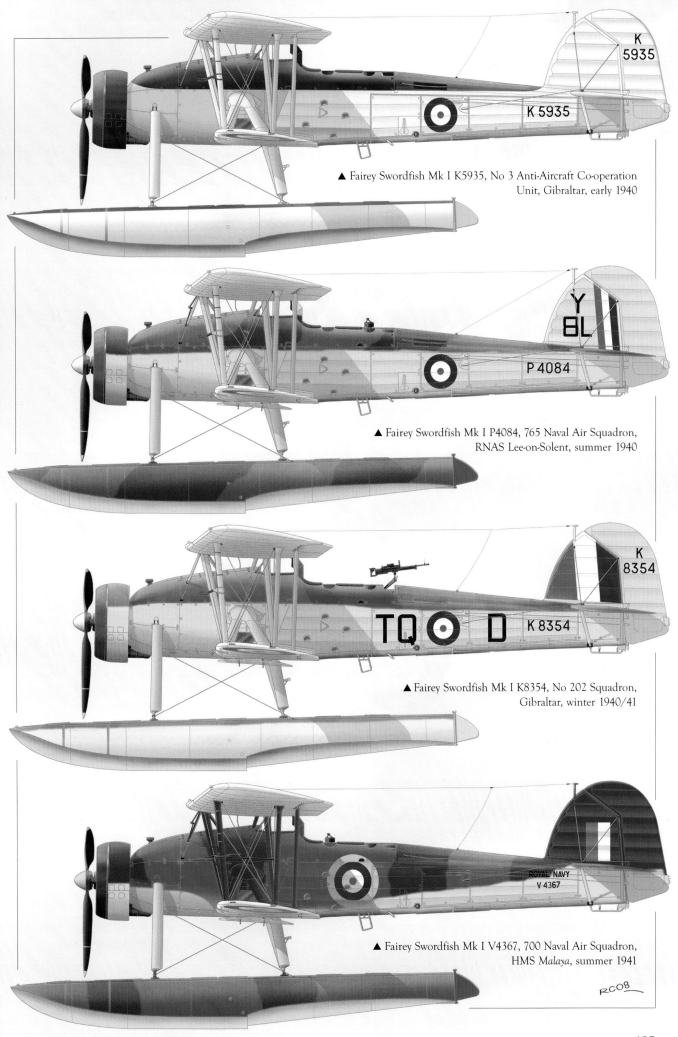

▲ Fairey Swordfish Mk I K5935, No 3 Anti-Aircraft Co-operation Unit, Gibraltar, early 1940

▲ Fairey Swordfish Mk I P4084, 765 Naval Air Squadron, RNAS Lee-on-Solent, summer 1940

▲ Fairey Swordfish Mk I K8354, No 202 Squadron, Gibraltar, winter 1940/41

▲ Fairey Swordfish Mk I V4367, 700 Naval Air Squadron, HMS *Malaya*, summer 1941

RC08

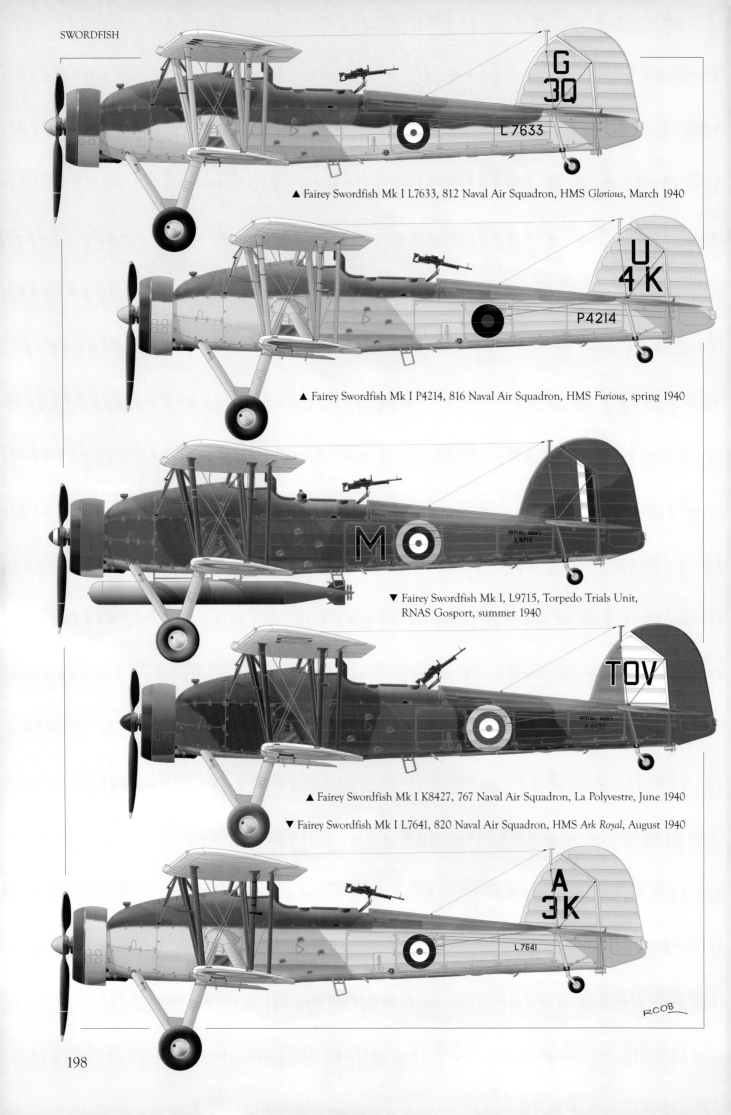

▲ Fairey Swordfish Mk I L7633, 812 Naval Air Squadron, HMS *Glorious*, March 1940

▲ Fairey Swordfish Mk I P4214, 816 Naval Air Squadron, HMS *Furious*, spring 1940

▼ Fairey Swordfish Mk I, L9715, Torpedo Trials Unit,
RNAS Gosport, summer 1940

▲ Fairey Swordfish Mk I K8427, 767 Naval Air Squadron, La Polyvestre, June 1940

▼ Fairey Swordfish Mk I L7641, 820 Naval Air Squadron, HMS *Ark Royal*, August 1940

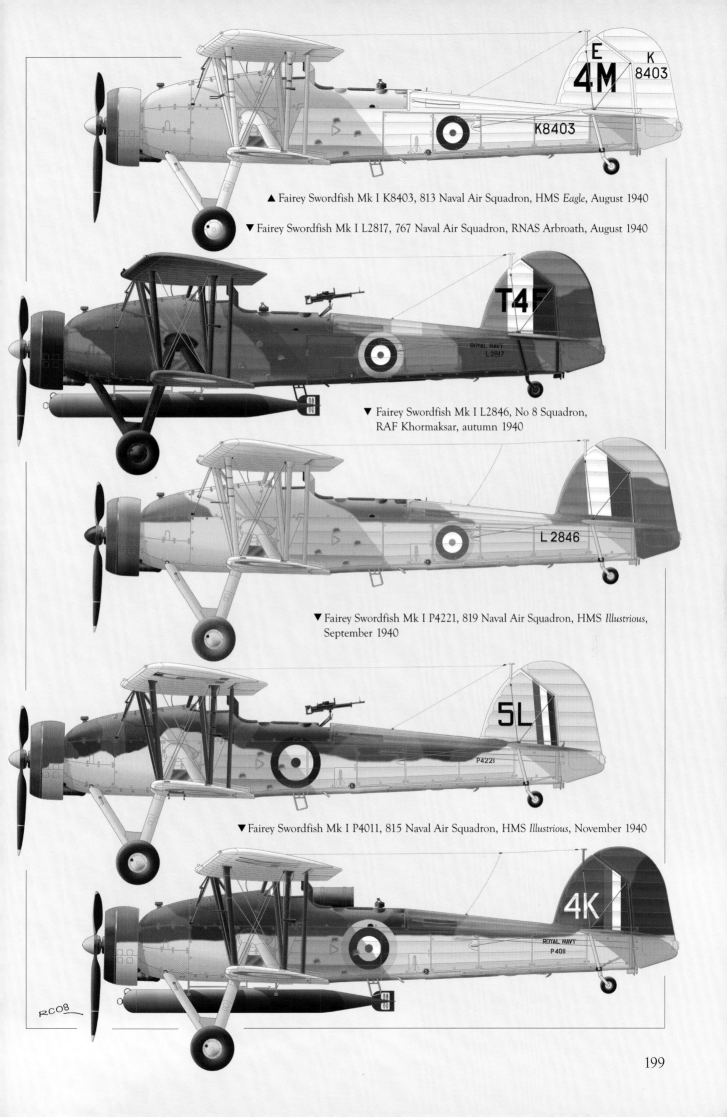

▲ Fairey Swordfish Mk I K8403, 813 Naval Air Squadron, HMS *Eagle*, August 1940

▼ Fairey Swordfish Mk I L2817, 767 Naval Air Squadron, RNAS Arbroath, August 1940

▼ Fairey Swordfish Mk I L2846, No 8 Squadron, RAF Khormaksar, autumn 1940

▼ Fairey Swordfish Mk I P4221, 819 Naval Air Squadron, HMS *Illustrious*, September 1940

▼ Fairey Swordfish Mk I P4011, 815 Naval Air Squadron, HMS *Illustrious*, November 1940

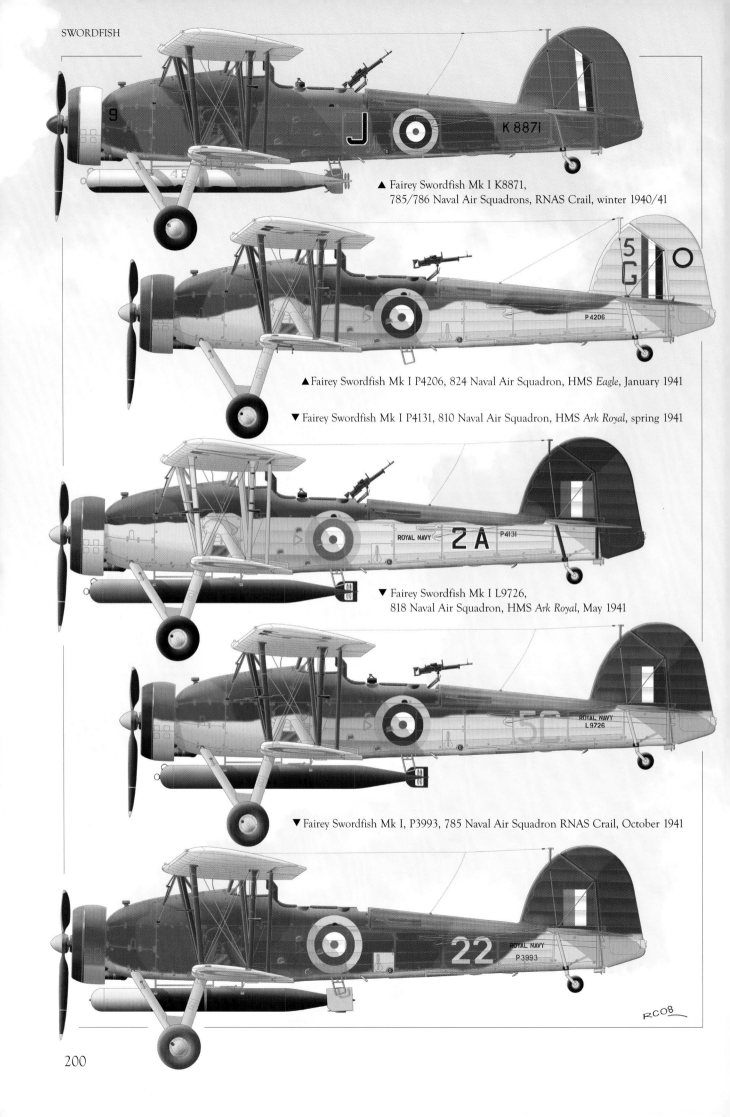

▲ Fairey Swordfish Mk I K8871,
785/786 Naval Air Squadrons, RNAS Crail, winter 1940/41

▲ Fairey Swordfish Mk I P4206, 824 Naval Air Squadron, HMS *Eagle*, January 1941

▼ Fairey Swordfish Mk I P4131, 810 Naval Air Squadron, HMS *Ark Royal*, spring 1941

▼ Fairey Swordfish Mk I L9726,
818 Naval Air Squadron, HMS *Ark Royal*, May 1941

▼ Fairey Swordfish Mk I, P3993, 785 Naval Air Squadron RNAS Crail, October 1941

RC08

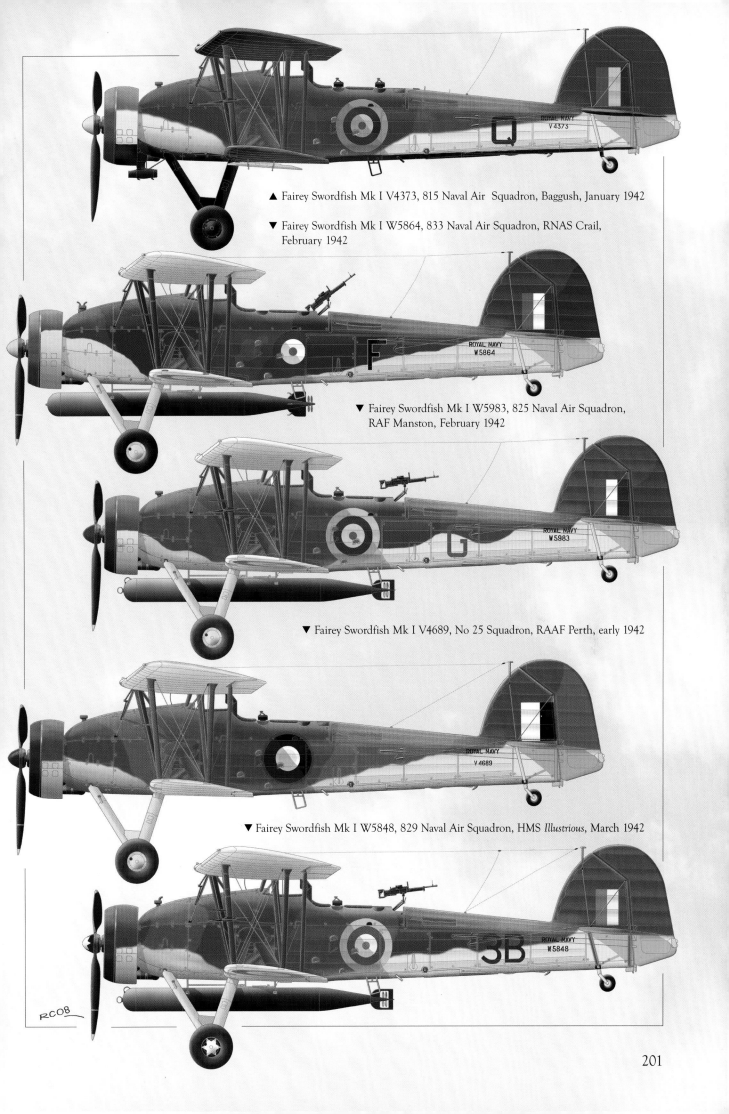

▲ Fairey Swordfish Mk I V4373, 815 Naval Air Squadron, Baggush, January 1942

▼ Fairey Swordfish Mk I W5864, 833 Naval Air Squadron, RNAS Crail, February 1942

▼ Fairey Swordfish Mk I W5983, 825 Naval Air Squadron, RAF Manston, February 1942

▼ Fairey Swordfish Mk I V4689, No 25 Squadron, RAAF Perth, early 1942

▼ Fairey Swordfish Mk I W5848, 829 Naval Air Squadron, HMS *Illustrious*, March 1942

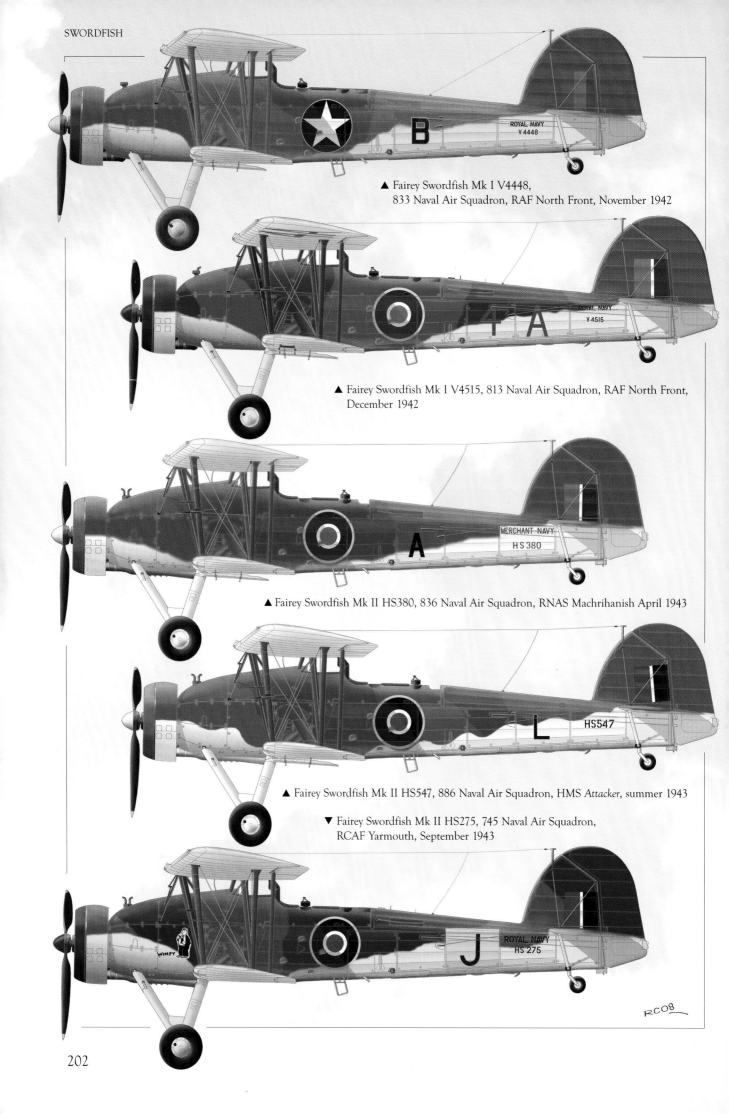

▲ Fairey Swordfish Mk I V4448,
833 Naval Air Squadron, RAF North Front, November 1942

▲ Fairey Swordfish Mk I V4515, 813 Naval Air Squadron, RAF North Front,
December 1942

▲ Fairey Swordfish Mk II HS380, 836 Naval Air Squadron, RNAS Machrihanish April 1943

▲ Fairey Swordfish Mk II HS547, 886 Naval Air Squadron, HMS *Attacker*, summer 1943

▼ Fairey Swordfish Mk II HS275, 745 Naval Air Squadron,
RCAF Yarmouth, September 1943

RC08

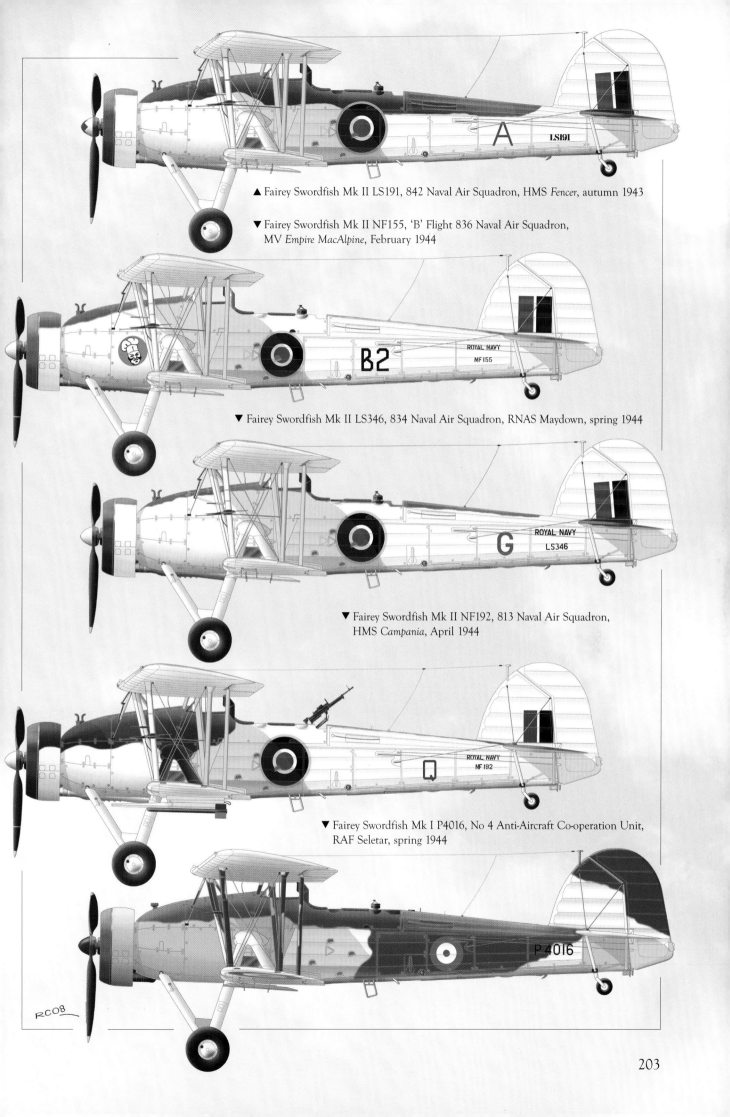

▲ Fairey Swordfish Mk II LS191, 842 Naval Air Squadron, HMS *Fencer*, autumn 1943

▼ Fairey Swordfish Mk II NF155, 'B' Flight 836 Naval Air Squadron, MV *Empire MacAlpine*, February 1944

▼ Fairey Swordfish Mk II LS346, 834 Naval Air Squadron, RNAS Maydown, spring 1944

▼ Fairey Swordfish Mk II NF192, 813 Naval Air Squadron, HMS *Campania*, April 1944

▼ Fairey Swordfish Mk I P4016, No 4 Anti-Aircraft Co-operation Unit, RAF Seletar, spring 1944

RC08

FLOWN BY THE AUTHOR

FAIREY SWORDFISH Mk III
NR864, 835 Naval Air Squadron, HMS *Nairana*, January 1945

RC08

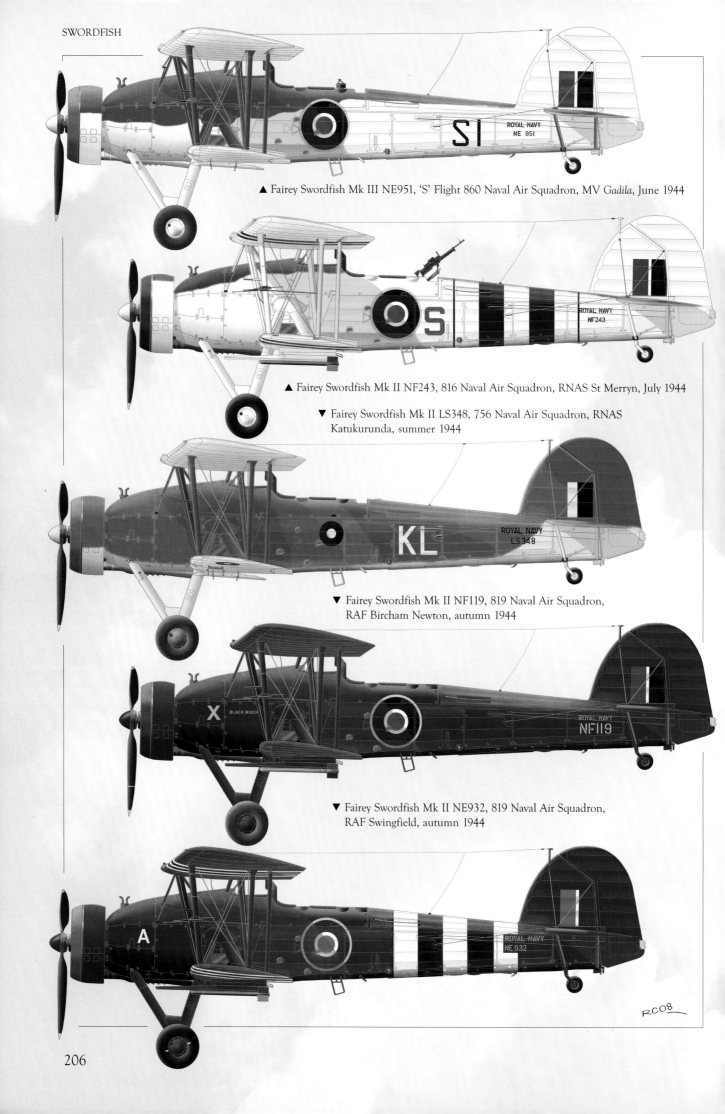

▲ Fairey Swordfish Mk III NE951, 'S' Flight 860 Naval Air Squadron, MV *Gadila*, June 1944

▲ Fairey Swordfish Mk II NF243, 816 Naval Air Squadron, RNAS St Merryn, July 1944

▼ Fairey Swordfish Mk II LS348, 756 Naval Air Squadron, RNAS Katukurunda, summer 1944

▼ Fairey Swordfish Mk II NF119, 819 Naval Air Squadron, RAF Bircham Newton, autumn 1944

▼ Fairey Swordfish Mk II NE932, 819 Naval Air Squadron, RAF Swingfield, autumn 1944